Richard Challoner

A Memorial of Ancient British Piety

A British Martyrology

Richard Challoner

A Memorial of Ancient British Piety
A British Martyrology

ISBN/EAN: 9783337413064

Printed in Europe, USA, Canada, Australia, Japan

Cover: Foto ©ninafisch / pixelio.de

More available books at **www.hansebooks.com**

A MEMORIAL

OF

Ancient BRITISH Piety:

OR, A

BRITISH MARTYROLOGY.

GIVING

A short Account of all such BRITONS as have been honoured of old amongst the Saints; or have otherwise been renowned for their extraordinary Piety and Sanctity.

To which is annexed,

A Translation of two ancient Saxon Manuscripts, relating to the Burying Places of the ENGLISH SAINTS. From the Library of Bennet College, Cambridge.

LONDON:

Printed for W. NEEDHAM, over against Gray's Inn Gate in Holborn. 1761.

THE
PREFACE.

ONE of the most interesting Parts of Church History, and which has usually the most Influence both on the Faith and on the Lives of Christians; is that which sets before their Eyes the Wonders of God in the Lives and Deaths of his Saints. The sacred Penmen, inspired by the Holy Spirit, set the first Example of this Kind of Writings: and many of the holy Fathers, and other learned and godly Men in all Ages, have copied after them, by publishing the Acts of the Martyrs, and of other more eminent Saints of God, whom the divine Grace has lighted up in every Age, and set upon the Candlestick of his Church as so many Lights to enlighten all that dwell in God's House, by the Splendor of their Works; to animate them to walk in their glorious Footsteps; and to inflame them with an heavenly Ardor to serve and love, with their whole Hearts, the God of all the Spirits of the Just; whose Love alone can make Saints.

But as the Multitude of these holy Martyrs, and these other Saints, who have illustrated the Church of Christ, by their Lives and by their Deaths, has been exceeding great; and withal the Acts of a great Number of them have been written at large, so as to fill many more Volumes than the Generality of Christians can either have the Means to procure, or the Leisure to read: there have been set forth from time to time Abridgments of their Acts, giving a short Account of what was most remarkable in the Lives and Deaths of these Christian Heroes, that the Faithful, by reading these Abridgments, might find every Day Lessons for the Conduct of their own Lives, in order to arrive at the same happy End by an Imitation of their Virtues. This was the Original of Martyrologies and Menologies; of which there has been published in the Church of God a great Variety; some more general; others
con-

PREFACE. 5

containing only the Saints of particular Nations, or particular Orders of Religious; for the Edification of the Faithful of that Nation, or the Religious of that Order.

Amongſt thoſe that were ſet forth for particular Nations, there was a *Britiſh* Martyrology, publiſhed about one hundred and fifty Years ago, by Mr. *John Wilſon*, an *Engliſh* Prieſt, (who lived abroad in the *Low Countries*) under the Title of *The Engliſh Martyrologe, containing a Summary of the Lives of the glorious and renowned Saints of the three Kingdoms, England, Scotland, and Ireland:* which, if the Performance had been anſwerable to the Title, might have diſpenſed with us from thinking of publiſhing the following Sheets; ſince the Work which we promiſe would have been already done to our Hands. But this Writer, beſides omitting the greater Part of the Saints of the *Scots* Calendar (which he never ſaw) and almoſt all the Saints of *Ireland*, has been guilty of many groſs Miſtakes in Hiſtory with regard to thoſe he has commemorated, and generally been very unhappy in the choice of the Materials he has made uſe of, omitting what would have been moſt edifying in the Summary he gives of the Lives of those Servants of God, and insisting chiefly on certain marvellous Events, for the most part destitute of any sufficient Authority to support them.

Wherefore we thought it would not be disagreeable to our Countrymen, more especially to as many of them as are Lovers of *British Antiquities*, or Friends to ancient Piety, to see a more accurate *British Martyrology*; which might take in the Generality of the Saints of all the three Nations, giving a short Account of their Virtues (where their Acts were known) and leaving out all that was apocryphal in their History; which is what we have endeavoured to aim at in the following MEMORIAL; concerning which it may be proper to acquaint our Readers, 1st. That we have not here given the Title of *Saints* to any but such as we found in possession of it, either in our *British* Calendars, or in the Names of our Churches and Parishes, or other ancient Monuments, testifying the religious Veneration formerly paid them by our Ancestors. 2dly. That if we have given a place in this *Memorial* to some other holy Persons who have not been thus enrolled amongst the Saints, it was not to bespeak them,

PREFACE.

them, or give any Sanction to, any public Veneration of them, till the Church should be pleased to declare them Saints, but merely as Historians, to record their Names with something of their Virtues, as Instances of ancient *British* Piety. 3dly. That with regard to many of our Saints, we have been able to give no more than their bare Names; because their Acts, if ever written, are long since lost: and as to others, we have sometimes been forced to join Numbers together in one Commemoration; because their very Names are at present unknown. 4thly. That as to the appointing our *British* Saints their respective Days throughout the Year, where our Calendars, or other Monuments, gave us Light, we have generally endeavoured to follow it: but where we could not find the Days, on which they were formerly honoured, we have commemorated them on such other Days, as otherwise might have been vacant: and thus we have not let so much as one Day in the Year pass without commemorating one or more Saints, or other Servants of God, illustrious for Christian Piety. Lastly, That as to those, who have preached the Faith of Christ in our Islands, or have otherwise promoted the Conversion of our Ancestors, though themselves no *Britons*; we have also given them a Place amongst our *British* Saints, on account of their Labours amongst us: as we have done also to some few others, who have had particular Connections with *Great Britain*; or whose Bodies have been translated hither; and from hence shall one Day be called forth to meet the Lord of Glory, and to live with him.

A MEMORIAL
OF
Ancient BRITISH Piety:
OR, A
BRITISH MARTYROLOGY.

JANUARY.

Jan. 1. AT *London*, the Commemoration of the holy Bishop *Thean*, whose Name stands the first in the Catalogue of the ancient Bishops of that City. He is said to have held his See in the Church of S. *Peter's*, *Cornhill*, and to have lived in the Time of King *Lucius*. See Abridgment of *Dugdale's Monasticon*, p. 331. Also a Commemoration of the other holy primitive Prelates of the second and third Century, who were the Fathers and Founders of our *British* Churches. *Remember*, says the Apostle, *your Prelates, who have spoken to you the Word of God: whose Faith follow; considering the End of their Conversation. Jesus Christ the same yesterday, and to-day: and he is the same for ever.* Heb. xiii. 7, 8. With these we may join the *British* Bishops, who flourished in the Beginning of the fourth Century; of whom *Eborius* of *York*, *Restitutus* of *London*, and *Adelfius* of *Camalodunum*, subscribed to the Council of *Arles*, anno. 312.

Jan. 2. At *London*, the Commemoration of the holy Confessors *Elvan* and *Medwyne*; who (according to divers *Historians and ancient Records) being sent to *Rome* by King *Lucius* to the holy Pope *Eleutherius*, to desire Missionaries from thence who might receive him and his People into the Church of Christ, returned home so well instructed in the Christian Faith, as to become both eminent Teachers, and great Saints. *Elvan* is said to have been the second Bishop of *London*, and to have converted many of the *Druids* or heathenish Priests to the Faith of Christ. In a little Island, on the East side of *Anglesey*, the Commemoration of St. *Cyriol*, whose Church and Monastery are mentioned in *Tanner's Notitia Monastica*, p. 699.

Jan. 3. At *Avallonia*, now *Glastenbury*, the Commemoration of the apostolick Missionaries *Fagan* and *Dwywan*, or *Deruvian*, honoured by

* See Usher's British Antiquities, p. 27. and Dugdale's Monasticon, vol. 3. p. 185.

the ancient *Britons* amongst their primitive Saints. They are called by the Lessons of the *Roman Breviary*, *May* 26, *Fugacius* and *Damianus*; and are there said to have been sent by S. *Eleutherius* the Pope for the Conversion of the *Britons*, which they happily effected. The *Antiquities of Glastenbury* further inform us, that S. *Fagan* and S. *Deruvian*, in their Progress through *Britain*, visited the Solitude of *Avallonia*, and found there the *Old Church*, supposed to have been built by S. *Joseph* of *Arimathea*; and that they there appointed twelve of their Disciples to lead a monastical, or eremitical Life, in the Neighbourhood of that holy Church: which Number of twelve, they say, was kept up by succession till the days of S. *Patrick*. See *Usher's Antiquities*, chap. 6.

Jan. 4. In the Territory of *Litchfield*, the Commemoration of many holy Martyrs, said to have been massacred there, under *Diocletian*: whose mangled Bodies that City bears in her scutcheon; and from them takes her name: *Litchfield* being the same as *Campus Cadaverum*, or *the Field of dead Bodies*. These Martyrs are supposed to have been Citizens of *Verulam*, lately converted to the Christian Faith by the means of the same holy Ecclesiastick who converted S. *Alban*; who upon occasion of the Martyrdom of this Saint, flying from the Heat of the Persecution, were overtaken at the Place, where *Litchfield* now stands; and all there slain, to the Number, as some Authors affirm, of about one thousand Persons: who having thus *washed their Robes in the Blood of the Lamb*, live now with him for ever. On this Day is also commemorated in

Wilson's

Wilson's Martyrology, S. *Croniack*, Confessor, illustrious for Sanctity amongst the *Scots*.

Jan. 5. In the Abbey of *Westminster* the Deposition of S. *Edward*, King and Confessor, renowned for the Innocence and Sanctity of his Life, and his virginal Purity, which he preserved, by a rare Example, even in the State of Matrimony. God made him also illustrious by the Gift of prophetick Light, and many Miracles; as well in giving Sight to the Blind, as in healing the King's Evil, and other Diseases. Obiit anno 1066. At *Westminster* the Commemoration also of blessed *Sebert*, the first Christian King of the *East-Saxons*; who first built the Church of S. *Peter* there, which some say was then consecrated by the Apostle himself. [See *Dugdale's Monasticon*, vol. 1. p. 55.] He passed to a better life anno 616; and lies buried in the southern part of the choir [b] of the Abbey Church.

Jan. 6. The *Epiphany*, or Manifestation of our Lord: the Christmas Day of all the Churches of the Gentiles. At the Abbey of S. *Peter* and S. *Paul* near *Canterbury* (commonly called S. *Austin's*) the Commemoration of blessed *Peter*, Disciple of S. *Gregory* the Great, and first Abbat of that Monastery, by the Appointment of S. *Augustin* our Apostle: who after a most Saint-like Administration of his Charge, being sent over to *France*, about some ecclesiastical Affairs, anno 607, was cast away upon the Coast of *Boulogne*.

[b] In australi parte sacrarii. Dugdale's Abridgment.

His Body was obscurely buried near the Shore; till the neighbouring People observing a heavenly Light, shining every Night over his Grave, and upon Enquiry finding how great and holy a Man he had been, taking up his Corpse translated it to the Church of *Boulogne*. S. *Bede*, l. 1. c. 33. *The Souls of the Just are in the Hands of God—to the Eyes of the Unwise they seemed to die, and their Departure from hence was looked upon as a Misery—but they are in Peace.* Wisd. iii. 1, 2, 3.

At *Canterbury* also the Commemoration of the holy Abbats *John*, *Rufinian*, *Gratiosus*, *Petronius* and *Nathanael*, Successors, one after another, of B. *Peter* in the Government of the same Monastery, all Disciples of the same S. *Gregory*; and all worthy of so excellent a Master.

Jan. 7. At *Lestingham* in *Yorkshire*, the Deposition of S. *Ced*, Bishop of *London*, Brother of S. *Chad* of *Litchfield*, and Disciple of the great S. *Aidan* of *Lindisfarne*, in whose Steps he walked, by a close Imitation of all his Virtues; for nothing of this World did he value or regard, but wholly consecrated himself to divine Love, and to the Service of the Souls of his Neighbours. His first apostolick Labours were dedicated to the Conversion of the *Midland English*: after which, he was sent to the Province of the *East-Saxons*, whom he brought over to the Faith of Christ. He founded, for the training up his Converts in Christian Perfection, the Monasteries of *Ithanchester* and *Tilbury* in *Essex*; laying the Foundations of them by forty Days Fasting and Prayer: as he did afterwards in founding, at the Desire of King *Edilwald*, a House of Saints at *Lestingham*

ham in the Mountains of *Deira* (*Yorkshire*). From whence he himself happily passed to the Mountain of Eternity, anno 664. His Body was deposited there in the Church of the Blessed Virgin. [S. *Bede*, l. 1. c. 21, 22, &c.] But his Soul is with him, whom he so entirely loved and served: according to that Promise of Truth, *If any Man minister unto me, let him follow me: and where I am, there also shall my Minister be.* S. John xii. 26.

Jan. 8. The Commemoration of the holy Priests, *Celin* and *Cynibil*, Brothers to S. *Ced* and S. *Chad*; and no less allied to them in Virtue than in Blood; and therefore jointly honoured with them by our Ancestors amongst the Saints. [*Sarum* Breviary, *March* 2.] Also at *London*, the Deposition of holy *Guithelin*, a zealous and godly Archbishop of that See, in the Time of the *Britons*. *Mat. Westminster*, anno 435. At *Tullicht* also, in the Diocese of *Aberdeen*, the Deposition of S. *Nethalen*, Bishop and Confessor, honoured on this Day in the *Aberdeen* Breviary.

Jan. 9. At *Canterbury*, the Deposition of S. *Brithwald*, the eighth Archbishop of that See, celebrated for his Learning and Sanctity. Obiit anno 731. S. *Bede*, l. 5. c. 9 & 24. In the Solitude of *Sirach*, not far from *Glendarchy*, in *Scotland*, the Deposition of S. *Filan*, or *Foilan*, Abbat, greatly honoured of old, both in *North Britain* and *Ireland*. Obiit anno 703. *Aberdeen* Breviary. Also in *Scotland*, the Commemoration of S. *Kentigerna*, Widow, said to have been Mother of S. *Filan*.

Jan. 10. At *Canterbury*, the Depofition of S. *Adrian*, Abbat of the Monaftery of S. *Peter* and S. *Paul* (commonly called S. *Auftin's*) who being fent over into *England* by Pope *Vitalian*, in the Company of S. *Theodore* the Archbifhop, anno 669, befides preaching every where, and inftructing the People, throughout the Land, in all the Rules of a Chriftian Life, and the right Way of eternal Salvation, opened in *Kent* an excellent School of all good Learning, and Chriftian Piety, in which he trained up many Saints; and brought fuch happy Days amongft us, as *England* had never known before. He departed to our Lord in a good old Age, *Jan.* 9. anno 710. S. *Bede*, l. 4. c. 1, 2. l. 5. c. 21. Alfo at *Canterbury*, the Commemoration of the holy Abbat *Albinus*, Difciple and worthy Succeffor of S. *Adrian*, and Affiftant to S. *Bede* in compiling his Church Hiftory. *They that inftruct many unto Juftice, fhall fhine as the Brightnefs of the Firmament, and as the Stars to all Eternity.* Dan. xii. 3.

Jan. 11. At *Worcefter*, the Feftivity of S. *Egwin*, the third Bifhop of that See, and Founder of the famous Monaftery of our Lady of *Evefham*: who thro' *many Labours, Trials* and *Tribulations*, made his way to the Kingdom of God anno 717, and was buried in his Monaftery of *Evefham*. *William* of *Malmfbury*, l. 4. de Pontif. Ang. &c. Alfo at *York* the Tranflation of the Body of S. *William* Archbifhop of that See, whofe Relicks were taken up (on occafion of the many illuftrious Miracles wrought at his Tomb) tranflated and enfhrined anno 1284. The Memory of which Tranflation was folemn-
ly

ly kept in the Diocese of *York*, on the Sunday within the Octave of the Epiphany. *Missale Eboracense*.

Jan. 12. At *Weremouth* in the Bishoprick of *Durham*, the Deposition of St. *Bennet Biscop*, Abbat, Founder of the sister Churches and Monasteries of S. *Peter* and S. *Paul* at *Weremouth* and *Jarrow*; where he trained up many excellent Religious; and amongst the rest, the great S. *Bede*: who has left us in writing the Lives of his Master, and the other first Abbats of the Monasteries by him established. He departed to our Lord, after being purified by a long and tedious Illness (which he qualified by divine Meditations) anno 690, and was buried in S. *Peter's* Church: from whence his Body was translated to *Thorney* Abbey anno 970. Also at the Abbey of *Rievale* or *Ridale* in *Yorkshire*, the Deposition of blessed *Aelred*, Abbat, illustrious for Learning and Sanctity. He was a close Imitator of his holy Father the great S. *Bernard*, both in his Manner of Writing, and in his Way of Living. Obiit anno 1166.

Jan. 13. At *Glasgow* in *Scotland*, the Festivity of S. *Kentigern*, alias *Mungho*, Bishop and Confessor. He was of the Royal Blood of the Kings of the *Cumbrian Britons*, who then inhabited the South-west of *Scotland:* and was brought up from a Child by S. *Servanus*, in his Monastery of *Culross*. Being afterwards made Bishop of that Province, he imitated both the Labours, and the Lives of the Apostles; and by his Preaching and Miracles brought over innumernumerable Souls to God. He also greatly promoted monastick Discipline, as well in his own Country, where he gathered together at *Glasgow*, a numerous congregation of devout Brethren, living according to the Form of the primitive Church; as in *North-Wales*, where he settled himself, (when forced from home by the Persecution of the Wicked) and founded the famous Monastery of *Llan Elwy* (now S. *Asaph's*) where he was spiritual Father to 965 Brethren; to whom he allotted their different Functions, of the active or contemplative Life; according to their Capacities and Dispositions; regulating also their Hours both of the Night and Day, in such Manner as never to suffer the divine Office to be discontinued; but that some or other of them should be always singing in the Church the Praises of God. At length being recalled to his former See, after many more Years of Apostolick Labours, he *entered into the Joy of the Lord*, anno 601: and was buried at *Glasgow*, where the great Church, now the Cathedral, was dedicated in his Name. See *his Acts in John of Tinmouth, in Usher's Antiquities*, &c.

Jan. 14. At *Clynnoc Vawr*, in *Caernarvonshire*, the Commemoration of S. *Beuno* or *Bennow*, Abbat, of whom there is ample mention in the Acts of S. *Winefrede*, and in the Lessons of the *Sarum* Breviary. He was of a most noble Extraction, in *Powis-Land*, Cousin German by the Mother to S. *Kentigern*; and an ardent Lover of God from his Childhood. After retiring from the World, and dedicating himself to a religious Life; he was for his Merit advanced

vanced to the Priestly Dignity; and by founding divers Churches and religious Communities, very much advanced the Glory and Kingdom of his Lord. His last Foundation was, after his departure from S. *Wenefrede*, the famous Monastery of *Clynnoc Vawr* anno 616. From whence he was called to the Land of the Living about the Year 623. *Clynnoc Vawr* was afterwards given to the *Bernardin* Monks; and a new Church built there, one of the noblest in *Wales*, under the Invocation of S. *Beuno*: but his Body continued in the old Church. See *Dugdale's Monasticon*, vol. 2. Also in the Isle of *Enlly* (*Bardsey*) the Commemoration of the Man of God, *Laudatus* (*Lowdhad*) first Abbat of a holy Congregation established in that Island; and nearly allied both to S. *Beuno* and to S. *Kentigern*. Also at *Llan-Ennian Vrenin*, the Commemoration of holy *Eneon Bhrenin*, King of *Cumbria*, who not long before the Foundation of *Clynnoc Vawr* by S. *Beuno*, leaving his Royalty, built a Church in that Country, which was afterwards called by his Name; where he spent the remainder of his Days in God's Love and Service. See concerning these Saints Mr. *Vaughan*, an Author well acquainted with the Antiquities of his Country, quoted in Dr. *Gibson's Cambden*, p. 825.

Jan. 15. At *Rosmede* in the County of *Waterford*, the Festivity of S. *Mida* or *Ita*, Virgin and Abbess, of the Royal Blood of the Monarchs of *Ireland*; who leaving all for Christ, by a constant Attention to divine Love, and a perpetual Recollection in God, arrived at so high a Pera Perfection in all Virtues, as to become, next to S. *Brigide*, the most illustrious of all the Women Saints of *Ireland*. Obiit anno 569. *Acta apud Bollandum*. In *Cornwall* the Commemoration of S. *Daye*, whose Church or Chapel at the Town of S. *Daye*, was in former Times a Place of great resort for Devotion. [*England's Gazetteer*.]

Jan. 16. At *Peronne* in *Picardy* the Deposition of S. *Furfey*, Abbat, of Royal *Irish* Blood, who from his very Childhood consecrated his whole Heart to Divine Love; and as he grew up, laboured with all his Power to impart to his Brethren, both by his Preaching and his Life, those bright Flames which were enkindled in his own Breast; being animated thereto by certain heavenly Visions, related at large in his ancient Acts. After having won many Souls to God in his own Country (where he could no longer endure the Crowds that were continually flowing in upon him) he came over to *Britain*; and preached Christ with great Zeal, and no less Fruit, in the Province of the *East Angles*; where also he founded the famous Monastery of *Burghcastle* in *Suffolk*. At length passing over into *France*, after establishing there the Abbey of *Lagny*, going to make another Foundation at *Peronne*; he was called from thence to a better Life, anno 650. His Body was found incorrupt four and twenty Years after his Death; and deposited in the Church of *Peronne*, which is dedicated to God in his Name. S. *Bede*, l. 3. c. 19. Likewise in *Ireland* the Festivity of S. *Nennidhius*, Abbat, Father and Teacher of many

many Saints, whom he trained up in his Monastery, in an Isle of the Lake of *Erne*. At *Tinmouth* the Deposition of S. *Henry*, Hermit, who following a Divine Call, leaving *Denmark* his native Country, with all his worldly Friends, and whatever he seemed to possess; embraced a Life of wonderful Austerity and Sanctity, in the Isle of *Cocket*, near the Coast of *Northumberland:* which he continued for a long Space of Years, till his dying Day; suffering, for a great Part of the Time, a most loathsome and painful Ulcer in the Knee; which even swarmed with Vermin; but hindered him not from still working for his poor Living, and perpetually praising God, with a most remarkable Alacrity : till he arrived at last at the end of all his Sufferings, and the happy beginning of a Repose and Life, that never ends, *Jan.* 16, anno 1127. He was buried in the Church of our Lady at *Tinmouth*, near the Body of S. *Oswin* King and Martyr. His Acts in *Capgrave*, &c.

Jan. 17. At *Menstrey* in the Isle of *Thanet* the Commemoration of the Royal Virgin S. *Milwyde*, Sister to the Saints *Mildred* and *Milburge*, and a close follower of their Purity and Sanctity. Also the Commemoration of S. *Meresin* Brother to these Saints : whose eminent Piety in a tender Age, has entitled to a Share in the Glory of the Saints. To whom we may apply that of the Wise Man, *Wisd.* iv. 13, 14. *Being made perfect in a short Space, he filled up a long Time : for his Soul pleased God : Wherefore he hastened to bring him out from the midst of Iniquities.* These Saints flourished in the Seventh Century. In *Ireland*
the

the Commemoration of S. *Kenan*, Confeſſor, renowned for Sanctity in the ſixth Century.

Jan. 18 In *Britain* the Feſtivity of S. *Deicola*, Abbat, Diſciple of S. *Columban* ſays the Roman Martyrology on this Day. He followed that great Saint from *Ireland* into *Britain*, and from *Britain* into *France* and *Burgundy*, where he founded the Abbey of *Lutra* (*Lure*) and eſtabliſhed it in great Perfection. In the latter Part of his Life, he retired to a private Oratory to prepare himſelf by continual Prayer and divine Contemplation for a happy Eternity, into which he entered in the former Part of the ſeventh Century. See his Life by *Chifflet*. 'Tis related of this Saint, that he always ſmiled: and that being aſked the Reaſon, he returned this Anſwer: I ſmile becauſe no man can take away my God from me. There were alſo two other holy Men, of the Name of *Deicola* or *Dicul*, of the ſame *Iriſh* Nation; who flouriſhed in *England* in the ſeventh Century: the one a Companion and Diſciple of S. *Furſey*, to whom he committed the Care of his Monaſtery at *Burghcaſtle*, when he betook himſelf to an eremitical Life, in the Company of his Brother S. *Ultan*, S. *Bede*, l. 3. c. 19. The other Abbat of *Boſeham* in *Suſſex*, when S. *Wilfrid* came to preach Chriſt to the *South Saxons*. S. *Bede*, l. 4. c. 13.

Jan. 19. At *Worceſter* the Feſtivity of S. *Wolſtan*, who from an humble Monk was, by compulſion, made Biſhop of that See; which he adminiſtered worthily of a Succeſſor of the Apoſtles. His preaching, like that of the Apoſtles,
with-

without the Pomp of secular Learning, or human Eloquence, carried with it an Unction of the Spirit, which made its Way into the most hardened Hearts: the more because his Life was a continual Sermon, and a perpetual Prayer. He had also a particular Talent in bringing Souls to God in the Sacrament of Penance, which attracted to him, from all Parts of the Kingdom, such Penitents as had not the Courage to declare their Sins to any other. He had the Charity of a Father to all; more especially to the Poor, and was generally loved by all, as a Father. He built the Cathedral of *Worcester*; and went to our Lord in a good old Age, anno 1095. On the same Day in *Finland* the Martyrdom of S. *Henry* an English Man, Bishop of *Upsal*, and Apostle of *Finland*. 'He settled and confirmed *Swedeland* as yet young in the Faith, (saith *John Magnus*, in the Lives of the Archbishops of *Upsal*) and brought it over from the filth of the Sins, with which it was defiled, to the Works of Christian Piety: he instructed the Nation, ignorant before, both in divine and human Laws: he helped King *Eric* to become a Saint, &c.' He converted to the Christian Faith a great Part of *Finland*; which also received his Blood, anno 1151. He has a Place in the *Swedish* Breviary.

Jan. 20. At *Fower* in the County of *Westmeath*, the Festivity of S. *Fechin*, Abbat, Founder of divers Churches and Monasteries, Father of above three hundred Monks, and Converter of a great Number of Infidels and Sinners. After a Life of wonderful Mortification and Sanctity, he he was taken to our Lord, in the Time of the great Mortality anno 664. Also at *Tegh Molagga* in the County of *Cork*, the Festivity of S. *Molacus*, Confessor, Patron of that Church. Also in the Monastery of S. *Columkille* in the Isle of *Hy*, the Martyrdom of S *Blathmac* Abbat, and his Companions, put to Death by *Danish* Pirates, in hatred of their Faith, towards the beginning of the ninth Century. Their Passion was written by *Walafridus Strabo*, a learned Abbat of the same Century: by which it appears that *Blathmac* was a Saint from his Childhood; and had long been ambitious of the Happiness of dying for Christ; and therefore he met with Joy that Death, which was to unite him with his true Life for evermore.

Jan. 21. In *Swedeland* the Commemoration of S. *Ulfrid* or *Wolfred*, an Apostolick Preacher of the *English* Nation, and one of those to whom under God, *Swedeland* stands indebted for the Faith of Christ. He suffered Martyrdom there at the Hands of the Infidels, about the Year 1028. In *Scotland* the Festivity of S. *Vinin*, Bishop, marked in the *Aberdeen* Breviary to have passed to a better Life anno 715. At the Monastery of S. *Michael* in *Tierarche* on the Confines of *Haynault*, the Festivity of S. *Malcallan* first Abbat of that Community, and of that of *Wazor* in the Territory of *Liege:* a Man of admirable Sanctity. Of whom thus writes *Flodoardus* a cotemporary Historian. ' Anno 978, the Man of God *Malcallan*, an Irishman by Nation, (*Jan.* 21) left this transitory Life, which he hated; and happily began to live with that

Lord, whom in his life Time he had continually served.'

Jan. 22. At *Wilton* the Comemoration of holy *Brithwald*, Bishop, eminent for the Sanctity of his Life, and his prophetic Spirit, of whom a most honourable mention is made in the Lessons of S. *Edward* the Confessor, in the *Roman* Breviary. Obiit anno 1007. At *Hertland* Abbey in *Devonshire* the Commemoration of S. *Nectan*, Confessor, Patron of that Church and Monastery. In *Cornwall* the Commemoration of S. *Just* Confessor, held heretofore in great Veneration amongst the *Cornish* Britons, as appears by the Places which to this Day bear his Name.

Jan. 23. At *Rumsey* in *Hampshire* the Commemoration of S. *Elfleda* or *Elfreda*, a noble Virgin, trained up in the Discipline of Christ, by S. *Merwenna*; and third Abbess of the Monastery of sacred Virgins at *Rumsey*. She flourished in all Sanctity in the tenth Century. Her Body was enshrined in the Church of the blessed Virgin at *Rumsey*, together with that of her Mistress S. *Merwenna*. Where also a Number of other Saints reposed in our Lord. *Saxon Manuscript.* At *Calcaria* (now *Tadcaster*) in *Yorkshire* the Commemoration of holy *Heiu*, Virgin and Abbess, said to have been the first Woman amongst the *Northern* English, that consecrated herself to our Lord, in the Life and Habit of a Nun, being dedicated to God by S. *Aidan.* She first founded the Monastery of *Hartlepool* (of which S. *Hilda* was afterwards Abbess) and then the Monastery of *Calcaria*;

from

from whence she passed to the happy society of the saints, some time in the seventh century. S. *Bede* l. 4. c. 23.

Jan. 24. At *Llancarvan* three miles from *Cowbridge* in *Glamorganshire* the festivity of S. *Cadoc* abbat; son of S. *Gundleus* prince of that country, by *Gladusa*, daughter of *Braghan*, or *Brecan*, who gave name to *Brecknockshire*, and was the father of four and twenty children, all saints. *Cadoc* following the example of his father, left his earthly principality, for the love of Christ, and put himself under the discipline of S. *Tathai* in the school of all good learning and piety, which he had lately opened at *Caer-Gwent* in *Monmouthshire*: till having learnt of this great master the science of the saints, he laboured to impart the same to many others, by the foundation of the school and monastery of *Llancarvan*, one of the most celebrated of all *Britain*; where he trained up many saints: and as he had always lived the life of the saints himself, so he died the death of the saints, sometime in the former part of the sixth century. At *Beneventum* in *Italy* the festivity of S. *Sophias*, called also *Cadoc*, a noble Briton, who going abroad into *Italy* was for his eminent merits made bishop of *Beneventum*, and ended his days by martyrdom. At *Llancarvan* also the commemoration of the holy abbat *Ellenius* disciple and successor of S. *Cadoc*, who no way degenerated from the virtues of his master.

Jan. 25. The conversion of S. *Paul*, the apostle and general doctor of all the churches of of the Gentiles: who also, as some authors affirm, personally preached in *Britain.* In the monastery of S. *Hilda* at *Streanshall* (now *Whitby*) in *Yorkshire,* the commemoration of holy *Trumwine* bishop of the *Picts,* who being expelled his see, when that nation shook off the *English* yoke, spent the remainder of the days of his mortality in religious solitude and devotion: instructing in the mean time in the ways of true life, and directing the men and women servants of God, who lived in community, in the famous monastery of *Streanshall,* governed at that time by the royal Virgin *Elfleda,* and her mother queen *Eanfled.* He was called from hence to our Lord about the year 700.

Jan. 26. In the isle of *Ycombkille* (*Hy*) the commemoration of holy *Eochoid* (or *Eoglodius,*) one of the twelve apostolick preachers, disciples of S. *Columkille,* who accompanied this saint, when he came over into *Britain,* and joined their labours with his, in converting the *Picts,* and propagating in *North Britain* monastick discipline. At *Barking* in *Essex* the commemoration of holy *Torchgyth* virgin, disciple of S. *Ethelburga,* and one of the superioresses of that saintly community: who as venerable *Bede* relates l. 4. c. 9. was favoured with a vision, in which she saw her holy mistress taken up to heaven: to which blessed place of eternal repose, she was also herself invited, after having been purified like gold in the furnace, with a course of long and painful infirmities, which exercised her, without intermission, for the space of nine years.

Jan.

Jan. 27. In the monaſtery of *Chelles* the depoſition of S. *Bathildes* (or *Baldchild*) queen of *France*, who being an *Engliſh Saxon* by birth, and carried away young into *France*, was for the beauty of her ſoul and body, advanced from the condition of a ſervant, to be the conſort of king *Clouis* II. to whom ſhe brought forth three ſons, all ſucceſſively kings of *France*, *Clotaire*, *Childeric*, and *Thierry*; and during their minority governed the kingdom with great wiſdom, juſtice and religion, ever guiding herſelf by the counſel of the moſt eminent in ſanctity, amongſt the biſhops. She founded the famous abbeys, of *Corby* for religious men; and of *Chelles* for religious women; in which latter many noble *Engliſh* virgins, in the infancy of our *Saxon* church, conſecrated themſelves ſpouſes to Jeſus Chriſt. S. *Bede* l. 3. c. 8. In this monaſtery alſo the holy queen herſelf as ſoon as her eldeſt ſon came to age, quitting the world, and all that the world is fond of, took up the ſweet yoke of religious obedience and humility, and there at length ended her days in ſanctity, anno 680. Her body was found uncorrupt, above a century after her death. She has a place both in the *Sarum* and *York* calendars *Jan.* 30. Some part of her relicks was kept in the monaſtery of *Rumſey* in *Hampſhire*. *Saxon Manuſcript,* of the burying places of the *Engliſh* ſaints.

Jan. 28. At *Coldingham* in the marches of *Scotland*, the commemoration of holy *Adamnan* an illuſtrious penitent, who touched with remorſe for a ſin committed in his youth condemned himſelf to ſuch a perpetual penance, as to eat but on two days in the week; and to spend both night and day, in prayers and penitential tears. God was pleased to reveal to him the judgment by fire which consumed that monastery, anno 686, in punishment of their irregularities. S. *Bede*, l. 4. c. 25.

Jan. 29. At *Glastenbury*, the festivity of S. *Gildas* confessor, surnamed the *Elder* and the *Albanian* from being born in *North Britain*: who after opening publick schools, for training up saints, both in *Britain* and *Ireland* (where he regulated the liturgy, and was honoured like a second S. *Patrick*) and illustrating both kingdoms with his wisdom and sanctity; retired to *Avallon*, now *Glastenbury*; and there after some years of an eremitical life reposed in our Lord, anno 512. *Usher's* Antiquities. Also at *Ruy* in *Little Britain* the deposition of S. *Gildas* the *Younger* surnamed *Badonicus*, disciple of S. *Iltutus*; and schoolfellow of S. *Samson* and S. *Paul de Leon*, illustrious for his learning and holiness of life, and his zealous labours in God's service. He passed over into *Little Britain*, and there became an hermite in an island called *Horata:* but many disciples resorting to him, he went over to the mountain of *Rewys* or *Ruy*, and there founded in their favour a famous monastery, afterwards from him called S. *Gildas's*. In the neighbourhood of which, he made himself a little oratory, where he devoted his solitary hours to divine love, till he was called to a happy eternity, anno 570. He is honoured as patron in the diocese of *Vannes* in *Little Britain*. In *Scotland* the festivity of S. *Makwolok* bishop,
honoured

honoured in the *Scottish* breviaries; where his happy death is marked anno 720.

Jan. 30. In *North Britain* the commemoration of holy *Mailoc*, brother to S. *Gildas*, the *Albanian*; a man excellently instructed in the divine letters: who leaving his father's house and all his worldly pretensions, built a monastery in a place called *Luihes*, where he lived and died in great sanctity. Also the commemoration of two other brothers of the same S. *Gildas*, *Egreas* and *Alloecus*; who with their sister *Peteona*, in like manner left the world, and choosing a retired place, in the furthest extremity of that country, built themseves separate oratories, where by watching, fasting and fervent prayer, they continually tended towards their heavenly home; till they were called at last to the joys of the Lord, some time in the sixth century. [See the acts of S. *Gildas*, published from an ancient manuscript, by *John de Bosco*.] Also in *Scotland*, the deposition of S. *Macglastian* bishop, who went to our Lord anno 814. Also in the abbey of *Fulden* in *Germany*, the deposition of S. *Amnichade* an *Irish* monk; who lived there for many years a recluse, immured between four walls; in the exercises of continual prayer and penance. Obiit anno 1043.

Jan. 31. In *Scotland* the festivity of S. *Modoch* bishop, who has a place this day in the *Aberdeen* breviary. Also at *Ferne* in the province of *Leinster* in *Ireland*, the feast of S. *Ædan* alias *Maidoc* bishop: a child of prayer; and trained up from his youth, by the great S. *David*

David of *Menevia*, in monastick discipline, and all christian perfection. He afterwards founded divers churches and monasteries in *Ireland*, and imparted to innumerable souls the lessons of perfection, he had learnt from so excellent a master. His chiefest foundation was that of *Ferne*, where he was both abbat and bishop. He departed to our Lord in a good old age, anno 632. *Usher*.

FEBRUARY.

Feb. 1. AT *Kildare* in *Ireland* the deposition of S. *Brigide* or *Bride* virgin and abbess: whose extraordinary sanctity and miracles have made her name renowned; not only in all our *British* churches, but in the whole church of Christ. Her feast is set down, on this day in the *Sarum*, *York*, and *Aberdeen* calendars, and in the *Roman* Martyrology; where also notice is taken, that when (at the time of her consecrating herself to God) she bowed down her head to kiss the dry wood, at the foot of the altar, it immediately grew green, in token of her purity. She gave a rule to religious virgins, which was followed afterwards by most part of the nuns of *Ireland*. She exchanged her mortal life for a happy immortality anno 523. Also at *Kildare* the deposition of the holy abbess *Darlugdacha*, the favourite disciple, and successor of S. *Brigide*, in the government of the monastery; who according to the prediction of the saint, was associated with her in the heavenly Paradise, on that very day twelve-month, after the death of her blessed mother.

Feb. 2. At *Canterbury* the deposition of S. *Law-*

Lawrence, the second archbishop of that see. He was a disciple of S. *Gregory* the Great, and next to S. *Augustin* the chiefest of those apostolical missionaries, who brought the light of faith to the *English* nation; and by their doctrine, sanctity and miracles brought over many thousands to Christ. He succeeded S. *Augustin* in the archiepiscopal see, and strenuously laboured, says S. *Bede*, l. 2. c. 4. 'to advance the foundations of the church, which he had seen so gloriously laid; and strove to bring this spiritual edifice to its full perfection; as well by his frequent and holy exhortations, as by the continual examples of his godly works, &c.' He converted king *Eadbald*, with his people, to the faith of Christ, and to a life worthy of christian piety; and not long after was called to receive the reward of his labours, *Feb.* 2, anno 619. Also at *Kildare* in *Ireland* the commemoration of B. *Conlaeth* first bishop of that city; illustrious for his sanctity and miracles: whom S. *Brigide* called out of his solitude, to be the director and father of the religious men, who embraced her institute.

Feb. 3. At *Hanbury* in *Huntingtonshire*, the deposition of S. *Wereburge* virgin and abbess, daughter to *Wulfhere* king of the *Mercians* by his queen S. *Ermenilda*: and nearly allied to many great saints. She consecrated herself, when very young, to Christ the spouse of virgins, in the monastery of *Ely*, founded by her aunt, S. *Audry*: and after arriving here at great perfection; she founded for herself with the help of her uncle king *Ethelred*, the monasteries of *Wedun*, *Trickingham* and *Hanbury*; and in them trained

trained up many holy virgins, in the ways of perfect purity, and divine love. She died towards the close of the seventh century, and was buried at *Hanbury:* from whence her body was afterwards translated to *Chester:* the cathedral of which city is dedicated to God in her name. Also in the same province of *Mercia*, the commemoration of a latter S. *Wereburge*, queen and abbess: who after the death of her husband king *Ceolred* (anno 716) retiring into a monastery; there like the holy widow *Anna* the prophetess, for the space of sixty-five years, constantly attended in the temple of God, serving night and day, with fasting and prayer, till her happy death, anno 782. *Hoveden.* This is also the day of S. *Blasius* bishop and martyr: whose relicks were brought from *Rome*, by holy *Plegmund* archbishop; and enshrined in the cathedral of *Canterbury.*

Feb. 4. At *Sempringham* in *Lincolnshire* the festivity of S. *Gilbert* confessor, founder of the religious order of the *Gilbertins*; who formerly had many monasteries in these kingdoms. He lived to be above one hundred years old; pursuing to the end the saint-like course of life, which he had entred upon in his youth. Obiit anno 1190, and was renowned for miracles, both alive and dead. See an abstract of his life in *Dugdale's Monasticon.* Also at *Rosneth*, near *Dunbarton*, in *Scotland*, the festivity of S. *Modan* abbat, honoured on this day in the *Aberdeen* breviary; and of his brother S. *Medan* or *Midan* confessor. Also in the territory of *Cambray*, the martyrdom of S. *Luitphard*, or *Liephard*,

phard, a *British* prelate, who returning from a pilgrimage he had made to *Rome*, was slain by certain *Pagan* robbers, in a wood near *Cambray* anno 642. His relicks are kept in the abbey of *Hannaw* in the same diocese.

Feb. 5. In the territory of *Glastenbury*, the passion of S. *Indractus* martyr, son to one of the kings of *Ireland:* who leaving his country and friends, came over into *Britain*; and there in the neighbourhood of *Glastenbury*, led a solitary life, in great abstinence and continual prayer, with seven other companions. Where at length they were all murdered, by some wicked men, in hopes of meeting with a booty. Their bodies, which the murderers had cast into a deep pit, were discovered by a light from heaven, and translated to the church of *Glastenbury*, in the days of king *Ina*: where their festivity was formerly kept on this day. W. *Malmesbury.* Also in *Cornwall* the commemoration of S. *Probus* confessor, in whose name a collegiate church was there formerly dedicated. See *Brown Willis Mitred Abbeys*, vol. 2. and *Tanner's Notitia Monastica*, p. 69.

Feb. 6. At *Ardachadh* in the county of *Longford* in *Ireland* the festivity of S. *Mel*, first bishop of that see, to which he was consecrated by his uncle S. *Patrick*. Where after a most saintly life, he reposed in our Lord anno 466. Also in *Ireland* the commemoration of the saints *Melchu*, *Munis* and *Rioch*, all *Britons* by birth, brothers of S. *Mel*, nephews of S. *Patrick*, and his coadjutors in his apostolical labours in *Ireland*.

land. Also the commemoration of S. *Macalleus* bishop and confessor, who gave the sacred veil to S. *Brigide*, and her companions, and was illustrious for his sanctity, in the fifth century.

Feb. 7. At *London* the passion of S. *Augulus*, bishop and martyr, who suffered under *Diocletian.* At *Lucca* in *Italy*, the deposition of S. *Richard* king and confessor, whose tomb has been illustrated by many miracles. He was father to the saints *Willibald*, and *Winibald*, and the virgin S. *Walburga.* In *Scotland* the festivity of S. *Ronan* bishop.

Feb. 8. At *Peronne* in *Picardy*, the festivity of S. *Meldan* an *Irish* bishop and confessor, honoured as patron of that town; where his relicks were deposited by S. *Fursey.* Also in *Ireland* the commemoration of S. *Bean* bishop and confessor. Of these two saints there is ample mention in the life and visions of S. *Fursey :* by whom, they were seen in glory; and to whom, they gave excellent lessons of life, recorded in his ancient acts. At *Stening* in *Sussex* the deposition of S. *Cuthman* confessor; whose burying place is mark'd in the ancient *Saxon* Manuscript, at *Stening*, and whose church in that borough is mentioned in *Tanner's Notitia*, p. 550.

Feb. 9. At *Landaff* the festivity of S. *Theliau*, second bishop of that see, and principal patron of that diocese; whom the *Welch* for the eminence of his learning and sanctity call the *Great Theliau.* He flourished in the sixth century; and had many disciples illustrious for their learning

BRITISH PIETY. 35

ing and sanctity: amongst whom the *Landaff* register names S. *Hismael*, S. *Tyfhei*, S. *Oudoc*, *Lunapeius*, *Gurmaet*, *Cynmur*, &c. Also at *Kill-Attracta* in the territory of *Lugne* in *Connaught*, the festivity of S. *Attracta* virgin, who received the sacred veil from S. *Patrick*, and lived and died a great pattern of sanctity.

Feb. 10. At *Worcester*, the translation of S. *Wilfrid* the younger, disciple of S. *John* of *Beverley*, and his successor in the see of *York*; whose body was on this day translated by S. *Oswald* from *Rippon* to the cathedral of *Worcester*: together with the venerable remains of the holy abbats, *Tilbert*, *Boruin*, *Albert*, *Sigred*, and *Wilden*. Also at *Altmunster* in *Bavaria* the festivity of S. *Alto* abbat, a *Scot* by nation, who after leading for some time an eremitical life of wonderful sanctity in that neighbourhood, founded with the help of king *Pippin*, the abbey which takes name from him: where he is honoured to this day with a solemn office, on the ninth of *February*, as patron of that church.

Febr. 11. In *Brecknockshire* of *Wales* the commemoration of S. *Canocus* confessor, son to *Braghan* a *British* prince, who gave name to *Brecknock*. He was the eldest of four and twenty children, all saints, and honoured with churches, erected in their name in that part of *Britain*. S. *Canocus*, with some others of his brethren, went over to *Ireland*, and there founded divers churches and monasteries for propagating the kingdom of Christ. He flourished in the fifth century. Also at *Cluainfode*, in the
southern

southern parts of *Meath* in *Ireland*, the festivity of S. *Etchen* bishop, godson to S. *Brigide:* who after a most holy life, departed to our Lord, full of years and good works, *Febr.* 11. anno 577. Also at *Oxford* the translation of S. *Fridefwide* virgin, patroness of that city, celebrated on this day in the *Sarum* breviary.

Feb. 12. At *Lindisfarne*, now *Holy Island*, on the coast of *Northumberland*, the deposition of S. *Ethelwold* bishop of that see, formerly disciple of S. *Cuthbert:* Obiit anno 740. Also at the monastery of S. *Hilda* near *Whitby* in *Yorkshire*, the commemoration of holy *Cedmon* monk, who being a plain illiterate rustick, was suddenly favoured with a miraculous gift of divine poetry; which he wholly employed, to the praise and glory of the giver: to whom also he consecrated his whole life. S. *Bede*, l. 4. c. 24.

Feb. 13. At *Ely*, the deposition of S. *Ermenilda* queen, third abbess of that monastery, after her aunt S. *Audry*, and her mother S. *Sexburga*, who had also both of them been queens. She was wife to king *Wulfhere*, and after his death, consecrated herself to God, in the aforesaid monastery, of which her mother was then abbess. Where, both in obedience, and in superiority she shewed such great examples of all virtues; and both lived and died in so holy a manner, as to be enrolled by our ancestors amongst the saints. Also in *Glamorganshire* of *Wales* the commemoration of S. *Donat* confessor. At the abbey of *Fescamp* in *Normandy*, the festivity of S. *Barforarius* abbat: a native of *England*. Also in in *Ireland* the festivity of S. *Dominic* bishop, disciple of S. *David*.

Feb. 14. At *Dormundcaster* in the neighbourhood of *Peterborough*, the commemoration of S. *Kynedride* and S. *Kyneswide* virgins, daughters of king *Penda*, and sisters of *Peoda*, *Wulfhere*, *Ethelred* and *Merowald* kings of the *Mercians:* who from their tender years wholly dedicated themselves to divine love, in perfect continency, and all other observances of religion, and kept their glorious resolution to their old age. *William* of *Malmesbury*, l. 4. de pontif. Who adds that the younger [S. *Kyneswide*] was also so happy as to induce the young king *Offa*, the *East Saxon*, to whom she had, against her will, been promised in marriage, to embrace in like manner a single life; and even to leave his kingdom for the love of Christ. Which grace she is said to have obtained, by the intercession of the queen of virgins.

Feb. 15. At *Vexow* in *Swedeland* the deposition of S. *Sigefrid* bishop, apostle of *Swedeland*. He was archdeacon of *York*, and sent into *Sweden*, in the days of king *Edred*; where by his preaching and labours, he converted many thousands, and established the christian faith. He went to our Lord, anno 1002. Also in *Swedeland* the commemoration of the saints *Sunaman*, *Unaman* and *Wiaman*, nephews of S. *Sigefrid*, and coadjutors in his apostolical labours; in the course of which, they were slain by certain wicked men; and have deserved to be honoured among the martyrs.

Feb. 16. At *Lindisfarne*, in *Northumberland*, the commemoration of S. *Finan:* who from a monk of *Hy*, was made second bishop of that see; and greatly promoted the kingdom of Christ, amongst the northern *English*. He reposed in our Lord Sept. 10. anno 661. S. *Bede*, l. 3. c. 17, 21, &c. Also at *Lindisfarne* the commemoration of holy *Tuda*, fourth bishop of that see, whom our venerable historian (l. 3. c. 26.) calls *a good and religious man; and one who diligently taught all men, both by word and work, those things that appertain to faith and truth.* Obiit anno 664.

Feb. 17. In the monastery of *Cluain Ædnech* in *East-Meath*, the deposition of S. *Fintan* abbat, illustrious for sanctity and miracles. Also the commemoration of holy *Brandubh*, a bishop of the province of *Leinster*; who resigning his bishoprick, put himself under the discipline of S. *Fintan*; and as the saint had promised, was called to our Lord, soon after the decease of his holy abbat, anno 603. In *Ireland* also the commemoration of S. *Corpreus* bishop and S. *Dymma* confessor, who flourished in the fourth century.

Feb. 18. In the monastery of *Feppingham* amongst the Midland *English* the commemoration of holy *Diuma* first bishop of the *Mercians*, (ordained by S. *Finan* of *Lindisfarne*) who after bringing over, in a great measure, that province to the faith of Christ, reposed in our Lord anno 650. Also the commemoration of the holy priests *Adda*, and *Betti*, co-adjutors of bishop *Diuma*, in his apostolick labours, for

the

the conversion of the *Mercians*: as also of the holy prelates *Kellach*, *Trumbere*, and *Jaruman*; who succeeded in the bishoprick of the *Mercians*; and were all of them strenuous labourers, in the vineyard of the Lord. In *Ireland* the festivity of S. *Culan* bishop.

Feb. 19. In *Northumberland* the commemoration of S. *Balther*, priest of the church of *Lindisfarne*, and anchoret; who concluded a saintly life with a happy death, anno 756. Our historians relate, that *Analaf* the *Dane*, having burnt the church of this saint, anno 951, was thereupon struck by God, and carried off by a sudden death. Also the commemoration of S. *Bilfrid* goldsmith, afterwards anchoret of *Lindisfarne*; cotemporary with S. *Balther*. The bodies of these two saints, after the *Danish* devastations, were translated to *Durham*, anno 1040.

Feb. 20. In the isle of *Thanet*, the deposition of S. *Mildred* a royal virgin, and abbess of *Menstrey*, highly honoured by our ancestors for the eminence of her sanctity; as two churches in the city of *London*, and many other monuments abundantly testify. She flourished in the seventh century. In *Yorkshire* the commemoration of S. *Ronald*; of whose parish, see *Browne Willis*, *Mitred abbies*, vol. 2, p. 295. In *Ireland* the festivity of S. *Olcanus* bishop; a *Briton* by birth; and a disciple of S. *Patrick*; illustrious for his sanctity and miracles, *Usher*, p. 492.

Feb. 21. At *Haselborough* in *Dorsetshire* the commemoration of S. *Ulrick* or *Wulfrick* priest and recluse; who led a life of wonderful austerity and sanctity, in a little cell near adjoining to the church of that place, where also he was greatly favoured with spiritual gifts, and stupendous miracles. Obiit *Feb* 20, anno 1154. His life was faithfully written by *John* prior of *Ford* his cotemporary; followed by *Matthew Paris* and other historians. At *Athelinghay* the memory of the holy abbat, *John* the *Saxon*, preceptor to king *Aelfred*, and assistant in restoring both learning and piety, in the *English* nation.

Feb. 22. At the abbey of S. *Peter's* in *Ghent*, the festivity of S. *Gudwal* a *British* bishop, renowned for sanctity. Whose body was carried over to *France* at the time of the *Danish* devastations; and at length, on this day, translated to *Ghent* anno 959. In *Cornwall* the commemoration of S. *Allan* confessor, who formerly illustrated that province with his sanctity; and has left his name to the place, where his body reposes, in expectation of a happy resurrection.

Feb. 23. At *Wenlock* in *Shropshire* the festivity of S. *Milburge* virgin and abbess, marked on this day in the *Roman* Martyrology. She was daughter of *Merowald* a *Mercian* prince, by S. *Ermemberga*, of the blood royal of *Kent*; and was sister to S. *Mildred* and S. *Milwithe*. She was from her childhood an ardent lover of Christ; to whom also she presented many virgin spouses, whom she trained up for him, in her monastery of *Wenlock*. Her body was found in a vault of her church, anno 1101; i. e. above four hundred years after her death; and being taken up, up, yielded a moſt odoriferous exhalation, which perfumed the whole church; and was the inſtrument of God, for the working of many great miracles; as *William* of *Malmeſbury*, who wrote about the ſame time, has left upon record, l. 4, *de Pontif.*

Feb. 24. At *Canterbury* the depoſition of S. *Ethelbert*, the firſt chriſtian king of the *Engliſh* nation; renowned for his royal munificence, and love of religion; who after a life worthy of a truly chriſtian prince, exchanged his earthly diadem for a heavenly crown, anno 616, and was buried in the church of the monaſtery of S. *Peter* and S. *Paul*, vulgò S. *Auſtin's*, which he had founded. The body of his devout queen *Berta* was buried in the ſame church near her royal conſort. At *Canterbury* alſo the commemoration of the holy prelate *Lethardus*, ſpiritual director of queen *Berta*, who was buried in the ſame church, and honoured by our forefathers amongſt the ſaints. *William* of *Malmeſbury de Pontif.* l. 1.

Feb. 25. At *Faremoutier* in *Brie* the commemoration of S. *Ercongote* virgin, daughter of *Ercombert* the religious king of *Kent*, by S. *Sexburga* his wife, and ſiſter to S. *Ermenilda*. Whoſe life was ſo eminently holy; as to have left behind her, in that famous monaſtery, a name which no length of time can ever obliterate. She was illuſtrious for miracles, both in her life, and at her death; at which time, a heavenly harmony was heard by the religious of that ſame community; and an exceeding great light was

ſeen

seen descending from heaven, and conducting that holy soul, now set loose from the prison of the body, to the eternal joys of her heavenly home. S. *Bede*, l. 3. c. 6. At *Fescamp* in *Normandy* the festivity of S. *Frothmund* an *Englishman*, honoured as a martyr in the abbey of *Fescamp*.

Feb. 26. At *Eychstadt* in *Germany* the festivity of S. *Walburga* virgin and abbess; daughter to the holy prince S. *Richard*, and sister to SS. *Willibald*, and *Winibald*. She was one of the chiefest of those sacred virgins, which were sent over from *England*, at the desire of S. *Boniface* apostle of *Germany*, to promote the kingdom of Christ amongst those of their sex. She was made abbess of *Heideinheim* in *Bavaria*: and after a most saintly life, passed to a happy immortality, *Feb.* 24. anno 779. Her relicks now repose in the cathedral of *Eychstadt*, to which city they were translated eighty years after her death: where also a certain oily liquor is said to distill from them, found to be a sovereign remedy for all diseases. Many churches have been erected in her honour, both in the higher and lower *German*; and her festival, in divers places, is ordered to be observed, as a holiday of obligation.

Feb. 27. At S. *Decombes* in *Somersetshire* the commemoration of S. *Decuman*, who leading there an eremitical life, was slain by a child of *Belial*, and honoured after his death, amongst the martyrs. Also in the isle of *Barry*, near the coast of *Glamorganshire*, the commemoration

tion of S. *Baruck* a hermit renowned for sanctity; from whom that island took its name. *Cambden.*

Feb. 28. At *Worcester* the deposition of S. *Oswald* bishop of that see, and archbishop of *York.* He was one of the principal restorers of ecclesiastical and monastical discipline in *England*, and of christian piety in general; which had suffered very much, by occasion of the pagan *Danes.* His whole life was dedicated to the promoting the glory of God, and the salvation of his neighbour; and in pronouncing those words on his knees, *Glory be to the Father,* &c. he gave up his spirit into the hands of Christ (*Febr.* 29 anno 992) expiring at the feet of the poor, which according to his custom he had just then been washing. He was buried in the church of S. *Mary* at *Worcester,* which he himself had built: where he was illustrated by divers miracles.

MARCH.

March 1. AT *Menevia*, the festivity of S. *David* archbishop, patron of *Wales*; who was in his life time *a burning and a shining light* to *Great Britain.* Before he was bishop, he is said to have founded twelve monasteries; to which he gave an excellent rule, agreeable to the institutes of the ancient fathers. After he was bishop, he purged *Britain* from all the relicks of the *Pelagian* heresy; and greatly contributed to the establishing christian piety, and all good discipline, in the churches both

of

of *Britain*, and of *Ireland*; as well by himself, as by the many saints of both nations, whom he had for his disciples. He went to our Lord anno 544. Also the festivity of S. *Swibert the Elder*, bishop and apostle of the *Frisons* and *Boructuarians*; (*Bede* l. 5. c. 11. 12.) As likewise of S. *Swibert the Younger*, the first bishop of *Werden*; and one of those apostolical preachers of the *English* nation, who were the fathers and founders of the churches of Christ amongst the *Germans*. In *North Britain*, the festivity of S. *Marnan* bishop, and of S. *Minnan* archdeacon; who are commemorated on this day, in the *Aberdeen* breviary.

March 2. At *Litchfield* the deposition of S. *Chad* bishop, renowned for his extraordinary sanctity. He was a disciple of the great S. *Aidan* of *Lindisfarne*; and partly under his discipline, and partly in the company of S. *Egbert* and other holy solitaries, to whom he associated himself in *Ireland* in the study of true wisdom, he learnt with great perfection the science of the saints. Returning into *England*, he was first made abbat of *Lestingham*; and then consecrated bishop of *York*: which see after some years he humbly resigned to S. *Wilfrid*; but soon after was obliged by S. *Theodore* of *Canterbury* (who was charmed with his humility) to take upon him the charge of the whole province of *Mercia* and *Lindsey*, fixing his bishop's see at *Litchfield*. 'As soon as he was made bishop, he zealously devoted himself says S. *Bede*, to the ecclesiastical truth and purity; applying himself to humility, mortification, and spiritual lectures;

visiting

visiting his diocese (which was vastly extended) after the manner of the apostles on foot; preaching the gospel, and seeking after souls, not only in towns, castles, and villages, but even in the meanest hutts, and in the very fields: for he was a true follower of S. *Aidan*; and endeavoured to instruct his people, with the like zeal, and by the same methods and conduct, as he had learnt from his, and his brother *Cedd's* example.' He was called to the eternal reward of his labours *March* 2, anno 673; to which he was invited, and conducted by a company of heavenly spirits; as may be seen in our venerable historian, l. 4. c. 2, 3. Also in *South Wales* the festivity of S. *Nonna*, mother of S. *David*, and spiritual mother of many religious women. There is a church in the neighbourhood of S. *Davids*, which still bears her name; and is commonly called S. *Nones*. Likewise in the lower *Germany* the festivity of S. *Willeick* confessor; who went over from *England* to preach the gospel in those countries; and died there renowned for sanctity.

March 3. In *Little Britain* the deposition of S. *Wimvaloc* abbat of *Tauracum*, whose wonderful sanctity has made his name illustrious, not only in *Britain*, where he was born; but also in *France* and *Flanders*. His relicks are kept in the church of the famous abbey of S. *Peter* in *Ghent*. Also in *South Wales* the festivity of S. *Lily* confessor, the beloved disciple and companion of S. *David*.

March 4. In *Scotland* the festivity of S. *Adrian* bishop of S. *Andrews*, and his companions, martyred by the *Danes* in the isle of *May* anno 874. At *Litchfield* the commemoration of holy *Owini* confessor, who from *Major Domo* to the holy queen S. *Audry*, became an humble and laborious lay-brother, in the monastery of *Lestingham*; and made such progress in sanctity, as to be the favourite disciple of S. *Chad*, whom he followed to *Litchfield*; where he was found worthy to hear that heavenly harmony by which S. *Chad* was invited to his eternal home. S. *Bede* l. iv. c. 3.

March 5. In *Cornwall* the festivity of S *Piran* hermit, illustrious for miracles. He is supposed to be the same as is honoured in *Ireland*, under the name of *Kiaran*, or *Keran the Elder*, esteemed the most ancient saint of that nation, and therefore called by the *Irish* the father of the saints of *Ireland*. At *Sier-keran* in *Ireland* the commemoration of S. *Carthac* the elder, disciple and successor of S. *Kiaran*, both as abbat and bishop. Likewise in *Cornwall* the commemoration of divers saints, natives of *Ireland*, who to withdraw themselves further off from their worldly friends and acquaintance, and to consecrate the days of their mortality, in a more perfect manner, to the exercises of a religious life; came over into *Cornwall*; and there lived and died in so great sanctity; as to have left their names to the places, where their bodies lie in expectation of a glorious resurrection. These were S. *Mewan*, S. *Erben*, S. *Eval*, S. *Wenn*, S. *Enedor*, &c. &c.

March 6. In the monastery of *Weremouth* in the bishoprick of *Durham* the deposition of holy *Easterwin* abbat, kinsman and disciple of S. *Bennet Biscop*: whose sanctity is attested by his scholar S. *Bede* in his lives of the first abbats of *Weremouth* and *Jarrow*. At *Dormundcaster* near *Peterborough* the festivity of S. *Kynebůrge*, queen and abbess, daughter to *Penda* king of the *Mercians*, and sometime wife to *Alchfrid* king of the *Northumbrians*. She founded the famous monastery of *Dormundcaster*, called from her *Kyneburgecaster*, where also she was made abbess; and after a most saintly life, departed to our Lord, in the latter part of the seventh century. In *Scotland* the festivity of S. *Baldred* bishop and confessor, honoured on this day in the *Scottish* calendars.

March 7. At *Seckingen* on the borders of *Switzerland* the commemoration of S. *Fredolin* abbat, a *Scotsman* by birth, who founded the monastery of that place, in the sixth century; and is there honoured amongst the saints. In the county of *Westmeath* in *Ireland*, the commemoration of S. *Corpreus* bishop of *Cluain micnois*, illustrious for sanctity in the ninth century. In the monastery of *Wazor* in the territory of *Liege*, the festivity of S. *Kadroe* abbat, companion of S. *Malcallan*, who went to our Lord in the tenth century; and for his extraordinary virtues, was enrolled after his death amongst the saints. At *Assisium* in *Italy* the memory of that venerable servant of God, *Frier William* surnamed *Anglicus* or the *Englishman*, one of the first companions and disciples of S. *Francis*; who was

so

so eminent for the sanctity of his life, and for the miracles, which God wrought by him, both before, and after his death, that he seemed to vie with, or even to out-do his holy father himself. He passed to a better life anno 1232.

March 8. At *Dummock* in *Suffolk*, the deposition of S. *Felix* bishop, and apostle of the *East-Angles*, of whom S. *Bede* l. 2. c. 15. writes that ' with the help of king *Sigebert* (whom he had converted to Christ) he founded churches, monasteries and schools; and in a short time quite changed the face of that nation: and according to the *happy* omen of his name (for *Felix* signifies *happy*) brought over the whole province from its former *infelicity* and iniquity, to the true faith, to the works of christian justice, and to the rewards of eternal *felicity*.' He entered into the joy of his Lord anno 650. His body after the *Danish* devastations was translated to the abbey of *Ramsey* in *Huntingtonshire*. In *Ireland* the festivity of S. *Senan* bishop, disciple of S. *David*; and founder of the famous monastery of *Inys-Cathaigh*, in the sixth century. In *Scotland* the festivity of S. *Duthacus* bishop of *Ross*: who was illustrious for miracles, both alive and dead. Obiit anno 1249.

March 9. At *York* the commemoration of blessed *Bosa* bishop of that see, *a man of great sanctity, and humility*, says S. *Bede* l. 5. c. 3. He was the first of five prelates, all men of *singular merit and sanctity*, that were trained up in the monastery of S. *Hilda*: as we learn from the same venerable historian, l. 4. c. 23. The other

other four were S. *John of Beverley*, *Hedda*, *Ostfor* and *Wilfrid* the younger. S. *Bosa* went to our Lord anno 705.

March 10. In *Scotland* the deposition of S. *Kessog* or *Mackessog* bishop, who flourished in the seventh century; and was illustrious for sanctity and miracles. His relicks formerly reposed in a church dedicated to God in his name at a place called *Lus*. At *Wissenaken* near *Tillemont* in the *Netherlands*, the festivity of S. *Hemelin* a *Scottish* priest, who returning from a pilgrimage he had made to *Rome*, departed this life at the place above-named; our Lord manifesting his sanctity by many miracles.

March 11. In the monastery of *Govane*, near the river *Cluyd* in *Scotland*, the festivity of S. *Constantine* martyr, a *British* prince, who after the death of his queen, being disgusted with the world, resigned his dominions to his son, and privately withdrew himself into *Ireland*; where unknown to any he served for some time as a lay-brother in the monastery of S. *Carthag* at *Rathene*; till being discovered, and fully instructed in the Holy Scriptures, he was found worthy to be promoted to the priesthood; and was sent over to preach the faith amongst the *Picts*: many of whom he converted to Christ, especially in the land of *Kentire*; till at length he met with the crown of martyrdom, towards the end of the sixth century; and was buried in the monastery which he himself had established at *Govane*. In *Ireland* the festivity of S. *Ængus* surnamed *Kele De* or the *worshipper of God*, a pre-

prelate illustrious for his learning and sanctity in the ninth century.

March 12. The festivity of S. *Gregory the Great*, bishop of *Rome*: whose charity and zeal for the conversion of our ancestors, which he brought about by the means of the missionaries he sent over into *Britain*, has procured him the glorious title of *Apostle of England*. Also in *Little Britain* the festivity of S. *Paul* bishop and confessor: who being born in *Great Britain* of noble parentage, retired very early from the world, and embraced a most saint-like life, in his own country: where also he was advanced to holy orders. Afterwards passing over into *Little Britain*, and leading there an eremitical life, he was at length drawn out of his solitude, and compelled to accept of the bishoprick of *Oxism*, now from him called S. *Paul de Leon*. He departed to our Lord full of days, and virtues, anno 579. In *Ireland* the festivity of S. *Murus* or *Muranus* abbat of *Fathene*, five miles from *Derry*, famous for sanctity, in the seventh century.

March 13. At *Mayo* in *Ireland* the festivity of S. *Gerald* an *English Saxon*, abbat of the monastery founded there by S. *Colman* of *Lindisfarne* for the *English* nation, and afterwards bishop of *Mayo*: where there is to this day a church dedicated to God in his name. In this monastery of S. *Gerald*, our Lord was served with so great perfection, that according to ancient *Irish* records, quoted by *Usher*, there flourished here of old no fewer than one hundred
English

English Saxon faints. S. *Gerald* departed to our Lord anno 732. Alſo in *Ireland* the commemoration of the holy men *Ballon*, *Biriket*, and *Hubriton*, brothers of S. *Gerald*, and cloſe imitators of his virtues: as alſo of holy *Segretia* virgin, their ſiſter, abbeſs of a religious community of ſacred virgins founded by S. *Gerald*; and honoured in *Ireland* amongſt the ſaints. In *Scotland* the feſtivity of S. *Kennocha* virgin, honoured this day in the *Aberdeen* breviary. She went to our Lord anno 1007; and repoſes as to her mortal remains in the church at *Kyle*, formerly called S. *Kinnocks*.

March 14. In *Ireland* the commemoration of S. *Mochoemoc* or *Pulcherius* abbat, diſciple of the great S. *Comgall*, and very illuſtrious for ſanctity. Obiit anno 655. At *Abernethi* in *Scotland*, the memory of S. *Brigide* virgin and abbeſs: whoſe relicks were honoured of old in the collegiate church of that place. The *Scots* ſuppoſe this ſaint to have been the ſame as the great S. *Brigide*, honoured *Feb.* 1. But the *Iriſh* make them two different ſaints. See *Uſher* p. 461.

March 15. The feſtivity of S. *Ariſtobulus* diſciple of the apoſtles; who as ſome writers affirm, was ſent by S. *Barnabas* to preach the faith of Chriſt in *Britain*. At *Canterbury* the commemoration of S. *Salvius* or *Selvius* biſhop, and of S. *Woolgam* confeſſor, whoſe bodies were anciently enſhrined in the cathedral of that city: as alſo of the holy virgin *Siburgis*, who by reaſon of the eminence of her ſanctity, was depoſited

sited by S. *Dustan* in the same church: See *Dart's* cathedral of *Canterbury*.

March 16. In *North Wales* the commemoration of S. *Deifer* hermit, illustrious for sanctity, amongst the ancient *Britons*. He was cotemporary with S. *Wenefride*, and visited by her. In *Scotland* the festivity of S. *Kyrinus* surnamed *Boniface* bishop of *Ross*; who by his preaching and miracles propagated the kingdom of Christ in *North Britain*, in the seventh century. In *Ireland* the festivity of S. *Finian* abbat, surnamed the *Leper*: who by a long course of sufferings, endured with an unwearied patience, and a perfect conformity to the will of God, was prepared for the kingdom of heaven; which he went to take possession of, anno 615.

March 17. The festivity of S. *Patrick* bishop, and apostle of the *Irish* nation; a great part of which he converted to the christian faith, by his preaching; and by the sanctity of his life; as well as by the great signs and wonders, which he wrought amongst them. He went to our Lord towards the latter end of the fifth century. Also the commemoration of many holy prelates, partly *Britons*, and partly of other nations, assistants of S. *Patrick* in his apostolical labours; men full of the Spirit of God, and fathers and founders of the churches of *Ireland*. These in an ancient catalogue of the saints of that island published in *Usher's Antiquities*, p. 473. make up the *first Class* of *Irish* saints: and are said to have been no fewer in number than three hundred and fifty, all men of extraordinary sanctity. The saints of the *second Class* came after the death of S. *Patrick*; and were also men of eminent holiness; being about three hundred in number, some few of them bishops, the rest priests. These flourished in the sixth century, and greatly propagated both monastick discipline, and sacred learning, amongst the *Irish*; having been themselves instructed by *British* masters; particularly by S. *David of Menevia*, S. *Gildas*, and S. *Docus*. The saints of the *third Class* succeeded these; and flourished during four reigns, down to the time of the great pestilence (anno 664): These were about one hundred in number, for the most part priests, living in desarts, on roots and herbs; and leading most mortified and abstracted lives. So far the catalogue.

March 18. The festivity of S. *Edward* king and martyr, who being killed by the treachery of his step-mother anno 979 was illustrated by many miracles. His day was appointed to be kept holy throughout *England*, in a synod held at *Winchester*, in the reign of king *Canutus*. In *Ireland* the commemoration of S. *Lactin* abbat, illustrious for sanctity, who departed to our Lord anno 622.

March 19. At *Derby* the festivity of S. *Alchmund* martyr, son of *Alred* king of the *Northern English*; who was drove into banishment by his subjects, anno 774. The young prince following his father, on this occasion, into the land of the *Picts*, made such good use of his temporal afflictions, as to purchase an eternal crown. Returning afterwards into his native country, he

he was slain by orders of king *Eardulf*, about the year 800. Many miracles were wrought at his tomb; so that his body was taken up, and translated to *Derby*: where a magnificent church was built in his honour, called to this day the church of S. *Alchmund*; which was formerly much resorted to by the people of the *North*; and illustrious on account of the miracles wrought there. There is also a church, erected in his name in the town of *Shrewsbury*.

March 20. At *Durham* the festivity of S. *Cuthbert* bishop of *Lindisfarne*, patron or tutelar saint of the bishoprick of *Durham*. He was divinely called, to a saint-like life, from a child, by the voice of a child: and was afterwards determined to leave the world, and become a monk; by a vision, in which he saw the soul of S. *Aidan* the first bishop of *Lindisfarne*, at the time of his death, carried up to heaven by angels. His admirable virtues and stupendous miracles are recorded by St. *Bede*, who has wrote his life both in prose, and in verse.

March 21. In the isle of *Aran* the festivity of S. *Enda* abbat, illustrious amongst the *Irish* saints, and father, or master of many saints. He built divers churches and monasteries in that island: the chief of which, is from him called *Kill-Enda* to this day: he flourished in the beginning of the sixth century. Also in the same Island, the commemoration of many holy solitaries, disciples and followers of S. *Enda*; who by the eminence of their sanctity, have given to that island the appellation of *Aran of the saints*.

Info-

Insomuch that in the church-yard of *Teglath-Enda*, in which is the sepulchre of that holy abbat; no fewer than one hundred and twenty saints are said to repose, in expectation of a happy resurrection. In *Ireland* the commemoration of S. *Fanchea* a noble virgin abbess of *Kill-aine* at the foot of mount *Bregh*, in the confines of *Meath*. She was sister to S. *Enda*, and by her pious exhortations, first reclaimed him from a worldly to a religious life. See the acts of S. *Enda* in the collections of F. *Colgan*.

March 22. In the neighbourhood of *Carlisle*, the commemoration of the man of God *Herebert* priest, united in a most holy band of friendship with the great S. *Cuthbert*; and called on the same day with him, as the saint had foretold, to a happy eternity. He led an eremitical life in a little island encompassed by the lake, from which the river *Darwent* flows: but frequently visited S. *Cuthbert*, to receive from him the lessons of eternal life and truth, by which he was more and more inflamed with divine love, and with a longing desire after a happy union with his sovereign good: to which he was at length admitted (after his soul had been duly purged, and prepared for it, by the sufferings of a long and painful illness) *March* 20 anno 687. S. *Bede*, l. 4. c. 29. On this day is also commemorated in *Wilson*'s martyrology *Hamund* bishop of *Sherborn*, slain by the *Danes* anno 871.

March 23. In the isle of *Farne*, on the coast of *Northumberland*, the happy death of S. *Edilwald*

wald priest and hermit: who after the death of the man of God *Cuthbert*, succeeded him in the exercises of a solitary life, in his lonesome mansion in that desert. To whose extraordinary sanctity S. *Bede* gives ample testimony. l. 5. c. 1.

March 24. At the monastery of *Barking* in *Essex*, the festivity of S. *Hildelid* virgin and abbess. She was one of the first *English* virgins, who going abroad before we had many nunneries here, consecrated herself in *France* a spouse to Christ: from whence she was invited over by S. *Earkonwald*, to instruct and direct his sister S. *Ethelburga* (for whom he had founded the monastery of *Barking*) in the holy discipline of a religious life. To whom she also succeeded in quality of abbess; and for many years had the superintendency of that saint-like community. S. *Bede* l. 4. c. 10. Amongst other saints whom she trained up to religious perfection, was S. *Cuthburga* sister to king *Ina*; who afterwards founded the famous monastery of *Winburn* in *Dorsetshire*; and there established that excellent discipline, which she had learnt from so great a mistress; and which from that family of saints, was afterwards propagated through *Germany*, by S. *Lioba* and her companions. At *Barking* also the commemoration of many holy nuns slain by the *Danes* in the ninth century. At *Canterbury* the deposition of the holy archbishop *Lanfrank*, eminent for his learning and piety. In *Ireland* the deposition of S. *Domangart* bishop, illustrious amongst the ancient *Irish* saints.

March 25. The *Annunciation* of the blessed Virgin; and the *Incarnation* of the Son of God, for the redemption of all nations. At *Norwich* the passion of S. *William*, a boy of twelve years old, put to death in that city by the *Jews*, on *Good Friday*, 1144, in hatred of Christ, and the christian religion; and illustrated by divers miracles. There was also another child crucified by the *Jews*, in the same city, in hatred of Christ, anno 1235. At *Sherborn* the memory of the holy bishop *Alfwold*; who flourished in the eleventh century. *William of Malmesbury.* De Pontif.

March 26. In *Ireland* the festivity of S. *Cammin* abbat, who has a place in *Usher's Antiquities*, amongst the most celebrated saints of the *Irish* nation. He retired young from the world into the solitude of the isle of *Inish-Kealtair*; where there is still a church that bears his name, called *Tempul Cammin*. Here the fame of his sanctity brought him many disciples; for whom he built a famous monastery, which was held of old in great veneration by the *Irish*, by reason of the eminent holiness of its inhabitants. S. *Cammin* passed to a better life, about the year 653. At *Munster* the festivity of S. *Ludger* bishop, apostle of the *Saxons*: educated at *York*, under the famous *Alcuin*.

March 27. In *South Wales* the commemoration of S. *Hismael* bishop, illustrious for sanctity. He was a disciple of the great S. *Theliau* of *Landaff*, and was consecrated bishop by him. Also in *South Wales* the commemoration of S. *Tysbei*, another

another disciple of the same S. *Theliau:* honoured of old as a martyr, at *Pennalun.* These saints flourished in the sixth century. In the territory of *Kellock* in *Ireland* the festivity of S. *Kellen* alias *Mochelloc* confessor; who flourished with sanctity in the seventh century.

March 28. At *Coventry* the commemoration of S. *Osburga* virgin and abbess, patroness of that church: whose day by reason of her *frequent miracles* was ordered to be kept festival there. See *Dugdale's Warwickshire.* Also in *Yorkshire,* the commemoration of S. *Athilda,* or *Alkilda:* in whose name the collegiate church of *Middleham,* in that county, was formerly dedicated. See *Dugdale's Monasticon,* vol. 3. In *France* the deposition of S. *Stephen Harding* abbat of *Citeaux,* and principal author of the *Cistercian* institute. 'Tis also the day of the translation of S. *Fremund* martyr, much revered by our *Saxon* ancestors.

March 29. In *South Wales* the festivity of S. *Gundleus* prince of that province, and father of S. *Cadocus:* who retiring from the world, crowned a life of admirable continency and sanctity, with a most holy and happy death, towards the close of the fifth century. In *Scotland* the commemoration of the ancient *Culdees, Modoc* the elder, *Calan, Ferran, Ambian* and *Carnoc,* who are said to have flourished in *North Britain,* in the fourth century. *Hector Boeth.*

March 30. At *Rumsey* in *Hampshire* the commemoration of S. *Merwenna* virgin, first abbess
of

of the monastery founded there, by king *Edgar*, in honour of the blessed Virgin, and eminent for sanctity of life; in which also she trained up many holy virgins; and among the rest S. *Elfleda*. At *Werdt* in *Germany*, the deposition of S. *Patto* a *Scot*, bishop of that see in the eighth century. He succeeded S. *Swibert* in that bishoprick; and for his sanctity was highly esteemed by *Charlemagne*.

March 31. The translation of S. *Aldelm* abbat of *Malmesbury*, and first bishop of *Sherborn*, most illustrious for sanctity and learning in the seventh century. Also the commemoration of many holy martyrs, who suffered under the *Pagan Danes*, about the year 870; when laying *England* waste, they shewed a particular malice to all religious places and persons. At which time they destroyed amongst others the famous monasteries of *Bardney*, *Croiland*, *Peterborough* and *Ely*, putting all the monks and nuns to the sword. *Ingulphus*, &c.

APRIL.

April 1. AT *Rome* the commemoration of holy *Ina*, king of the *West Saxons*: who after a long and successful reign, and many acts of religious munificence, quitting the world took a journey to *Rome*, and there put on a religious habit, in which he made a holy end anno 727. In *Scotland* the festivity of blessed *Gilbert*, who from archdeacon of *Murray* was made bishop of *Cathness*: which see he administred, for twenty years, in so worthy and saint-like a manner,

manner, as to be honoured after his death amongſt the ſaints; with whom he has a place on this day in the *Aberdeen* breviary. Obiit anno 1240.

April 2. At S. *Ricquiers* in *Picardy* the commemoration of the ſaints *Caidoc* and *Adrian* two holy prieſts, natives of *Ireland:* who going over into the *Belgick Gaul*, in the reign of king *Dagobert*, to advance by their preaching the kingdom of Chriſt, met with very bad treatment from the rude barbarous people of that country; 'till they were reſcued out of their hands, by a noble Lord called *Richarius*, and were hoſpitably entertained by him. In recompence of which charity they preached to him and his, the word of life; by which, and by their ſaintly lives, they effectually perſuaded him to become a great penitent, and a great ſaint. They flouriſhed in the ſeventh century, and lye buried in the abbey of S. *Ricquier*. In *Ireland* the feſtivity of S. *Cuanus*, or *Mochua* abbat.

April 3. At *Chicheſter* in *Suſſex*, the depoſition of S. *Richard* biſhop of that ſee; a prelate of moſt admirable ſanctity; and an unbounded charity to the poor. He died to this world, to live for ever with his God, anno 1253; and by occaſion of his great miracles, was canonized by Pope *Urban* IV. nine years after his death. At *Faremoutier* in *Brie*, the feſtivity of S. *Fara* virgin and abbeſs, foundreſs of that famous monaſtery (which takes its name from her) in which many holy virgins of the *Engliſh* nation, in the earlieſt times of our chriſtianity, were happily

happily espoused to Christ; amongst which the most illustrious were S. *Sethird,* S. *Edilburga* and S. *Earcongota.*

April 4. At *Worcester* the memory of the holy prelate *Ostfor,* second bishop of that see, *a man of singular merit and sanctity.* S. Bede l. 4. c. 23. He was sometime disciple of the saints *Theodore* and *Adrian,* and trained up by them in all good learning, in their excellent school, in the company of *Tobias,* afterwards bishop of *Rochester,* and many other holy and learned men. In *Cornwall* the commemoration of S. *Guerir* confessor; near to whose church, S. *Neot* sometime led an eremitical life.

April 5. The festivity of S. *Vincent Ferrerius,* of the order of *Friers* preachers; who in the course of his apostolical progress through the greatest part of *Christendom,* illustrated also our *British* islands with his preaching and miracles. He flourished in the fifteenth century. In *Ireland* the deposition of S. *Tigernake,* bishop of *Clogher,* founder of the church of *Clunes:* who went to our Lord anno 550. Also in *Wales* in the monastery of S. *Davids,* in the vale of *Ross,* the memory of the holy abbat *Monennius,* by whom S. *Tigernake* was trained up in religious discipline. In *Scotland* also is honoured on this day in the *Aberdeen* breviary, a holy *Scottish* bishop of the name of *Tigernake,* said to have *entered into the joy of his Lord* anno 823.

April 6. At *Rome* the deposition of S. *Celestine* pope; who by the means of S. *Germanus*
delivered

delivered *Britain* from the *Pelagian* herefy, and fent S. *Palladius* to the *Scots*, and S. *Patrick* to the *Irifh*. In *Ireland* the feftivity of S. *Celfus*, or *Kellach*, archbifhop of *Armagh*, predeceffor to S. *Malachi*; and a ftrenuous labourer in bringing about a reformation of the difcipline of the church, and of the morals of the people, in that ifland. Obiit anno 1129.

April 7. In *Wales* the depofition of S. *Bernach* an ancient *Britifh* abbat, of admirable fanctity. In *Scotland* the feftivity of S. *Bercham* bifhop, honoured on this day in the *Scottifh* calendars, where alfo his death is marked anno 839. In *Ireland* the commemoration of S. *Congellus*, abbat of *Cambas*; in the fixth century. *Ufher ex Adamnano.*

April 8. In the monaftery of S. *Colum-kille* in the ifle of *Hy*, the commemoration of the holy abbat *Segenius*, difciple of that faint, who fent the great S. *Aidan* anno 634 for the converfion of the *Northern Englifh*. *Segenius* was the fourth abbat of that famous monaftery; and one of thofe faint-like men of whom S. *Bede* writes, l. 3. c. 4. fpeaking of S. *Colum-kille*, that he *left behind him fucceffors, renowned for much continency, or abftinence, for the love of God, and for regular difcipline:* men, as he fignifies c. 5. who taught no otherwife than they lived; and who neither loved nor cared for any thing of this world. In *Cornwall*, the commemoration of S. *Achebran*, patron of the church of *Lanachebran*. See *Tanner's Notitia Monaftica*, p. 66.

BRITISH PIETY. 63

April 9. At *Winchester* the commemoration of S. *Frithstane* bishop, a man of extraordinary sanctity. He voluntarily resigned his bishoprick, a year before his death, to give himself up to divine contemplation in solitude; and so passed to a happy eternity anno 933. At *Canterbury* the commemoration of the holy archbishop *Alfrick*, whose venerable remains were enshrined in the cathedral of that city. See *Dart*.

April 10. In *Swedeland* the passion of S. *Eskill* bishop and martyr. He was an *Englishman* by birth, a kinsman and disciple of S. *Sigefrid* the apostle of *Swedeland*; and a zealous preacher of the faith of Christ. He was stoned to death by the infidels on *Good Friday*, anno 1016: and by the miracles wrought at his tomb, converted many more than he had done in his life time. He was much honoured of old by the *Northern* nations; where his festivity was wont to be kept on the 12th of *June*. At *Paderborn* in *Germany* the memory of the man of God *Paternus*, a *Scot* by nation; who shut himself up between four walls in that city, and led there a life of great abstraction, and mortification, in the eleventh century.

April 11. In the isle of *Croyland* the festivity of S. *Guthlake* priest and hermit, renowned for sanctity and miracles. He first inhabited that desert; where in his honour was afterwards founded a famous monastery anno 719, by *Ethelbald* king of the *Mercians*; to whom he had foretold the kingdom. S. *Guthlake* went to our Lord anno 714. Also in *Croyland* the commemoration

moration of divers other saints; whose sepulchres were placed round the tomb of S. *Guthlake*, in the church of that monastery, before the *Danish* devastations: amongst whom were S. *Bettelm* his disciple, S. *Cissa* priest and hermit, S. *Egbert* priest, and S. *Tatwin* confessor. See *Ingulphus*, &c.

April 12. The commemoration of S. *Pega* virgin, sister of S. *Guthlake*, who by reason of her eminent virtues, was also after her death enrolled amongst the saints. In *France* the commemoration of holy *Mechthildis* a *Scottish* virgin of royal blood, who privately withdrawing herself, at the age of twenty, from her father's house, together with her younger brother *Alexander*, went beyond the seas; where *Alexander* became a lay brother, amongst the *Cistercians* in the diocese of *Laon*; whilst his sister made herself a little hut, in a village called *Lopion*, where she led a life of most admirable sanctity, maintaining herself by the labour of her hands; without asking or receiving alms from any one; and praying night and day. She went to our Lord about the year 1200, and was illustrious for miracles both alive and dead. See *Thomas Cantipratensis*, of the miracles of his own time.

April 13. In *Pembrokeshire* the deposition of the venerable servant of God *Caradoc* priest and hermit, who died in the sweet odour of sanctity anno 1124, after a most saintly life, and was buried in the cathedral of S. *David*: where his body was found many years after his death entire and uncorrupt. In *Scotland* the festivity of S. *Guinochus* bishop, who
flourished

flourished in the ninth century; and is commemorated on this day in the *Aberdeen* breviary. At *Hereford* the deposition of the holy bishop *Robert de Betun*; whose life full of great examples of all virtues, was written by his cotemporary *William* prior of *Lanthony*; abridged by *Harpsfield*, p. 379. Obiit anno 1148.

April 14. At *Glastenbury* the commemoration of holy *Ethelfleda*, a lady of the blood royal, who choosing for herself a dwelling-place in the neighbourhood of that church, there lived the life of a saint, under the conduct of S. *Dunstan*; and there died the death of a saint, about the middle of the tenth century. On this day is also commemorated the holy king *Ethelwolf*, renowned for his godliness, and religious munificence; who reposed in our Lord anno 857.

April 15. In *Wales* the commemoration of S. *Paternus* bishop and confessor, who with the bright rays of his sanctity illustrated both *Britain* and *France* in the sixth century. The place of his bishop's see in *Cardiganshire* was from him called S. *Patern's*; in *Welch*, Llan-Padernvaur, or the church of the great *Paternus*. In *Scotland* the festivity of S. *Mundus* abbat in *Argileshire* anno 962. In *Ireland* the festivity of S. *Rodan* abbat of *Lothra* in the county of *Tiperary*, anno 584.

April 16. The festivity of S. *Magnus* martyr, who suffered in the isles of *Orkney* anno 1106. He was greatly honoured of old, both in *England* and *Scotland*, as appears from the *Sarum*, *York* and *Aberdeen* breviaries: and his feast was kept

kept with solemnity in the isles of *Orkney*, as of the patron or tutelar saint of those islands. In *Ireland* the commemoration of S. *Ercus* first bishop of *Slane*, who went to our Lord anno 514. See *Usher* p. 412.

April 17. The festivity of S. *Stephen Harding* abbat, founder of the religious order of the *Cistercians*; who first received S. *Bernard* to the habit, flying from the contagion of the world, with thirty other young gentlemen; and through him quickly became the father of innumerable saints. This order within 150 years, by reason of the fervour and sanctity of its professors, (who observed during all that time much the same discipline as is now observed at the famous abbey of *La Trappe*) was so greatly multiplied through all *Christendom*, as to count no fewer than eighteen hundred monasteries. In *Scotland* the festivity of S. *Donan* abbat; celebrated on this day in the *Scottish* calendars; where he is said to have departed to our Lord anno 840.

April 18. In the monastery of *Cluain-Finchoil* in *Ulster* the commemoration of S. *Lugad* abbat, brother to S. *Fintan Munnu*; a man of admirable sanctity: who, as S. *Adamnan* relates in his life of S. *Colum-kille*, saw the soul of this saint, at the time of his departure (*June* 9 anno 597) carried up to heaven in great glory; attended by innumerable angels, and a celestial melody. In the monastery of *Leghlene* in *Leinster* the deposition of S. *Laisrean* bishop, abbat over 1500 monks, and eminent for his sanctity.

BRITISH PIETY. 67

April 19. At *Greenwich* the martyrdom of S. *Alphege,* or *Elphege,* archbishop of *Canterbury,* illustrious for his pastoral zeal, and charity: who was put to death by the *Danes* anno 1012; and both in his life, and after his death was honoured with great miracles. His body was found entire and incorrupt, eleven years after his death; and was translated from S. *Paul's,* where he was first buried, to the cathedral of *Canterbury,* and there enshrined near the high altar.

April 20. At *Erford* in *Franconia,* the translation of S. *Adelhare,* an *English* priest, and apostolick preacher; who was martyred, with S. *Boniface* apostle of *Germany,* anno 754; his body on this day was translated to *Erford:* where it is still kept with great veneration. At *Rome* the deposition of king *Ceadwall* the *West-Saxon;* who upon his conversion to the christian faith, quitting all for Christ, was baptized at *Rome,* by pope *Sergius*; and died before he had put off the white garments of his baptism, anno 689.

April 21. The festivity of S. *Anselm* archbishop of *Canterbury,* and doctor of the church; greatly renowned through the christian world, for his sanctity, learning and miracles. He died anno 1109, and lies buried in the cathedral of *Canterbury,* in a chapel bearing his name, near the altar of S. *Peter.*

April 22. The commemoration of blessed *Ethelred* the first of that name, king of *England,* a most religious prince; who was slain
in

in battle by the *Pagan Danes*, anno 872; and honoured as a martyr, at the place of his burial, which was at *Winborn* in *Dorsetshire*.

April 23. The festivity of S. *George*, a most illustrious martyr of Christ, under *Diocletian*; who for his piety, fortitude, and constancy in his sufferings, has been greatly revered by all the churches, both of the *East* and *West*: more especially by our *English* ancestors; who chose him for their tutelar saint, in their wars; and have ascribed great victories to his intercession. In *Ireland*, the feast of S. *Ibar* bishop, cotemporary with S. *Patrick*, and his fellow labourer in the conversion of that island. He went to our Lord about the year 500, and was interred in his monastery, in the isle of *Beckerin*; where he had opened a famous school both for divine and human learning.

April 24. At *Canterbury* the deposition of S. *Mellitus*, disciple of S. *Gregory* the Great, and sent by him into *England*, to the assistance of S. *Augustine* our apostle: he was soon after ordained bishop of *London*; where he converted king *Sebert* and his people to the faith of Christ: then upon the death of S. *Laurence*, he was made archbishop of *Canterbury*: which see when he had governed, with great wisdom and sanctity, for the space of five years, he happily reposed in our Lord anno 624. S. *Bede*, l. 1. c. 29, 30. l. 2. c. 3. &c. Also the translation of the body of S. *Wilfrid* the elder from *Rippon* to *Canterbury* anno 957; where it now reposes, as it is
believed,

believed, near the monument of *Cardinal Pool*. *Dart.*

April 25. The commemoration of S. *Egbert* prieſt, a man of admirable ſanctity; who ſent S. *Willibrord* and his companions, to preach the faith in Lower *Germany*; and brought over the monks of S. *Columb* in the iſle of *Hy* to the right obſervation of *Eaſter*; amongſt whom he alſo laid down the load of his mortal fleſh in the 90th year of his age, and with his ſpirit took his flight to our Lord, on *Eaſter* day, anno 739. S. *Bede*. Alſo the commemoration of holy *Edilhun* companion of S. *Egbert*; of whoſe happy death, in the monaſtery of *Rathmelfigi* in *Ireland*, at the time of the great mortality, anno 664; ſee S. *Bede*, l. 4. c. 27.

April 26. At S. *'Ives* in *Huntingtonſhire* the commemoration of S. *Ivo* biſhop and confeſſor: whoſe body was there diſcovered, anno 1001 (four hundred years after his death) being found whole and intire in his epiſcopal habit, as if he had been juſt then buried; his ſanctity alſo being atteſted by many miracles. His body was tranſlated to the abbey of *Ramſey*; where alſo the bodies of his companions *Sithius* and *Inthius* were at the ſame time depoſited.

April 27. In the abbey of *Wazor* in the territory of *Liege* the commemoration of S. *Forannan*, an *Iriſh* prelate of the tenth century, eminent for learning and virtue; who going over, with twelve companions, into the *Netherlands*, for the advancing the kingdom of Chriſt, was received by count *Eilbert* founder
of

of the abbey of *Wazor*, and desired to take upon him the charge of that monastery; of which he was the third abbat, after S. *Maccallan*, and S. *Cadroe*. This office he administred till his dying day, anno 982, with so much prudence, piety and sanctity, as to be judged worthy to be enrolled, after his death, amongst the saints; God also attesting his merit by evident miracles.

April 28. At *Roscree* in the county of *Tiperary* in *Ireland*, the festivity of S. *Cronan* abbat; honoured of old as patron of that church. He founded a famous monastery there, which he quickly stock'd with most religious monks; many resorting to him, attracted by the odour of his sanctity; and desiring to learn of him to be saints. He reposed in our Lord anno 640. *Usher* p. 502. In *Germany* the festivity of S. *Cortill* a *Scot*, bishop of *Werdt* in the ninth century.

April 29. At *York* the deposition of S. *Wilfrid* the younger, disciple of S. *John of Beverley*, and his successor in the see of *York*; a man of *singular merit and sanctity* [*Bede*] bountiful to the poor, a great lover of the beauty of the house of God; and greatly addicted to divine contemplation. Obiit anno 735.

April 30. At *London* the deposition of S. *Erkonwald*, fourth bishop of that see; and for the eminence of his sanctity, honoured as patron of the diocese; two festivals being kept yearly in his memory, *viz.* this day, and the 14th of *November*, which was the day of his translation. He founded out of his own patrimony, before he

was

was bishop, the famous abbeys of *Chertsey,* and *Barking:* and was illustrious for miracles both alive and dead. V. *Bede,* l. 4. c. 6. In *Little Britain* the festivity of S. *Briocus* bishop, a disciple of S. *Germanus,* and a zealous preacher of the word of life: who flying the fury of the *Saxons,* passed the seas, and founded a monastery on the coast of *Aremorica,* where now stands the episcopal city of S. *Brieu,* which takes its name from him: where he lived and died a great pattern of sanctity; in the beginning of the sixth century.

MAY.

May 1. AT *Llan Elwy* in *North Wales,* the festivity of S. *Asaph* bishop and confessor: he was the favourite disciple of S. *Kentigern,* and his successor, both in his monastery of 995 religious brethren, over whom he was abbat; and in the bishoprick of *Llan Elwy*; which now from his name is called S. *Asaph's.* He flourished in great sanctity in the latter part of the sixth century, and has a place on this day in the *Roman* Martyrology. In which also on this same day is commemorated the royal virgin and abbess S. *Walburga*; whose principal festivity is kept in *Bavaria* on the first of *May.* In *Ireland* the festivity of S. *Kellach* bishop, who flourished about the year 600.

May 2. In the monastery of *Fosses* in the territory of *Liege,* the commemoration of blessed *Ultan* abbat; brother of the great S. *Fursey:* who after having illustrated with the rays of his

his sanctity the province of the *East Angles*, going over into the *Belgic Gaul*, there founded, with the help of S. *Gertrude* of *Nivelle*, that famous abbey; where also he happily reposed in our Lord anno 680. At *Lindisfarne* the commemoration of another great servant of God, of the name of *Ultan*, who was a monk of the monastery there, and noted for his learning and holiness of life. In the *Netherlands* the festivity of S. *Germanus* a *British* prelate, who preached the faith of Christ in those parts; and was there crowned with martyrdom. *Rosweidus, in fastis Sanctorum.*

May 3. In *Lincolnshire* the commemoration of S. *Ethelwin* bishop of *Lindsey*, and of S. *Aldewin* abbat of *Peartney*: both of them illustrious for sanctity, in our primitive *English* church. S. *Bede*, l. 3. c. 11. In *Scotland* the commemoration of S. *Marnoc the black*; whose sanctity is celebrated by the *Scottish* historians.

May 4. In *Wales* the commemoration of S. *Docus* priest and abbat, one of the most illustrious for sanctity and learning amongst the doctors of the ancient *British* church; who jointly with S. *David* and S. *Gildas* greatly promoted christian piety, and religious discipline both in *Britain* and *Ireland*. See the ancient catalogue of saints, in *Usher's Antiquities*. In the monastery of S. *Hilda* at *Hakeness* in *Yorkshire*, the commemoration of holy *Begu* virgin, to whom God was pleased to shew, in a vision, the soul of S. *Hilda*, at the very hour she departed

parted this life (in her monastery of *Whitby*) ascending up to heaven in great glory. S. *Bede*, l. 4. c. 23.

May 5. At *Bardney* in *Lincolnshire*, the commemoration of S. *Ethelred*, king of the *Mercians*, who after a glorious reign of thirty years, resigning his earthly kingdom, for the gaining of a heavenly one, became a monk in the monastery of *Bardney*; and there made a holy end, anno 710. S. *Bede*, l. 5. c. 20. His successor king *Coenred*, after five years reign followed his example; and in like manner exchanged his crown and scepter for the habit and life of a monk, anno 709. In *Scotland* the commemoration of holy *Scandalius*, disciple of S. *Colum-kille*, and one of those twelve apostolical men, that came over with him from *Ireland*, to preach the faith of Christ to the nation of the *Picts*.

May 6. At *Lindisfarne*, now *Holy Island*, on the coast of *Northumberland*, the deposition of S. *Eadbert* bishop, renowned for his learning and sanctity. He was successor to S. *Cuthbert* in that see, and diligently walked in his blessed footsteps; and as his body was laid with him in the same sepulchre here on earth, so was his soul associated with him on this day in glory anno 697. S. *Bede*, l. 4. c. 29, 30. At *Landaff* the translation of the body of S. *Dubritius*, the first bishop of that see, from his sepulchre in the isle of *Enhly* or *Bardsey* to the cathedral of *Landaff*.

May 7. At *Beverley* in *Yorkshire* the festivity of S. *John* some time bishop of *York*, eminent for his sanctity, learning, and miracles; attested by S. *Bede* his cotemporary (L. 5. c. 2, 3. &c.) who received his holy orders both of deacon, and of priest at his hands. Obiit anno 721. At *Tinmouth* the memory of the holy abbat *Herebald*, disciple of S. *John of Beverley*. S. *Bede*.

May 8. In the monastery of S. *Odilia* near *Ruremond*, the deposition of S. *Wiro* bishop; who going out of *Britain* preached the faith of Christ in the *Low Countries*, about the beginning of the eighth century; and after reaping great fruits of his labours, there happily reposed in our Lord. In *Scotland* the festivity of St. *Gibrian*, confessor, marked on this day in the *Scots* Calendar; where he is said to have gone to our Lord, anno 532.

May 9. In *Switzerland* the festivity of S. *Beatus* confessor, said to have been a *Briton* by birth, and the first that preached the word of life to the *Switzers*. Amongst the ancient *Britons*, the commemoration of S. *Nennio*, a holy prelate, who held his see in a place called *the great monastery*; and was spiritual father to the famous S. *Winnin*. He flourished in the sixth century. See the Acts of S. *Winnin*.

May 10. At *Benchor* in *Ireland* the festivity of S. *Comgall* or *Congellus* abbat, who gave a rule to the great monastery there, the most renowned for religious discipline of any in *Ireland:* of which, and of its holy founder, thus writes the great S. *Bernard*, in his life of S. *Malachi*. ' This monastery of *Benchor*, says he, had been most

most famous before, under its first father *Congellus*, bringing forth many thousands of religious; and being the head of many monasteries. A place truly holy, and fruitful in saints, ... insomuch that one of the sons of that holy congregation, by name *Luanus*, is reported alone to have been the founder of a hundred monasteries, &c. In short its offspring filled in such manner *Ireland* and *Scotland*, that those verses of Psalm 64 seem to have foretold these days: *Thou hast visited the earth, and thou hast plentifully watered it: thou hast multiplied the enriching of it. The river of God hath been filled with water: thou hast prepared their food*, &c. *Fill up plentifully the streams thereof; multiply its fruits; it shall spring up and rejoice in its showers*, &c. Neither did those swarms of saints only spread themselves through the aforesaid countries; but also, like overflowing waters, they poured themselves out into foreign lands. Of which number S. *Columbanus* coming through our parts of *France*, built the monastery of *Luxeuil*; and grew up there into a great nation: so great, as it is said, that the solemnity of the divine office was there continued by choirs succeeding one another, so that not a moment of the day, or night, passed without the praises of God.' So far S. *Bernard*. S. *Comgall* came also over into *Britain*, to visit the saints who then flourished amongst the *Britons*: and founded here a monastery in a territory then called *Heth*: and after a life full of years and of good works, he was called to the rewards of a happy eternity, anno 601. Also in the same monastery of *Benchor*, the commemoration of many holy monks, to the number, as it is said, of nine hundred, who were there martyred in one day by the *Danes.* S. *Bernard.* At *Tarentum* in *Italy* the festivity of S. *Cataldus* bishop and confessor, honoured on this day in the *Roman* martyrology; and said, in his acts, to have been a native of *Ireland.*

May 11. The festivity of S. *Fremund* martyr, who retiring from the world, in the flower of his age, led a life of extraordinary devotion and penance in a lonesome solitude in the confines of *Wales*; where he was at length slain by the *Danes,* anno 862; and held in very great veneration by our ancestors. At *Canterbury* the deposition of archbishop *Athelard* anno 806; to whom our historians give the character, of *a very learned, pious and good prelate.* See *Dugdale's Abridgement.*

May 12. At *Thorney* in *Cambridgeshire,* the commemoration of S. *Huna* confessor, whose mortal remains reposed in the church of the abbey there: as did also the bodies of S. *Hereferth* and S. *Cissa.* See *Saxon Manuscript.* In *Scotland* the festivity of S. *Comgall* abbat of *Haliwood,* in the eleventh century; who is honoured on this day in the *Scottish* Calendars.

May 13. In *Wales* the commemoration of S. *Cathmael* confessor, cotemporary with the great S. *David*; and renowned for the sanctity of his life: of whom we read in the Acts of S. *Finian* of *Clonard,* (called *the master, or teacher of the saints of* Ireland) that during his stay in *Britain,* he was conversant with three eminent *British* saints,

saints, viz. S. *David*, S. *Gildas*, and S. *Cathmael*. In *Ireland* the commemoration of the saints *Bitheus* and *Genocus*; religious men of the *British* nation, who accompanied the same S. *Finian*, in his return from *Britain* to *Ireland*, and for their extraordinary sanctity, were held after their death in great veneration in the churches of *Ireland*. Also in *Ireland* the deposition of S. *Moelbod* alias *Maldod* abbat.

May 14. At *Lismore* in *Ireland* the festivity of S. *Carthac junior*, called also *Mochuda*, founder and first bishop of the church of *Lismore*; and father and teacher of many saints, whom he trained up in his celebrated school, and monastery of *Rathenin*. Also the commemoration of his twelve principal disciples; who were renowned above all the rest for the eminence of their sanctity: whose names may be seen in *Usher's Antiquities*, p. 503. In *Ireland* the commemoration of S. *Dunnius* abbat, disciple of S. *Patrick*.

March 15. At *Pollesworth* in *Warwickshire*, the commemoration of S. *Editha* virgin, daughter to king *Egbert*, (or as others say to king *Ethelwolf*) and recommended by him to the care of S. *Modwenna* of *Ireland*; by whom she was educated in all sanctity, in the company of S. *Osith*, and S. *Line*. She was the first abbess of *Pollesworth*, and patroness of that holy community. See *Dugdale's Warwickshire*. At *Gele* in *Brabant* the festivity of S. *Dympna* virgin and martyr, daughter to an *Irish* prince; who flying from the unnatural lust of her own father,

father, crossed the seas, under the conduct of a holy priest called *Gerebern*; and chose for her dwelling a lonesome solitude, where now stands the town of *Gele:* till her father, having got intelligence of the place of her retreat, coming thither, and finding her constant in her resolution, slew her with his own hands: having first murthered S. *Gerebern*, her spiritual director. The body of S. *Dympna* reposes in a collegiate church, dedicated to God in her name in the town of *Gele*, where it has been illustrated with many miracles. The body of S. *Gerebern* was translated from *Gele* to the church of *Sonsbeck*, in the dukedom of *Cleves*.

May 16. At *Clonfert* in *Ireland*, the festivity of S. *Brendan* the elder, abbat and founder of many monasteries and schools of piety, as well in *Britain*, as in *Ireland:* in which he had no fewer than three thousand religious of his institute; to whom he gave an excellent rule, said to have been dictated to him by an angel. He went to our Lord in the 93d year of his age anno 578. In *Ireland* also the festivity of S. *Carantac*, a *British* nobleman, who was called from leading an eremitical life in his own country, to go and join his labours with S. *Patrick*, in preaching the faith of Christ to the *Irish*. At *Bourdeaux* in *France* the happy death of S. *Simon* surnamed *Stock*; an *English* Carmelite, General of his order, and renowned for the wonderful sanctity of his life. Also on the same day at S. *Albans* in *Hertfordshire* the translation of the relicks of S. *Alban*, the most illustrious amongst our *British* martyrs.

May

May 17. In *Cornwall*, not far from the *Land's End*, the commemoration of S. *Madern* or *Maddren* confeffor: where there is a chapel, and a well called from his name, which by a remain of ancient devotion ufed to be particularly frequented on the *Thurfdays* in *May*, and more efpecially on *Corpus Chrifti* day. Here in the year 1640, *John Trelille*, who had been an abfolute cripple for fixteen years, and was obliged to crawl upon his hands, by reafon of the clofe contraction of the finews of his legs; upon three feveral admonitions, in his dream, wafhing in S. *Madern's* well, and fleeping afterwards on what was called S. *Madern's* bed, was fuddenly and perfectly cured: fo that *I faw him*, fays bifhop *Hall* (in his *Treatife of the invifible World*, l. 1. fect. 8.) *able to walk, and get his own maintenance.* This proteftant prelate, who was at that time the bifhop of the diocefe, in his vifitation, as he tells us in the fame place, *befides the atteftation of many hundreds of the neighbours, took a ftrict and perfonal examination* of the cafe, and found the whole to be unqueftionable: *here was neither art, nor collufion,* fays he, *the thing* was *done, the author invifible.*

May 18. In *Scotland*, the feftivity of S. *Convallus*, faid by the *Scottifh* breviary to have been a difciple of S. *Kentigern*, and to have greatly promoted, by word and work, the kingdom of Chrift in that part of *Britain*. His happy death is marked anno 612. At *Shaftfbury* the feftivity of S. *Ælgyve* queen, mother to king *Edgar*, a lady moft eminent for her piety and charity. Obiit anno 971.

May 19. The festivity of S. *Dunstan* archbishop of *Canterbury,* who from his childhood taking up the sweet yoke of Christ, by wholly addicting himself to devotion and divine love; became one of the brightest lights of the *English* church; a zealous reformer of monastick discipline; and a restorer of christian piety and purity. He was also illustrious for the gift of prophecy and of miracles: and was called to the reward of his labours, anno 988. At *Tours* in *France* the deposition of venerable *Alcuin,* disciple of holy *Egbert* archbishop of *York,* and his successor in the charge of the famous school, which that prelate had opened in that city. From whence he was invited over to *France* by the emperor *Charlemagne,* who honoured him with the title of his *Master;* and by his assistance and advice founded the university of *Paris.* He was the most learned man of his age, as his works testify. In the latter part of his life he withdrew from court, to the abbey of S. *Martin's* at *Tours;* where he died in the odour of sanctity, anno 804.

May 20. At *Hereford,* the festivity of S. *Ethelbert* king of the *East Angles,* a most religious and godly prince; who going to the court of *Offa* king of the *Mercians,* to demand his daughter *Alfreda* in marriage, was treacherously murthered at *Sutton Wallis;* and privately buried at *Marden.* But a pillar of light, which was seen in the night over his sepulchre, occasioned his body to be taken up, and translated to *Hereford;* where it was illustrated by many great miracles:
info-

May 21. At *Fynchal* in the bishoprick of *Durham*, the deposition of S. *Godrick* hermite, renowned for sanctity and miracles. Obiit anno 1170. At *Lucca* in *Italy*, the feast of S. *Silaus* an *Irish* prelate, eminent for holiness of life, who died there in his return from *Rome*, anno 1094.

May 22. At *Beverley* in *Yorkshire*, the commemoration of S. *Berethun* abbat, disciple of S. *John of Beverley*, and appointed by him the first superior of his monastery in *Deirwood*; who living and dying with such holiness as became the disciple of so great a master, went to join his company in glory anno 733. Also the commemoration of S. *Winewald*, successor to S. *Berethun*, and imitator of his virtues; who went to our Lord anno 751. On this day also is marked in the *Sarum* calendar, and in the *English Martyrology*, the decease of holy king *Henry* VI. whose life was so eminently godly, and his death, though violent, so precious in the sight of our Lord, that he was pleased to illustrate him with many miracles; to which, says Dr. *Harpsfield*, in his history, all *England* was witness. Obiit anno 1471.

May 23. At *Knaresborough* in *Yorkshire*, the commemoration of S. *Robert* hermit. At *Rochester* the deposition of S. *William* of *Perth*, a holy pilgrim murthered in that neighbourhood, by a youth, whom he had brought up out of charity: whose body being buried in the cathedral of that city, was honoured with divers miracles. *Capgrave.*

May 24. At *Barking* in *Essex*, the commemoration of holy *Ethelburga* queen, wife to king *Ina*; who after inducing her husband to quit the world, retired to the monastery of *Barking*; and there made a holy end about the year 740. There is a church in *London* dedicated in her name. On this day also is commemorated in some martyrologies the great king *Edgar*; who after repairing, by seven years penance, enjoined him by S. *Dunstan*, the scandal given by the sins of his youth; and like another *David*, promoting with all his power, the beauty of the house of God, and the general good of religion, went to receive his reward, anno 975. He was buried at *Glastenbury*; where his body was found incorrupt fourscore years after his death; and being enshrined, was placed over the high altar of the abbey church.

May 25. At *Sherborn* in *Dorsetshire*, the deposition of S. *Aldhelm* first bishop of that see, most illustrious, both for his learning, and for his sanctity. S. *Bede*, l. 5. c. 19. He was the first of the *English* nation, who for his godly and learned writings, both in prose and verse, has deserved to be ranked amongst the fathers, and doctors of the church. Obiit anno 709. At *Malmsbury* the commemoration of holy *Maidulf*, founder of the abbey there, and as some affirm, master of S. *Aldhelm*. He is called S. *Mæildun* in the old *Saxon* manuscript, of the burying places of the *English* saints.

May

May 26. At *Canterbury* the feſtivity of S. *Auguſtin* the monk, firſt archbiſhop of that ſee, and apoſtle of the *Engliſh*; who being ſent into *England*, by the holy pope S. *Gregory* the Great, and upheld by God by the working of miracles, joined with an extraordinary ſanctity of life, brought over king *Ethelbert* and his people, from the worſhip of idols to the faith and law of Chriſt. Obiit anno 608. At *Rome* the depoſition of S. *Eleutherius* pope; who ſent over into *Britain* the ſaints *Fugacius* and *Damianus*, for the inſtruction of king *Lucius* and his *Britons*; in the ſecond century.

May 27. In the monaſtery of *Jarrow*, in the biſhoprick of *Durham*, the depoſition of venerable *Bede* prieſt, and doctor of the church; who at the age of ſeven years being happily and holily offered and dedicated to God under the care of S. *Bennet Biſcop*; ſpent his whole life in the exerciſes of religion, in ſinging the divine praiſes, and in meditating on God's holy word; in ſuch manner as to make it his greateſt delight to employ all the leiſure time he could have from other neceſſary duties, in either learning, or teaching, or writing ſomething for the greater glory of his God. And as he lived, ſo he happily died in theſe holy exerciſes, on Aſcenſion Eve anno 735. His body was afterwards tranſlated to *Durham*.

May 28. In the famous monaſtery of *Faremoutier* in *Brie*, the commemoration of S. *Sethryd* a noble *Engliſh* virgin, who, for her ſingular virtue and ſanctity, after the death of S.
Fara

Fara was chosen, though a stranger, abbess of that community of saints, and there died the death of the saints. S. *Bede*, l. 3. c. 6. At *Fiesoli* in *Tuscany*, the commemoration of S. *Brigide* a *Scottish* or *Irish* virgin, who for the love of Christ, leaving her worldly friends and country, and going into *Italy*, led a most saintly life in a wood near that town, and dying in the sweet odour of sanctity, some time in the ninth century, is honoured there to this day among the saints.

May 29. In *Cornwall* the commemoration of S. *Buriene*, a most holy virgin: the place of whose earthly dwelling retains her name to this day. The great opinion our ancestors had of the eminent sanctity of this illustrious virgin, appears from king *Athelstan's* granting to her church the privilege of a sanctuary, anno 936. On this day also is marked in the *Scots* calendar the happy death of *David* king of *Scots*, a most religious and munificent prince, and son to the blessed queen S. *Margaret*. He died at *Carlisle May* 29, in great sentiments of piety, anno 1153.

May 30. At *Baber* near *Norwich*, the commemoration of S. *Walstan* confessor, whose veneration is very ancient in that neighbourhood. His acts are recorded in *Capgrave's* collection of the lives of *British* saints.

May 31. At S. *Edmunds Bury* in *Suffolk*, the commemoration of S. *Jurmin* confessor, son to the holy king *Anna*; and brother to the saints
Audry,

Audry, Sexburge, Edilburge, and *Walburge.* His body was tranflated, from his firft burying place, to the church of S. *Edmund,* and there kept with great honour, in the time of *William of Malmefbury,* who wrote not long after the conqueft. In the fame place, the commemoration alfo of S. *Botulph* bifhop, whofe body, as the fame author relates, repofed in the fame church. In the *Ifle of Man,* the commemoration of the holy prelate *Patricianus,* who flying from the fwords of the *Saxons,* and retiring into that ifland, made there a holy end. *Hector Boeth.*

JUNE.

June 1. AT the abbey of *Evefham,* the feftivity of S. *Wiftan* king of the *Mercians,* martyred anno 849. Of whom it is recorded, that in token of his fanctity, the place where he fuffered was for thirty nights illuftrated with a heavenly light, where afterwards a chapel was built in his honour: his body was buried in the royal abbey of *Repondon,* the burying place of the *Mercian* kings; from whence it was tranflated to the famous monaftery of *Evefham.* In *Scotland* the commemoration of holy king *Malcolm* III. a devout and religious prince, who was hufband to the bleffed queen S. *Margaret,* an imitator of her virtues, and a partner in her charities. He was interred at the abbey of *Dumfermlin,* in the fame church with his holy confort, anno 1093: from whence, upon the change of religion, their relicks were carried abroad, and given to *Philip* II. of *Spain;* who depofited them in the new church of his

palace

palace of the *Escurial*; with this inscription on the shrine, S. *Malcolm* king, and S. *Margaret* queen.

June 2. In a little island upon the coast of *South Wales*, the commemoration of S. *Piro* abbat, illustrious for sanctity in the fifth century: to whose monastery S *Samson* retired from the continent; and for some time directed the religious there. In the *North* of *England*, the commemoration of *Herefrid the man of God*: whose happy death is marked in the appendix to S. *Bede's* chronological table, anno 747.

June 3. In the abbey of *Milton*, or *Middleton*, in *Dorsetshire* the commemoration of S. *Branwalador* bishop, patron of that church and monastery. See *Tanner's Notitia*. p. 104. At *Gleandeloch* in *Ireland*, the deposition of S. *Coemgen* alias *Keivin* abbat, illustrious for sanctity and miracles, who went to our Lord anno 615. Also in *Ireland*, the commemoration of S. *Cronan* a holy priest, who flourished in the fifth century, by whom S. *Coemgen* was baptized: as also of another S. *Coemgen* abbat of *Gleanussen* in the sixth century.

June 4. At *Padstow* (olim *Petrocks-stow*) in *Cornwall*, the festivity of S. *Petrock* an abbat, eminent for sanctity; who founded a college or monastery there in the sixth century, in which amongst others, he had three most holy men for his disciples, *Credan*, *Medan*, and *Dachan*. His tomb and shrine, in *Leland's* time, was in the east part of the church of *Padstow*. Also at *Bodmin* in *Cornwall* the festivity of another S. *Petrock* bishop of *Cornwall*, in the ninth century; whose

body

body reposed in a church dedicated to God in his name in *Bodmin:* the ancient name of which was *Bosmana,* that is the *mansion of Monks,* so called from S. *Petrock's* monastery. *Dugdale.* Also in *Cornwall* the commemoration of S. *Guronus* hermit, who led a solitary life in great sanctity, in a small cottage, which he gave up to S. *Petrock,* when he came into that neighbourhood.

June 5. In the famous abbey of *Fulda* in *Germany,* the festivity of S. *Winfrid,* alias *Boniface,* archbishop of *Mentz,* and apostle of *Germany*; who finished the course of his apostolical life, and labours, by a glorious martyrdom at *Dockum* in *East Friseland* anno 755. His body was translated to his monastery of *Fulda,* where it has been illustrated with innumerable miracles. Also the commemoration of the saints *Eoban* bishop, *Wintrung, Walter* and *Adelhere* priests; *Hamund, Strichald* and *Bosa* deacons; *Waccar, Gunderhar, Williker* and *Hadulph* monks; with others of the laity to the number of about fifty in all; a great part of them of the *English* nation, who were martyred at the same time with S. *Boniface* by the barbarous infidels. At the abbey of S. *Vanarelleis* in *Normandy* the festivity of S. *Bagna* or *Baga* an *English* monk of that monastery. Obiit anno 720.

June 6. In *Scotland* the festivity of S. *Colm* or *Colmoc* bishop, apostle of the isles of *Orkney.* He flourished in learning and sanctity about the year 1000, in the days of king *Kenneth* III; and has a place on this day in the *Aberdeen* breviary.

In *Germany* the commemoration of holy *Agatha* virgin and abbess; who was one of those *English* nuns, whom S. *Boniface* invited over from the monastery of *Winborn* in *Dorsetshire*, for the establishing religious discipline amongst his *German* converts. She went to our Lord some time after the middle of the eighth century.

June 7. In the monastery of *Newminster*, of the *Cistercian* order, near *Morpeth* in *Northumberland*, the deposition of S. *Robert* abbat, renowned for sanctity and miracles. He went to our Lord *June* 7, anno 1159: at which time S. *Godrick*, who was then praying in his hermitage at *Finchal*, saw his soul, in the shape of a globe of fire, carried up by angels into the heavenly paradise, in spite of a troop of infernal spirits, who sought to obstruct his way. He also saw, at the same time, the soul of a holy woman of *Hastings* in *Sussex*, whose name was *Editha*, take the same happy road. At *Worcester* the translation of the body of S. *Wolstan* bishop of that see; which being taken up above an hundred years after his death, was found, in all his pontifical attire, as whole and incorrupt, as when it was first laid in the grave. In *Ireland* the festivity of S. *Colmoc* first bishop of *Dromore*, celebrated for sanctity.

June 8. At *York*, the festivity of S. *William* archbishop, honoured of old as one of the principal patrons of that church. He died anno 1154, and was illustrious for many great miracles. On the same day is honoured in the *Scots* calendar, S. *Syra* or *Cyra* virgin, sister to the great

great saint *Fiaker*, in whose name divers churches have been anciently dedicated to God.

June 9. In the famous monastery of the isle of *Hy* (now called *Ycombkille*) the deposition of S. *Columb* abbat; who from the number of the *cells*, or monasteries by him established, and to which he gave a peculiar rule, is commonly called S. *Columkille*. He was born in *Ireland* of the noble race of *Neil*, anno 521; and was brought up in the company of many great saints, in the school of S. *Finian* of *Clonard*. From his youth he devoted himself, with his whole soul, to the love and service of his God; continually beging three kinds of graces, of his Divine Majesty; which were all plentifully bestowed upon him, viz. *Purity* of soul and body; the heavenly light of true *wisdom*, for his direction in all things; and a *disengagement* of his heart, from all earthly affections, that it might freely fly up to God. Being ordained priest, after having made many holy foundations in *Ireland*, following a divine call, he passed over into the *North* of *Britain*, with twelve apostolical men, out of the number of his disciples, and there he preached the faith to the *Northern Picts*; whom he converted to Christ, together with their powerful king *Bridius*, by his doctrine and miracles: from whom also he received the isle of *Hy*, for the place of his residence; and established there that congregation of saints; to whom under God not only the churches of the *Picts* and *Scots*, but those of the *Northern English* also are greatly indebted for their instruction and sanctification. S. *Columb* happily reposed in our Lord
anno

anno 597. His life and miracles are recorded in three books by S. *Adamnan* abbat of *Hy*, in the following century. On this day is also celebrated in the *Sarum* calendar, the translation of S. *Edmund* archbishop of *Canterbury*, illustrious for innumerable miracles: whose body being taken up on this day, seven years after his death, was found entire and uncorrupt, with all the joints as flexible as when the saint was alive; and was solemnly translated to a more honourable sepulchre, in presence of S. *Lewis* king of *France*, and a great number of prelates and noblemen.

June 10. The festivity of S. *Margaret* queen of *Scots*: whose life written by her *Confessarius Theodorick*, a monk of *Durham*, is full of admirable lessons and great examples of all christian virtues; but more especially of an extraordinary piety, self-denial, humility and charity. She died the death of the saints, anno 1093. At *Rochester* the deposition of S. *Ithamar* bishop, celebrated for the sanctity of his life, and his erudition. S. *Bede*, l. 3. c. 14. Obiit anno 671.

June 11. In the monastery of S. *Columb* in the isle of *Hy*, the commemoration of S. *Baithen* abbat; trained up from his youth in the discipline of that great saint, a close imitator of all his virtues, and his immediate successor in the charge of that monastery, and of the many others both in *Britain* and *Ireland*, which depended on it. He followed his holy father to heaven, anno 601. In the monastery of *Bobbio* in *Lombardy*, the commemoration of S. *Cumian*

mian an *Irish* prelate; who following an extraordinary call, left his bishoprick and native country; and going into *Italy* embraced a strict monastick life, at the age of seventy-five, in the monastery of S. *Columbanus* at *Bobbio*; and there, for twenty years, lived, in the close observance of regular discipline, a perfect model of all virtues, to his dying day; which was some time in the eighth century.

June 12. In *Scotland* the festivity of S. *Ternan* bishop, who has a place on this day in the *Aberdeen* breviary. He is said to have been a disciple of S. *Palladius*, and by him to have been ordained bishop of the *Picts*, anno 431. At *Peblis* in the same kingdom the memory of S. *Nicolaus* bishop and martyr; who is supposed to have suffered under *Dioclesian*. His relicks were discovered in that neighbourhood anno 1261. See *Usher's Antiquities*, p. 334.

June 13. In *North Wales*, the commemoration of S. *Elerius* abbat, trained up in piety and learning, in the monastery of S. *Asaph*; from whence he retired into the wilderness; and there led an eremitical life; till preferring the benefit of many before his own private satisfaction which he took in solitude, he founded a monastery of religious men in the vale of *Cluyd* of which he was abbat: and another for sacred virgins; in which he received S. *Wenefride*; whom also he continued to direct in the ways of the most sublime perfection till her happy death.

June 14. In *South Wales* the festivity of S. *Dogmael* abbat, who flourished in the sixth century. There was an ancient church dedicated in his name in the land of *Kemes* in *Pembrokeshire*, which was given after the conquest to a priory of monks, which subsisted under the name of S. *Dogmael* till the days of king *Henry* VIII. At *Oxford* the commemoration of S. *Aldate*, of whose church and monastery there, see *Tanner's Notitia Monastica*, p. 419.

June 15. At *Winchester*, the festivity of S. *Edburge* virgin, daughter to king *Edward the Elder*, who from a child despised the world, and all its empty toys; and when she was grown up, devoted herself to be a spouse of Christ, in the nunnery of *Winchester*: Her sanctity, says our great historian *William of Malmesbury*, grew with her age, ' and her humility ripened with her years..... because all her works were begun by charity; and finished by humility. In short the devotion of her breast, and the virginal purity of her body, were both in her life, and after her death, demonstrated by very many miracles.' l. 2. *de Regibus.* Obiit anno 960. In *Little Britain* the festivity of S. *Vouga* or *Vio*, an *Irish* prelate, in the sixth century, who passing over the seas, became an *hermit*, and lived and died in so great reputation of sanctity, as to have divers churches dedicated to God in his name.

June 16. In *Little Britain* the commemoration of S. *Main*, a *British* prelate of extraordinary sanctity, some time disciple of the great S. *Brendan*; honoured to this day in that province,

BRITISH PIETY. 93

vince, by an abbey and church bearing his name. At *Chichester* the translation of S. *Richard* bishop of that see, renowned for many miracles. Amongst the religious of our Lady of *Mercy* (instituted for the redemption of captives) the commemoration of S. *Serapion* an *Englishman*, disciple of S. *Peter Nolasco*; who was martyred in *Africa* by the *Moors* anno 1240.

June 17. The festivity of S. *Botulph* abbat, honoured on this day in the *York* calendar; whose name has been very illustrious, on account of his extraordinary sanctity, throughout all *England*; at least from the ninth century and downwards. In *Ireland* the deposition of S. *Moling*, alias *Dairchilla* bishop of *Fernes*; greatly renowned amongst the *Irish* saints. He died in a good old age, anno 687.

June 18. In the *Netherlands* the commemoration of S. *Adulph* bishop, brother of S. *Botulph*; who going over from *England*, when young, into the *Belgick Gaul*, embraced a monastick life, and became so great a proficient in all virtue, as to be advanced, though a stranger, to the bishoprick of *Trajectum*, which he administered in so saint-like a manner, as to be honoured after his death amongst the saints. In *Scotland*, the commemoration of holy *Malcolm* IV. king of the *Scots*, surnamed the *Maiden*, grandson to the blessed king *David*, and great grandson to S. *Margaret*: whose admirable virtues, and unblemished purity, are highly extolled by our historians. *William of Newbridge.*

June 19. At *Hexham* in *Northumberland*, the commemoration of S. *Alchmund*, confecrated bifhop of that fee, anno 767, a prelate exceedingly religious, and renowned for his holinefs of life. *Hoveden.* At *Ely*, the commemoration of the holy bifhop *John*, who being firft a monk, and afterwards abbat of *Fountains* in *Yorkfhire*, of the *Ciftercian* order, then flourifhing in its primitive fervour; was made bifhop of *Ely:* in which dignity his extraordinary humility, charity and fanctity, recommended him to the higheft efteem and veneration of all true lovers of virtue and religion. He went to our Lord anno 1225.

June 20. At *Rome* the commemoration of the holy priefts *Timotheus* and *Novatus*, fons of S. *Pudens*; and fuppofed to have had fome particular connections with the *Britifh* nation; and the former of them to have for fome time preached in *Britain*. See *Ufher's Antiquities*, p. 17. At *Shaftfbury* the tranflation of the body of S. *Edward* king and martyr, which being taken up three years after his death was found as frefh and entire as if it had been buried the fame day. At *Winocfbergen* in *Flanders*, the tranflation of the relicks of S. *Ofwald* king and martyr.

June 21. At *Harlem* in *Holland*, the feftivity of S. *Engelmund* abbat, who went over from *England* to the affiftance of S. *Willibrord*, in his apoftolick labours, in the converfion of the *Netherlands*; where after bringing many fouls to God by his preaching, he went to receive the reward of his labours, fome time in the eighth century.

Or

On this day also S. *Leufred* abbat is honoured in the ancient *Missal* of the church of *York*.

June 22. At *Verulam* the passion of S. *Alban*, the most illustrious amongst our *British* martyrs, who after suffering cruel torments for the faith of Christ, was beheaded anno 286, under the emperor *Dioclesian*. With him also suffered the soldier, who was to have been his executioner; but being converted upon the spot, by the sight of the wonderful works of God, and confessing Christ, became the companion of his martyrdom, being baptized in his own blood. It is also the day of the passion of that eminent servant of God, *John Fisher*, cardinal and bishop of *Rochester*, beheaded on *Tower Hill* by orders of K. *Henry* VIII. for denying his ecclesiastical supremacy, anno 1535.

June 23. At *Ely* the festivity of S. *Ethelreda* or *Ediltrude* vulgo S. *Audry* queen, virgin and abbess; renowned for her love of purity and sanctity; and the perpetual incorruption of her body after death. Obiit anno 680. S. *Bede*, l. 4. c. 19.

June 24. At *Guitherin* in *Denbighshire*, the deposition of S. *Wenefride* virgin and martyr, illustrious for sanctity and miracles. At *Mechlin* in *Brabant* the passion of S. *Rumwold* bishop and martyr, principal patron of that church, who going out from *Britain*, laboured in propagating the kingdom of Christ in those countries; where at length he met with the crown of martyrdom, anno 775. In the isle of *Farne* the happy

happy death of holy *Bartholomew* hermit, who served our Lord in that solitude, above two and forty years, with extraordinary sanctity, about the middle of the twelfth century. *Capgrave.*

June 24. At *Egmond* in *Holland* the festivity of S. *Adelbert* confessor, of the blood royal of the *Northumbrian* kings; a disciple and companion of S. *Willibrord*, who converted many thousands to the faith of Christ: he flourished in the eighth century; and was honoured after death in a great church and monastery dedicated to God in his name, at the town of *Egmond*. In *Scotland* the festivity of S. *Molonach* bishop, disciple of S. *Brendan*. Obiit anno 629. *Aberdeen* breviary. In *Ireland*, the festivity S. *Nessan* deacon of S. *Patrick*, honoured as patron in the monastery of *Mungarret*.

June 26. At *Redburn* in *Hertfordshire*, the martyrdom of the holy clergyman, the spiritual father of S. *Alban*, commonly known by the name of S. *Amphibalus*. His relicks were found in the church of *Redburn* (which is dedicated in his name) and solemnly translated to the abbey S. *Albans*; not without many illustrious miracles, anno 1178.

June 27. At *Caion* in the diocese of *Tours* in *France*, the deposition of S. *John* a *British* priest of admirable sanctity. Of whom writes S. *Gregory* of *Tours*, l. *de Gloria Confessorum*, c. 23. At S. *Omers* the commemoration of S. *Ortrude* virgin, whose body at the time of the *Danish* devastations, was translated from *Eng-*
ana

land to the church of the abbey of S. *Bertin's*, and is there kept with great veneration.

June 28. In *North Wales*, the commemoration of the saints *Chebeus* and *Senan* illustrious confessors of Christ: whose bodies were found in the church of *Guitherin*, near the sepulchre of S. *Wenefride*, at the time of her translation. At *Pontoise* in *France*, the commemoration of holy *William* an *English* priest, who died there in the odour of sanctity, anno 1192: whose tomb was illustrated with many miracles. S. *Antoninus, Titulo* xvii.

June 29. The feast of the glorious apostles S. *Peter* and *Paul*; to whose preaching and labours (either by themselves, or by their successors) all the churches of the *West*, and especially those of *Great Britain*, stand indebted for their faith in Christ. In *Ireland*, the commemoration of divers holy bishops, abbats, and other religious men of the name of *Colman*, to the number, says *Usher*, p. 501, of two hundred and thirty; all honoured of old amongst the saints, in that *island of saints*.

June 30. At *Canterbury*, the deposition of S. *Deusdedit* or God's gift, the sixth archbishop of that see, and not inferior in merit to the five illustrious saints, who went before him. Obiit anno 664. In *Britain*, S. *Leonorius* bishop, commemorated in some ancient martyrologies, on the first of the following month. In the isle of *Hy*, the commemoration of holy *Diermit*, disciple and individual companion of the great S. *Columba*,

Columba, who also at his death saw the place, where that saint lay, encompassed with heavenly light. S. *Adamnan*.

JULY.

July 1. AT the city of the *Legion* (*Caerlion*) formerly the metropolis of *Britannia Secunda*, the festivity of the saints *Julius* and *Aaron*, who by a glorious martyrdom, in the persecution of *Dioclesian*, anno 286, washed their robes in the blood of the Lamb; and are now before the throne of God, in the happy society of all the faithful witnesses of his truth, who are led by the Lamb to the living fountains of the waters of *Paradise*. *Apoc*. vii. They had formerly each of them a church in the city of *Caerlion*. At *Mechlin* the translation of S. *Rumwold*, or *Rumoldus* bishop and martyr. Amongst the *Northern Britons*, the festivity of S. *Servanus* bishop, illustrious for sanctity; who baptized S. *Kentigern*; and educated him from a child in that saint-like discipline, which made him afterwards so eminent in the house of God. In *Little Britain*, the festivity of S. *Golven* third bishop of *Leon*, renowned for sanctity.

July 2. At *Winchester*, the deposition of S. *Swithin* bishop; who after a life of extraordinary sanctity, entered into the joy of his Lord, *July* 2, anno 862. At *Landaff*, the festivity of S. *Ouaoceus* bishop and confessor; who succeeded S. *Theliau*, in that see; and no ways degenerated from the virtues of that excellent prelate; whose memory

memory will always be in benediction amongst the ancient *Britons* of *South Wales.*

July 3. In the isle of *Man*, the festivity of S. *Germanus*, a *Briton*; a wise and holy man disciple of S. *Patrick*, and first bishop of that island. (*Usher* p. 335.) Also the commemoration of the saints *Romulus* and *Conindrius*, disciples of the same saint, who after the death of S. *Germanus*, were by him consecrated, and sent to be bishops of *Man* and the islands. These two holy prelates concluding a saintly life with a saintly death, had for their successor S. *Maguil* or *Macaldus*, a prelate eminent for sanctity and miracles; and honoured with many churches after his death. These four saints were the fathers and founders of the church of *Man*. In the same island, the commemoration also of the saints *Conan*, *Contentus*, *Bladus* and *Malchus*, who were all successively bishops of *Man* and the islands; and were all found worthy to be ranked, after death, among the saints. On the same day, at *Oostkerk* near *Bruges* in *Flanders*, the festivity of S. *Guthagon* confessor, patron of the church there, said to have been of royal *Scottish* blood; who despising this world and its cheating vanities, went over into *Flanders*, and led a solitary life at *Oostkerk*, in great sanctity; insomuch that his burying-place was much frequented after his death, on occasion of the great miracles, wrought by his intercession. He is believed to have flourished in the eighth century.

July 4. At *Canterbury*, the deposition of S. *Odo* archbishop of that see, surnamed *the good*;

a prelate of extraordinary sanctity. He went to our Lord anno 958. At *Battle* in *Sussex* the commemoration of another eminent servant of God, whose name also was *Odo:* who flourished in the eleventh century; and was first a monk of *Canterbury*, and afterwards abbat of *Battle:* whose life and death was so remarkably holy, that he was also honoured by our ancestors amongst the saints.

July 5. At *Burton* upon *Trent*, the festivity of S. *Modwenna* virgin and abbess, who first founded the famous nunnery of *Pollesworth* in *Warwickshire*, where she trained up S. *Editha*, S. *Ositha* and other saints; and established a holy discipline, which was kept up in that community, till the days of *Henry* VIII. Then after other religious foundations, she retired into a little island, in the river *Trent*, where she employed the latter part of her life in a more close and uninterrupted application to God, and preparation for eternity. She was illustrious for miracles both alive and dead. At *Canterbury*, the translation of S. *Anselm* archbishop of that see, and doctor of the catholic church. At *Durham* the festivity of S. *Boisil* priest, spiritual father and master of the great S. *Cuthbert:* to whom S. *Bede* gives this character, that he was a man of wonderful sanctity, of *sublime virtues*, and of a *prophetick spirit, to whose direction* Cuthbert *humbly subjecting himself, received from him,* says he, *both the knowledge of the holy scriptures, and the examples of all good works.* He departed to our Lord in the time of the great pestilence (anno 664) which he had foretold three years before;

before; and was interred in his monastery of *Mailross*; his body was translated to *Durham* anno 1030; and deposited near that of his disciple S. *Cuthbert*.

July 6. In *Scotland* the festivity of S. *Palladius* bishop, apostle of the *Scots*, to whom he was sent by the holy pope S. *Celestine* about the year 430. He is called by the *Scots* S. *Padie*; and his festival is marked on this day in the *Aberdeen* calendar. At *Ely*, the deposition of S. *Sexburge* queen and abbess, who succeeded her sister S. *Audry*, in the government of that holy community; and was succeeded by her daughter S. *Ermenilda*, who had also been a queen: so that the three first abbesses of *Ely* were all queens. For such was the faith and fervour of that golden age of the *English Saxon* church; that the greatest princesses in those days thought themselves happy, when they could exchange the toys of worldly honours, riches, and pleasures for the sweet yoke of religion and devotion, and the securing to their souls a happy eternity. On this day also that great and good man Sir *Thomas More*, sometime Lord High Chancellor of *England*, suffered death for the catholick religion, anno 1535.

July 7. At *Canterbury*, the translation of the body of S. *Thomas* archbishop and martyr, whose shrine was illustrated with innumerable miracles. At *Winchester* the deposition of S. *Hedda* bishop, renowned for his wisdom and holiness of life. He translated the see of the bishoprick of the *West Saxons* from *Dorchester* to *Winchester*;

and after most worthily administring his episcopal office for thirty years, reposed in our Lord anno 705; his sanctity being evidenced also after his death by many miracles. S. *Bede*, l. 5, c. 19. In *Ireland*, the festivity of S. *Medran* and S. *Odhrain* brothers, illustrious for sanctity in the sixth cenury.

July 8. At *Eystadt* in *Germany*, the deposition of S. *Willebald* bishop, son to the holy prince S. *Richard*; kinsman of S. *Boniface* apostle of the *Germans*; and his assistant in his apostolick labours. He went to rest anno 786. At *Wurtzburg*, the festivity of S. *Kilian* a *Scottish* or *Irish* bishop, apostle of *Franconia*, and of his companions, S. *Colman* and S. *Totman*, who after bringing over many thousands to the faith of *Christ*, were martyred in that neighbourhood, anno 689. At *Winchester* the festivity of S. *Grimbald* abbat, principal assistant of king *Ælfred* the Great, in the reformation of his kingdom. Obiit anno 904.

July 9. At *York* the festivity of S. *Everildis* a noble virgin, who with two other saint-like companions, served our Lord with great perfection, at a place afterwards called from her *Everildesham*; and by reason of her eminent sanctity, was highly honoured after her death: especially in the church of *York*; in the breviary of which she has an office of nine lessons. Also the commemoration of holy *Ælgar* hermit, whose life is quoted in *Usher's Antiquities*, p. 275.

July 10. In the famous abbey of *Lieſſy* in *Hainault* the feſtivity of S. *Etto* an *Iriſh* prelate, who with ſix other companions, went over into the *Low Countries* ſome time in the ſeventh century, to carry the light of Chriſt to them that *as yet ſat in darkneſs and in the ſhadow of death:* where at length in a good old age, illuſtrious for ſanctity and miracles, he departed to our Lord at the monaſtery of *Feſcau:* from which his body was tranſlated to that of *Lieſſy*, where it is now kept with great veneration. This monaſtery of *Lieſſy* was reformed by the venerable abbat *Lewis Bloſius,* about the middle of the ſixteenth century.

July 11. In divers parts of the *Netherlands,* the commemoration of many apoſtolical men, who being ſtrongly moved with a zeal for the glory of God and the ſalvation of ſouls, about the ſame time with S. *Etto,* going out of our *Britiſh* iſlands, dedicated their labours and their lives to the propagating both the faith and the life of the goſpel amongſt infidels and ſinners. Amongſt theſe, ſome of the moſt eminent were S. *Bertuin* biſhop, whoſe body waits for a happy reſurrection at the abbey of *Maloigne* upon the *Sambre.* S. *Eloquius,* who repoſes in the monaſtery of *Wazor.* S. *Adalgiſus,* who reſts in the monaſtery of S. *Michael* in *Tierarche.* S. *Mombul* abbat, employed by S. *Eligius,* in preaching through his whole dioceſe of *Tournay* and *Noion,* &c. &c. *Miræus in Faſtis Belgicis, July* 10.

July 12. In the monastery of S. *Fara*, in the forest of *Brie*, the commemoration of S. *Edelburge* virgin, daughter to king *Anna*, and third abbess after S. *Fara*, and S. *Sethrid*, of that illustrious congregation. She was renowned for her extraordinary sanctity, and most perfect purity both of soul and body; evidenced by the incorruption of her body after death. S. *Bede*, l. 3. c. 6. She is honoured in the *Roman* Martyrology on the seventh of *July*; which was the day on which she died; or rather on which she began to live in that region where she shall never die: anno 660.

July 13. At *Canterbury*, the translation of the body of S. *Mildred* virgin and abbess, from *Menstrey* in the isle of *Thanet*, to the abbey of S. *Austin*, anno 1033. Also a commemoration of those holy spouses of Christ, who were slain by the *Danes*, when they burnt the church and monastery of *Menstrey*, anno 1011; and laid the whole island waste with fire and sword.

July 14. At *Daventer*, in the province of *Overyssel*, the festivity of S. *Marchelm* an *English* priest, and apostolical preacher, in the eighth century. He was a disciple of S. *Willibrord*, and sent by him, in the company of S. *Lebwin*, to preach the faith of Christ in *Overyssel*; where they converted many thousands; and have been honoured ever since as apostles and tutelar saints of the city and diocese of *Daventer*. S. *Marchelm* is commemorated on this day in the *Roman* Martyrology, under the name of *Marcellinus*.

July 15. At *Winchester* the translation of S. *Swithin* bishop, so renowned amongst our ancestors for his sanctity and miracles, that the cathedral of that city for some time bore his name. In *Swedeland*, the festivity of S. *David* abbat, an *Englishman* by birth, eminent for sanctity, in the eleventh century; and honoured with a proper office in the *Swedish* breviary. On the same day, the deposition of S. *Editha* queen, daughter to *Edward* the elder, and married to *Sithricke* the *Danish* king of *Northumberland*; who after the death of her husband, entered into a monastery, which she had begun at *Tamworth*; and there died in the odour of sanctity, anno 926. In *Scotland*, the commemoration of S. *Donevald*, and his nine virgin daughters, honoured on this day in the *Scottish* calendars. See *Usher*, p. 372.

July 16. At *Salisbury*, the translation of S. *Osmund* bishop of that see, in the time of the *Conqueror*, the first compiler of the *Sarum* office. His body still lies in the cathedral of that city, where it has been honoured with many miracles. Obiit anno 1089. At *Wilton*, the commemoration of S. *Ivy* bishop; whose relicks formerly reposed in that church. *Saxon Manuscript.*

July 17. At the abbey of *Winchelcomb* in *Gloucestershire*, the festivity of S. *Kenelm* king of the *Mercians*, treacherously murdered anno 819, and honoured with great miracles after his death. He has a place this day in the *Sarum* calendar. In the *Netherlands*, the feast of S. *Fredegand* an apostolical preacher, and companion of S. *Foillan:*

Ian: whose relicks are now kept in the collegiate church of S. *Peter* at *Monstier* upon the *Sambre*. In the territory of *Ruremond*, the commemoration of S. *Odilia*, a *British* virgin and martyr.

July 18. At *Ailesbury* in *Buckinghamshire*, the festivity of S. *Eadgithe*, or *Editha*, virgin and abbess, daughter of *Frithwald* a *Mercian* lord, by *Wiltiburge* daughter to king *Penda*; who rejecting the marriage of *Sigher* king of the *East Saxons*, consecrated her whole soul and body to God; and became an eminent saint. Also the commemoration of her sister S. *Eadburge* or *Edburge*, who made the like consecration of herself to God; accompanied her sister in her retirement, and all her religious exercises, and at length was associated with her in glory. These saints flourished in the seventh century. See *Mahew's Trophæa*. At *Glasgow*, the festivity of S. *Thenaw* a *British* matron, mother of S. *Kentigern*; and honoured on this day in the *Scottish* calendars.

July 19. At *Derham* in *Norfolk*, the commemoration of S. *Withburge* virgin, daughter to king *Anna*, and the youngest of four sisters all eminent saints. She was very young, when after the death of her father, slain by king *Penda*, she consecrated herself wholly to divine love; and choosing for herself the solitude of *Derham*, there continued to serve God with wonderful devotion, till her dying day anno 743. Her body was translated to *Ely*; and in the year 1106, deposited near her sister S. *Audry:* at which time (which was above three hundred and sixty years
after

BRITISH PIETY. 107

after her death) she was found not only entire and uncorrupt; but with her limbs as flexible as if she were living, her cheeks beautifully red, and her very garments entire and fresh. Cardinal *Baronius* in his church annals, on the year 725, commemorates also another noble *English* lady of the name of *Withburge*, who for the love of God, shut herself up for life in a small cell, in S. *Peter's* church at *Rome*; where she wholly devoted herself to divine contemplation.

July 20. In the diocese of *Ruremond*, the commemoration of S. *Plechelm* a *British* prelate of admirable sanctity; who preached the faith of Christ with great fruit in *Guelderland*, and the neighbouring provinces, in the eighth century: and is honoured to this day with a proper office in the diocese of *Ruremond*.

July 21. At *Strasburgh* in *Germany*, the deposition of S. *Arbogast* a *Scot*, or *Irishman* by birth, who leading a hermit's life in *Alsatia*, was by reason of his great sanctity, drawn out of his solitude, and made bishop of *Strasburgh*. He departed to our Lord anno 658, illustrious for miracles; amongst which 'tis recorded, that he recalled to life, by his prayers, prince *Sigebert* son to king *Dagobert*, who in hunting had been slain by a wild boar.

July 22. In *Ireland*, the commemoration of S. *Luman* bishop, nephew and coadjutor to S. *Patrick*, and founder of the church of *Trim*: also the commemoration of the holy bishops *Brochadius*, *Brochanus* and *Mogenochus* brothers

of

of S. *Luman*, all *Britons* by birth, nephews of S. *Patrick* by his sister *Tigridia*, and employed by their uncle in propagating the kingdom of Christ in *Ireland*. See *Usher*, p. 824. Also the commemoration of S. *Darerca* sister to S. *Patrick*, and no ways unworthy of such a brother.

July 23. In the territory of *Nandesi* in the county of *Waterford*, the festivity of S. *Declan* bishop, one of the first preachers of the faith of Christ in *Ireland*. He founded the church of *Ardmore*; and opened a school for piety and learning, in which he had many illustrious disciples. Seven of these are honoured amongst the saints, viz. *Mochelloc, Bean, Colman, Lachnin, Mobius, Findlug* and *Caminan*; who built the seven famous *cells*, in the plain called *the field of the shield*, near *Lismore*. These saints flourished in the fifth century.

July 24. At *Stone*, in *Staffordshire*, the festivity of the saints *Ulfhad* and *Ruffin* martyrs; who having been privately instructed in the faith of Christ, and baptized by S. *Chad*, were upon that account slain by their pagan father, in the neighbourhood of *Stone*; where a church was not long after built in their honour.

July 25. At *Berg* S. *Winoc* in *Flanders*, the translation of S. *Lewine* a *British* virgin and martyr, from a monastery at *Seaford* near *Lewes* in *Sussex*, to the abbey of *Berg* anno 1058. God was pleased to honour this translation with many evident miracles, recorded by a cotemporary historian, an eye-witness, and acknowledged by
the

the century writers of *Magdeburg*, in these words: 'When the body of *Lewine* the virgin was carried anno 1058, through the villages and towns on the sea coast of *Flanders*, the paralyticks, the deaf, the lame, and such as were otherwise diseased, were suddenly cured.' *Centur.* xi. fol. 274. In the same abbey of *Berg*, the commemoration of S. *Idaberga* virgin, whose relicks were translated at the same time.

July 26. At *Dendermond* in *Flanders* the festivity of S. *Christiana* an *English* virgin, honoured as patroness, or tutelar saint of that town: where her relicks are kept in the collegiate church; to which they were translated, in the ninth century, from her burying place at *Dikelven* a village upon the *Scheld*, where she had crowned a saintly life with a happy death in the foregoing century.

July 27. At *Glastenbury*, the festivity of S. *Joseph* of *Arimathea*, the noble counsellor who buried our Lord: who, according to the tradition of that place, agreeable to some ancient records, came over into *Britain* with eleven other companions, and settled himself in the isle of *Avallonia* (now *Glastenbury*) where he built the first christian church, in honour of the blessed Virgin; and after a most saintly life, reposed in our Lord, leaving behind him a succession of saints in that holy solitude. At *Lincoln*, the passion of S. *Hugh* a child of ten years, crucified by the *Jews*, in hatred of Christ, anno 1255.

July 28. At *Dole* in *Little Brittany*, the feast of S. *Samson* bishop; honoured on this day in

the

the *Sarum*, *York* and *Paris* breviaries; who with the bright rays of his extraordinary sanctity, very much illustrated both *Britain* and *France*. Obiit anno 565 *Mabillon*. In *Swedeland*, the festivity of S. *Botuid* martyr, who being baptized by a holy priest in *England*, and taught to be a saint, returning into *Swedeland*, by his doctrine and miracles converted great numbers to Christ, in the twelfth century.

July 29. At *Troyes* in *France*, the festivity of S. *Lupus* bishop, a man of most sublime virtues and apostolick spirit, who coming over into *Britain* with S. *Germanus* of *Auxerre*, by his sanctity and miracles greatly contributed to the extirpation of the *Pelagian* heresy; which had taken deep root amongst the *Britons*. Obiit anno 472. In *Norway*, the festivity of S. *Olave* king and martyr, who having learnt the faith of Christ in *England*, or by the ministry of the *English*; embraced it with all the affections of his soul; and zealously labouring to propagate it through his dominions, was at length slain by the enemies of it; and so received the crown of martyrdom anno 1030. He was greatly honoured by our ancestors; four parishes in *London*, and many others throughout *England*, being dedicated to God in his name.

July 30. At *Canterbury*, the deposition of S. *Tatwyne*, the ninth archbishop of that see, and no ways unworthy of his predecessors; who were all of them saints. Obiit anno 734. In the isle of *Thanet*, the commemoration of S. *Ermengithe* virgin; who consecrated herself to God,
together

together with her niece S. *Mildred,* in the monastery of *Menstrey;* and was illustrious for miracles. Saxon *MS.*

July 31. At *Auxerre* in *Burgundy,* the festivity of S. *Germanus* bishop of that see, one of the greatest prelates that ever illustrated the *Gallican* church. He twice came over into *Britain* to oppose the *Pelagian* heresy, and enlightened the whole island with the rays of his sanctity; working also wonderful miracles amongst us. S. *Bede,* l. 1. c. 17, &c. He died at *Ravenna* anno 448. Many churches in *Britain* have been dedicated in his name. In *Cornwall,* the deposition of S. *Neot* priest; renowned for sanctity in the days of king *Ælfred.* Obiit anno 890.

AUGUST.

August 1. AT *Winchester,* the feast of S. *Ethelwold* bishop, cotemporary with S. *Dunstan;* a zealous reformer both of the clergy and religious, and an ardent lover and promoter of the beauty of the house of God: whom he went to enjoy, anno 948. In *South Wales,* the feast of S. *Kined* or *Kinedvau* hermit, cotemporary with and an intimate friend of S. *David* of *Menevia;* whose name was very illustrious of old amongst the *Britons* of *South Wales.*

August 2. In *Brecknockshire,* the festivity of S. *Almedha* virgin and martyr, daughter to *Bragan,* who gave name to that county, and sister to the saints *Canocus* and *Keyna.* At *Canterbury,* the deposition of the holy archbishop *Plegmund.*

He

He was called from his hermitage, to the pastoral charge; and made archbishop of *Canterbury* in the days of king *Ælfred*; and was highly instrumental in the restoration of learning and piety under that reign; after the confusion and profanation of all that was holy, which had been occasioned by the *Danes*: in which he was also assisted by *Werefrid*, the holy bishop of *Worcester*. Obiit anno 923.

August 3. In the abbey of *Mailross* in the Marches of *Scotland*, the festivity of S. *Waltheof* abbat, of the *Cistercian* or *Bernardin* institute; who despising his high birth (being allied both to the kings of *England*, and of *Scotland*) and all that this world could give or promise him; embraced the strict discipline, poverty and abstraction of that holy order: in which he lived, and died a most perfect pattern of all christian and religious perfection. Obiit anno 1160.

August 4. In *Ireland*, the festivity of S. *Luan* or *Molua* abbat, disciple of S. *Comgall* of *Benchor*, and founder of a hundred monasteries; to whom he gave a particular rule, said to have been highly applauded by S. *Gregory* the Great. He is numbered amongst the chiefest fathers of the churches of *Ireland*, by abbat *Cummian* in his epistle to *Segenius* abbat of *Hy*. He departed to our Lord anno 622. He is also called *Lugidus*, or *Lugeus*.

August 5. The festivity of S. *Oswald* king and martyr, a most zealous and religious prince, slain by the *Pagan Penda* anno 642, and glorified after his

his death by many miracles. S. *Bede*, l. 3. c. 6, 9, 10, 11. He is honoured on this day, both in the *Sarum* and *York* missals; as well as in the *Roman* Martyrology. At *Bardney* in *Lincolnshire*, the burying place of S. *Ostrytha* queen of the *Mercians*, sister to S. *Oswald*. *Saxon MS.*

August 6. At *Dover*, the passion of *Thomas* a holy monk; slain by the *French*, when they plundered that town, anno 1295, because he would not discover to them the sacred vessels, &c. and honoured by miracles after his death. *Capgrave*. In the monastery of *Bredan* in *Leicestershire*, the commemoration of S. *Hardulf* confessor, honoured as patron or tutelar saint of that abbey. See *Dugdale's Monasticon*.

August 7. At *Westminster Abbey*, the memory of holy *Matildes* or *Maude*, queen of *England*, a most religious princess, wife to king *Henry* I. daughter to S. *Margaret* of *Scotland*; and a close follower of all her virtues; especially of her extraordinary charity and humility. She reposed in our Lord anno 1118. In *Dean Forest*, the memory of S. *Briavel* confessor, of whose hermitage there, see *Dugdale's Abridgment*, p. 107.

August 8. The commemoration of S. *Colman*, who from a monk of S. *Columb's* monastery in the isle of *Hy*, was made third bishop of *Lindisfarne*. He was a prelate of a most amiable character in regard to his perfect disinterestedness, his moderation and humility; as well as his fervour in the service of God, and his zeal for the salvation of souls. S. *Bede*, l. 3. c. 26.

c. 26. He resigned his bishoprick anno 664, and retired into *Ireland*; where he founded the monastery of *Inys-bo-finde* for the *Scots*; and that of *Mayo* for the *English*; which was so renowned of old for piety and religion, as to count at once no fewer than one hundred saints; all *living in great continency and simplicity by the labour of their hands, under a rule and canonical abbat, by the example of the venerable fathers*. S. *Bede*, ibidem. S. *Colman* went to our Lord anno 676: and is honoured in the *Aberdeen* calendar, on the 18th of *February*.

August 9. In the isle of *Croyland*, in *Lincolnshire*, the commemoration of holy *Alfreda* alias *Etheldritha* virgin, daughter to *Offa* king of the *Mercians*; who after the base murder of S. *Ethelbert* king of the *East Angles*; who came to her father's court, to seek her in marriage; detesting the world, and its wicked ways, withdrew herself into the solitude of *Croyland*, and there lived a recluse, and most holy life, for about forty years, in a cell, in the south part of the church. Obiit anno 934.

August 10. At *Dumblain* in *Scotland*, the festivity of S. *Blaine* bishop. He was renowned for faith and sanctity in the tenth century; and had for his bishop's see a college or convent of the *Culdees*, or ancient *Scottish* canons, in the place where *Dumblain* now stands; the cathedral of which is dedicated to God in his name. He is honoured on this day in the *Aberdeen* breviary.

August

August 11. At *Canterbury*, the deposition of the holy archbishop *Janbercht*, or *Lambert*, who went to our Lord anno 701. At *Chichester*, the commemoration of holy *Gilbert de S. Lifard* bishop of that see; whose sanctity is highly extolled by our historians; who also record divers miracles to have been wrought at his sepulchre. Obiit anno 1305. *Matthew Paris*, &c.

August 12. At *Winborn* in *Dorsetshire*, the commemoration of holy *Tetta*, abbess of a double community there; renowned for her own sanctity; and a mother to many great saints. She was cotemporary with S. *Boniface*, apostle of *Germany*; and at his request, sent over divers of her children to his assistance; by whom the work of God was carried on, with great benediction in those countries. She flourished in the eighth century.

August 13. In *Germany*, the festivity of S. *Wigbert* priest and abbat, one of the chiefest of those apostolical men, who went over from *England* to the assistance of S. *Boniface*, in the work of the gospel. He was made by that saint, abbot of *Fritzlar*, and afterwards of *Ortdorff*; and after labouring with great fruit for many years, for the glory of God, and the sanctification of souls, he was called to the reward of his labours, anno 747; and has a place on this day in the *Roman* Martyrology. In *Normandy*, the festivity of S. *Walter* an *Englishman*, abbat of *Fontanelle*, who departed to our Lord anno 1150.

August 14. In *Holland*, the deposition of S. *Werenfrid*, an apostolical priest and missionary of the *English* nation; and one of those to whom the *Hollanders*, under God, stand principally indebted for their christianity. He converted the isle of *Batavia*, and divers other territories to Christ, and went in a good old age to receive the reward of his labours, some time in the eighth century. His mortal remains were interred amongst his converts at the town of *Elst*; where a collegiate church was erected over them; and dedicated to God in his name.

August 15. At *Clogher* in *Ireland*, the festivity of S. *Kertennus* or *Mactarthen*, disciple and inseparable companion of S. *Patrick*; and made by him the first bishop of *Clogher*: where his memory is in great veneration to this day. He went to our Lord anno 506. *Usher*, p. 445.

August 16. In the monastery of *Cateby* in *Northamptonshire*, the commemoration of the holy spouses of Christ *Margaret*, and *Alice*, sisters to S. *Edmund*, archbishop of *Canterbury*, and successively prioresses of the aforesaid community: in which they lived and died in the sweet odour of sanctity, (in the thirteenth century,) as became the sisters of such a brother.

August 17. At *Hertford*, the deposition of the venerable servant of God *Thomas* the archdeacon, disciple of S. *Edmund*, archbishop of *Canterbury*; celebrated by our historians for the eminent holiness of his life, and for the many miracles, wrought by his intercession after his death. Obiit anno

anno 1253. *Matt. Weſt. & Paris.* anno 1253. In *Holland*, the feſtivity of S. *Jeron*, a native of *Great Britain*, and apoſtolick preacher in that province, where he was martyred by the *Danes* in the ninth century.

Auguſt 18. At *Rome*, the depoſition of S. *Helen* the empreſs, mother of *Conſtantine* the Great, illuſtrious for her royal munificence, and unbounded charities; as well as for her ſingular piety, and humility. At *Irvine* in *Scotland*, the feſtivity of S. *Evan* or *Inan* confeſſor, renowned for ſanctity. Obiit anno 839. In *Ireland*, the depoſition of S. *Dega*, ſurnamed *Mac Caryll*, biſhop and confeſſor, who repoſed in our Lord anno 586.

Auguſt 19. In *South Wales*, the commemoration of S. *Clitanc*, king of that province; a prince moſt amiable for his great virtue, and his admirable endowments both of body and mind, joined with a ſingular love of purity: who being ſlain by a wicked courtier in hunting, was for the innocence of his life, and the prodigies that accompanied his death, honoured amongſt the ſaints and martyrs, a church being erected over his grave, by the biſhop of *Landaff*, and dedicated in his name. *Dugdale's Monaſticon*, vol. 3. In *Scotland*, the memory of that ſaint-like prelate *John Scot*, an *Engliſhman*, biſhop of *Dunkeld*: who after a moſt worthy adminiſtration of that ſee, retired to the *Ciſtercian* abbey of *Newbottle*, and there died the death of the ſaints anno 1203. See *Fordun*, l. 4. c. 35, 36, &c.

August 20. At *Tinmouth*, the festivity of S. *Oswin* king of the *Deiri*, a prince of *exceeding great piety and religion*, says S. Bede, l. 3. c. 14. *beloved by all men, for the royal dignity of his mind, of his person, and of his merits —— but amongst the other glories of his virtue, and —— his extraordinary benedictions, his humility* was most particularly remarkable. He was basely murdered, after seven years reign, by his rival king *Oswin* the *Bernician*; and after his death was illustrated by many miracles: insomuch that the church and priory of *Tinmouth*, to which his body was translated, was dedicated to God, in his name.

August 21. At *Andria*, in the kingdom of *Naples*, the commemoration of S. *Richard*, an *Englishman*, bishop of that see, in the twelfth century; a zealous preacher of all holiness, both by word and work. He departed to our Lord, about the close of that century; and was solemnly canonized by pope *Boniface* VIII. after a juridical examination and proof of no fewer than one hundred miracles, wrought by his intercession. See the *Bollandists*.

August 22. At *Louth* in *Ireland*, the commemoration of S. *Mochteus* a *Briton*; the first bishop of that see, in the days of S. *Patrick*; with whom he was united in the bands of a most holy friendship. He was renowned for sanctity; and for the spirit of prophecy; and opened a great school of christian piety; in which he is said to have trained up no fewer than one hundred bishops, and three hundred priests: who afterwards wonderfully propagated

the

the kingdom of Chriſt amongſt the *Iriſh*. Obiit anno 535. At *Jarrow* in the biſhoprick of *Durham*, the depoſition of holy *Sigfrid* abbat, coadjutor of S. *Bennet Biſcop:* whoſe ſaint-like life and death is deſcribed by his diſciple S. *Bede*, in his hiſtory of the abbats of *Weremouth* and *Jarrow*.

Auguſt 23. In the iſle of *Ramſey*, the paſſion of S. *Juſtinian*; who led a ſolitary life in that iſland, in the days of S. *David* of *Menevia*, in great ſanctity; always employed, either in treating with God by prayer, or in bringing others to God, by his preaching and inſtructions: for many being drawn by the ſweet odour of his ſanctity reſorted to him, to learn of him the ways of *truth* and *life*. He was at length ſlain in his hermitage, by ſome children of *Belial* in hatred of his virtue; and was honoured by the *Britiſh* church, as a martyr. His body was tranſlated from the iſland to the oppoſite ſhore; to a port which ſometime bore his name, and a church was there built under his invocation. In the ſame iſland, the commemoration of the man of God *Honorius*, ſon of *Trefriauc* a *Britiſh* prince, who firſt conſecrated that ſolitude to Chriſt, and received S. *Juſtinian* at his coming thither. In *Ireland*, the feſtivity of S. *Eogain* biſhop of *Ardſrathen* (which ſee is now tranſlated to *Londonderry*) illuſtrious for ſanctity, in the ſixth century.

Auguſt 24. The feſtivity of S. *Audoenus* or *Owen* archbiſhop of *Rouen*, a prelate of extraordinary ſanctity; whoſe relicks were formerly enſhrined in the cathedral of *Canterbury*. In *Scotland*

land the festivity of S. *Irchard* or *Erchad* bishop and confessor, honoured on this day in the *Scots* calendar, which marks his happy death anno 933. At *Isselbey* in *Lincolnshire*, the commemoration of S. *Pandwyne* or *Pandania* virgin, whose relicks were kept in that church. Obiit anno 904.

August 25. At *Coludburgh* or *Coldingham*, in the *Marches* of *Scotland*, the festivity of the royal virgin S. *Ebba* (vulgo S. *Tabbe*) abbess of a double community in that town. She, was sister to S. *Oswald*, and from her tender years happily dedicated herself to divine love; insomuch that rejecting the suit of *Ædan* king of the *Scots*, who desired her in marriage, she fled from all the pomps and vanities of the world into the *Asylum* of religion: and taking along with her divers other virgins, who were of the same mind, she founded, with the help of her brother king *Oswi*, first the monastery of *Ebchester*; and afterwards that of *Coldingham:* where she shone forth in such manner by the lustre of her virtues, as to be most *honourable to all, no less for the religiousness of her life than for the nobility of her blood.* S. *Bede, vita S. Cuthberti,* c. 10. She departed to our Lord, in a good old age, anno 683. At *Monte Fiascone* in *Tuscany*, the deposition of S. *Thomas* bishop of *Hereford*, illustrious for sanctity and miracles. Obiit anno 1287.

August 26. At *Canterbury*, the deposition of S. *Bregwin*, the twelfth archbishop of that see: a man (says the abridgment of *Dugdale*) *profoundly devoted to religion.* He went to our Lord anno

anno 762. His relicks were afterwards enshrined, with those of the holy archbishop *Plegmund* and placed behind the altar of S. *Gregory*, in the cathedral of *Canterbury*. In the diocese of *Landaff*, the commemoration of S. *Budgualan;* whose church is mentioned in the synods of *Landaff*.

August 27. In *Scotland*, the festivity of S. *Malrube* hermit, martyred by the *Danes*, according to the *Scottish* calendars anno 1024. On this day also is honoured in the missals and breviaries of *Sarum* and *York*, S. *Ruffus* martyr. In *Cornwall*, the commemoration of S. *Kewe*, honoured of old in that province.

August 28. At *Winborn* in *Dorsetshire*, the commemoration of S. *Quenburge* virgin, sister to king *Ina:* who with the help of her sister S. *Cuthburge*, founded the famous monastery of *Winborn*, the nursery of many saints. At *Brackley* in *Northamptonshire*, the commemoration of S. *Rumbald* confessor.

August 29. At S. *Paul's* in *London*, the festivity of S. *Sebbi* king and confessor : *a man much devoted to God, and greatly addicted to religious exercises:* who after a most christian reign of thirty years, happily ended his days in the habit of religion, towards the close of the seventh century. S. *Bede*, l. 4. c. 11. At the abbey of *Cerne* in *Dorsetshire*, the translation of S. *Edwold* brother to S. *Edmund* king and martyr; who retiring into the province of the *West Saxons*, led there an eremitical life, in prayer and contemplation near *Shaftsbury*, feeding upon nothing but bread and

and water; till he was called from his lonesome cell, to an eternal kingdom, anno 871.

August 30. In the diocese of *Meaux* in *France*, the festivity of S. *Fiaker*, said to have been born of royal *Scottish* blood: who leaving his native country, and worldly friends, and all things that he seemed to possess, in order to secure to his soul the hidden treasure of the kingdom of heaven; going into *France*, addressed himself to S. *Faron* bishop of *Meaux*, for his direction; who appointed him a solitary place in his diocese, for an hermitage, in which he continued to his dying day a life of great austerity, and admirable sanctity. He was also most illustrious for miracles: insomuch, that to this day there is scarce any saint held in greater veneration by the people of *France*; or for whom they have more devotion, than S. *Fiaker*. He went to our Lord about the year 670.

August 31. At *Lindisfarne*, the deposition of S. *Aidan* first bishop of that see, and apostle of the *Northern English*. He was sent at the request of the holy king S. *Oswald*, from the famous monastery of the isle of *Hy*, for the instruction of the *English*, in the faith of Christ; for which God gave him very great graces; and in which he blessed his labours with admirable fruits! Whose doctrine, says S. *Bede*, l. 3. c. 5. nothing so much recommended to all men, as his teaching no otherwise than he and his lived. For nothing of this world did he either seek or love. Whatsoever was given him by the rich, he presently gave to the first poor he met.' He travelled over his vast diocese, (which was extended from the *Humber* to the *Frith*) generally on foot, employed all the way in prayer and meditation; or in spiritual conferences, with those that accompanied him, or in reciting the psalms. He was ever ready to run to the assistance of souls; not only in the towns and villages, and even in the poorest cottages; but also in the highways, and the very fields: for wheresoever he saw any persons, he went up to them; that if he found they were infidels, he might invite them to the faith of Christ; or if they already believed, he might confirm them in their faith, and exhort them to a life worthy of their faith. In these apostolical labours, and in the exercises of all the evangelical virtues, in their greatest perfection, as well as in the establishing of many churches, schools and monasteries, and in training up many saints, he employed seventeen years. At the end of which he was called to eternal rest, anno 651. S. *Cuthbert*, then a shepherd in the mountains, saw his departing soul, in exceeding great glory, carried up by angels to her everlasting home; which vision determined him to quit the world, and to become a monk. S. *Bede in vita Cuthberti.*

SEPTEMBER.

September 1. AT *Winchester*, the commemoration of S. *Elphegus*, or *Alphege the elder*, bishop of that see; illustrious for the holiness of his life, and for his spirit of prophecy. He went to our Lord anno 953. *William of Malmesbury*, l. 2. de Pontif. In *Scotland*, the deposition of S. *Murdoc* bishop and confessor. In the monastery of *Mailross* upon the river *Tweed*, the memory of holy *Drithelm* the servant of God, who having seen in a trance many extraordinary things with relation to the other world, retiring into that religious community, followed there a life of admirable austerity, and sanctity. S. *Bede*, l. 5. c. 13. It is also the feast of S. *Giles* a holy abbat, in whose name innumerable churches have been erected in *Britain*.

September 2. At *Roschild* in *Denmark*, the commemoration of S. *William* an *Englishman*, bishop of that see, in the beginning of the eleventh century; celebrated for his pastoral zeal, and the holiness of his life. *Saxo Grammaticus*, c. 11. In *Ireland*, the commemoration of S. *Senach* archbishop of *Armagh*; who went to our Lord anno 610.

September 3. In the island of *Hy*, the commemoration of blessed *Adamnan*, abbat of the monastery of S. *Columba*; whose wonderful acts and miracles he published in three books. He was a *wise and holy man*, who by conferring with S. *Ceolfrid* abbat of *Weremouth*, being himself convinced of the canonical time of celebrating *Easter*, brought over a great part of the *Scots* and *Irish* to the observance of the same. Obiit anno 698. S. *Bede*, l. 5. c. 16. In *Ireland* the commemoration of the holy bishops S. *Colman* founder of the church of *Clone*, S. *Murgeus*, S. *Loman Lachigili*, and S. *Loman Lachavoir*, who all flourished in sanctity in the seventh century. See *Usher*, p. 473.

September 4. At *Durham*, the translation of the body of S. *Cuthbert* bishop of *Lindisfarne*, the great *Thaumaturgus*, or wonder worker of *England*: whose body, after divers removals occasioned by the *Danish* devastations, was at length (together with the bishoprick) translated to *Durham:* where also it was found whole and incorrupt, above 800 years after his death, when his shrine was demolished by the visiters under K. *Henry* VIII. See *Ancient Rites*, &c. *of the Church of Durham*, p. 160. In *Scotland*, the deposition of S. *Mirinus*, bishop and confessor. In *Ireland*, the festivity of S. *Ultan* bishop of *Ardbrecan*, of the kindred and family of S. *Brigide*; who was in his days very illustrious for sanctity, and is named in the second place amongst the saints of the third *order* or *class*, in the famous manuscript catalogue published by *Usher* in his *Antiquities*, p. 473. Obiit anno 657. At *Triers* in *Germany*, the festivity of S. *Marcellus* bishop and martyr; said to have been of the *British* nation.

Sept. 5. At *Burton* upon *Trent*, the commemoration of S. *Athy* virgin, companion of S. *Modwenna*, who flourished in sanctity in the ninth century. In *Ireland*, the commemoration of S. *Petranus* bishop of *Luske*; whose name stands the first in the third class of *Irish* saints, in the ancient manuscript catalogue. Also in *Ireland*, the commemoration of the holy abbats *Airedan* and *Faillan*, illustrious for sanctity.

Sept. 6. In *Cumberland*, the commemoration of S. *Bega*, vulgo S. *Bee* virgin and abbess, whose

whose relicks were anciently kept, with great veneration, in a church called from her S. *Bees*, in the territory of *Coupland*, near *Carlisle*. In *Cornwall*, the commemoration of S. *Etha*, alias S. *Teath*, or *Theha*, in whose name there stands a church dedicated to God in that province. See *Tanner*'s *Notitia monastica*, in *Cornwall*.

September 7. At *Canterbury*, the translation of S. *Dunstan*, archbishop and confessor, who for the eminence of his sanctity has been greatly honoured by our ancestors; as appears from the many churches dedicated to God, in his name. At *York*, the commemoration of S. *Euurcius*, bishop, celebrated on this day in the *York* Missal. At *Winborn* in *Dorsetshire*, the commemoration of S. *Cuthburga*, virgin and abbess, sister to the glorious king *Ina*; who, being espoused to *Aldfred*, king of the *Northumbrians*, preferred the title of the humble hand-maid of Jesus Christ before that of a queen; and having obtained the consent of king *Aldfred*, to preserve her virginity, and enter into religion, she betook herself to the famous monastery of *Barking* in *Essex*; where, under the holy abbess S. *Hildelide*, she learnt to be a saint; and going thence, she founded, with the help of her sister *Quenburga*, the double monastery of men and women at *Winborn* in *Dorsetshire*, dedicated to the Queen of virgins, where she taught many others to be saints. She went to our Lord in the 8th century, and is commemorated in the *Sarum* calendar, on the 31st of *August*.

September 8. At *Difenburg*, in the diocese of *Mentz*, the festivity of S. *Difen* or *Difibode*, bishop, by nation an *Irish Scot*, a zealous preacher of the gospel, both at home and abroad; and founder of that famous monastery, which takes its name from him. He reposed in our Lord, being very illustrious for sanctity and miracles, about the year 700. His life was written by S. *Hildegardes*. At the monastery of *Menstrey* in the isle of *Thanet*, the commemoration of S. *Eadburge*, virgin and abbess, who succeeded S. *Mildred* in the charge of superior of that holy community; whose body also she translated to the new church which she built in honour of S. *Peter* and S. *Paul*. She was of the blood royal of *Kent*, but more renowned for the holiness of her life, than for the nobility of her extraction. Obiit anno 751. Her relicks were translated to *Canterbury*, anno 1055, and deposited in the church of S. *Gregory*.

September 9. At *Cluain-micnois*, in the county of *Westmeath*, the festivity of S. *Queranus*, or *Kieran* the younger, abbot, and first bishop of *Clanes*. He was disciple of S. *Finian* of *Clonard*; and in the acts of this saint has the first place amongst the twelve, who for their extraordinary sanctity were called the twelve apostles of *Ireland*, and were all trained up in the same school. He was the author of a monastick rule; and opened, in his monastery of *Cluain-micnois*, a school, which for divers ages was renowned for sacred letters. He went to our Lord anno 549;

and was honoured of old as patron, or tutelar saint, of the whole province of *Connaught.*

September 10. At *Kill-winnin* in *Cuningham* of *Scotland,* the feſtivity of S. *Finian* biſhop; whom the *Britons* call S. *Winnin.* He was of noble *Iriſh* blood, and trained up in piety and learning firſt at home, by a holy biſhop called *Colman*; afterwards in *Britain,* by S. *Nennio,* a *Britiſh* prelate, in his *Great Monaſtery.* He illuſtrated both *Britain* and *Ireland* with the rays of his extraordinary ſanctity, and the glory of his miracles; for he even raiſed four perſons from death to life, as his acts atteſt. He departed to our Lord ſome time in the ſixth century, and has the firſt place in the ſecond claſs of *Iriſh* ſaints in the ancient catalogue. He was honoured of old as tutelar ſaint of the whole province of *Ulſter.*

September 11. In the dioceſe of *Ruremond,* the commemoration of S. *Otger,* a holy deacon of the *Engliſh* nation; who aſſociated himſelf with the ſaints *Wiro* and *Plechelm,* in preaching the faith of Chriſt in the *Netherlands*; where he is honoured to this day in the dioceſes of *Ruremond* and *Groningen* as one of their apoſtles. In *Ireland* the commemoration of S. *Coelan,* abbat of *Noendrum,* who flouriſhed in ſanctity in the ſixth century.

September 12. In *Ireland* the feſtivity of S. *Ailbeus,* firſt biſhop of *Emely,* apoſtle, and ſpecial patron of the province of *Munſter.* He was inſtructed from a child and baptized by a *Britiſh* prieſt,

priest, whom divine providence conducted into *Ireland* for that purpose, before S. *Patrick* came thither: and going abroad, as far as *Rome*, after having made a great progress there in the study of the holy scriptures, and in all virtue and sanctity, he was ordained bishop, and sent by the pope to preach the gospel in his own country: which he did with great fruit, especially in his native province of *Munster*; confirming his doctrine with many miracles, and continuing his apostolick labours till his happy death, anno 527. See his acts in *Usher*'s Antiquities. He is named by the holy abbat *Cummian*, in his epistle to *Segenius*, fourth abbat of *Hy*, about the observance of Easter, the first amongst the most eminent fathers of the churches of the south of *Ireland*; in *Usher*'s *Sylloge Epist. Hibernic.* p. 33. and was the founder of a religious congregation, for which he composed a monastick rule, still extant.

September 13. In the famous monastery of *Daimh-Inys*, in the lake of *Erne*, in *Ireland*, the festivity of S. *Laisrean* the elder, commonly called S. *Molaissius*, abbat; who going out of the school of S. *Finian* of *Clonard*, being one of the twelve called the apostles of *Ireland*; by his doctrine and sanctity shone forth as a bright lamp, enlightening the whole kingdom, and directing innumerable souls in the ways of truth and life. Obiit anno 570.

September 14. At *Folkston*, in *Kent*, the commemoration of S. *Eanswide*, virgin and abbess, daughter to *Eadbald* king of *Kent*, who from her infancy

infancy despised all worldly toys, and consecrated her whole heart and soul to the love of God. Her father built for her a monastery by the sea-shore near *Folkston*, where she presided over a congregation of holy virgins; and after a most innocent and saint-like life gave up her soul to rest, some time in the seventh century. Her body was buried in her own monastery; where it remained till, by the sea's encroaching and destroying the buildings, the inhabitants were obliged to translate her relicks to the church of *Folkston*, which had been dedicated by king *Eadbald* in honour of S. *Peter*; but, by the devotion of the people to S. *Eanswide*, was afterwards called by her name.

September 15. In *Scotland* the commemoration of many saints, honoured of old by the *Scottish* nation; whose names are still retained by the places where their cells, or monasteries and churches anciently stood: such as S. *Cumin*, honoured at *Kilchimen* in *Invernefs*; S. *Linchin*, honoured at *Killinchan* in *Argile*; S. *Barchan*, honoured at *Kilbarchan* in *Renfrew*; S. *Ruvius*, honoured at *Kill-ru* in the isle of *Isla*; and many others; as may be seen in the table of the parishes in *Scotland*, published by Mr. *Robert Keith*, anno 1755: where also is mention of the churches, of S. *Boswall* in *Roxburgh*; of S. *Bothan's* in *Merse*, and E. *Lothian*; of S. *Madois* in *Perth*; of S. *Monan's* in *Fife*; of S. *Kibuts* in *Kile*; and of other saints, whose acts are written in the book of life, though very little known at present upon earth.

Sept.

Sept. 16. At *Withern* in *Galloway*, the festivity of S. *Ninian* (whom the *Scots* call S. *Ringen*) bishop, and apostle of the southern *Picts*. He was *a most holy man of the* British *nation, regularly instructed at* Rome *in the faith, and in the mysteries of the truth,* says S. *Bede,* l. 3. c. 4. *The seat of his bishoprick (where his body with those of many other saints reposeth) was called* Candida casa *or the* white house, *because the saint built there a church of* white *stone, which was at that time an unusual thing among the* Britons. He reposed in our Lord anno 432: and his sepulcher was illustrated with miracles. Also the commemoration of S. *Plebeias,* brother of S. *Ninian* and imitator of his virtues; as likewise of those many other saints, who, according to our venerable historian, reposed of old in S. *Martin's* church at *Withern.* At *Wilton* in *Wiltshire,* the deposition of S. *Editha,* daughter to king *Edgar,* who being from her tender years dedicated to God in the monastery there, may be said rather never to have known the world, than to have forsaken it. Obiit anno 984. At *Pollesworth* in *Warwickshire,* the commemoration of another S. *Editha,* virgin, sister of king *Edgar,* who consecrated her virginity to God in the nunnery of *Pollesworth;* she is different from the S. *Editha* disciple of S. *Modwenna,* and first abbess of that community.

September 17. The festivity of the glorious martyrs S. *Socrates* and S. *Stephen,* who suffered under the persecution of *Diocletian.* Also in divers places of *Great Britain,* the memory of many other holy martyrs, who about the same time
stood

stood in the field of battle, with invincible courage, says S. *Gildas*, and after having been tortured with unheard of cruelty, fixed their glorious trophies on the gates of the heavenly *Jerusalem*.

September 18. In the isle of *Thorney* in *Cambridgeshire*, the commemoration of the two holy anchorets S. *Thancred* and S. *Torthred*, the first inhabitants of that solitude; one of whom died a martyr, the other a confessor: as also of blessed *Toua* their sister, famed for the sanctity of her life. See king *Edgar*'s charter, in *Dugdale*'s Monasticon; and the *Saxon* MSS. of the burial places of the *English* saints.

September 19. At *Canterbury* the deposition of S. *Theodore*, the seventh archbishop of that see, a man of profound erudition and irreproachable life, and who, as S. *Bede* informs us, brought such bright days amongst us, as never shone before in *England*; as well by opening schools of divine letters, and gathering together a numerous congregation of disciples, to whom he plentifully imparted the waters of saving knowledge; as by diligently teaching all men the right way of living, in order to live for ever; and by setting over all our churches excellent bishops, and most eminent saints: insomuch that the time of his administration might be justly stiled the *golden age* of the *English* church. He departed to our Lord anno 690, being 88 years old. S. *Bede*, l. 4. c. 1, 2, &c. & l. 5. c. 8. where he applies to him, and to the six archbishops that went before him, that saying of *Ecclesiasticus* xliv. 14. *Their bodies*
are

are buried in peace, and their names shall live for all generations.

September 20. In *Lincolnshire*, the commemoration of S. *Hygbald*, abbat, *a most holy and most mortified man*; S. *Bede*, l. 4. c. 3. At *Hulm* in *Norfolk*, the commemoration of holy *Suneman*, hermit, who led a most faintly life, in a marshy place in that neighbourhood, for above fifty years; where also some disciples resorting to him, who were desirous to lead a penitential life under his direction, formed themselves into a kind of religious community: but when the *Danes* under *Inguar* and *Hubba* laid waste the province of the *East-Angles*, they put them all to the sword. See *Dugdale*'s account of the abbey of *Hulm*, which was afterwards founded upon the same spot.

September 21. In the monastery of *Chelles* in *France*, the commemoration of blessed *Herefwide* queen, sister to S. *Hilda*, and widow to the holy king *Anna*; who after the death of her husband, going abroad, consecrated her widowhood to divine love; choosing for her place of abode, during the remainder of her transitory life, that holy monastery, in which she lived a great pattern of sanctity till she was called from this temporal banishment to an eternal crown. S. *Bede*, l. 4. c. 23.

September 22. In *Scotland*, the festivity of S. *Lolan*, bishop of *Whitern*, honoured on this day in the *Scots* calendar; where he is said to have departed to our Lord, anno 1034. In S. *Columb*'s monastery,

monastery, in the isle of *Hy*, the commemoration of holy *Cobthack* or *Cybthake*, kinsman and disciple of S. *Columb*; and holding the first place after his brother S. *Baithen*, in the list of the twelve saints who were associated with S. *Columb* in preaching the faith of Christ to the *Picts*.

September 23. In *Scotland*, the festivity of S. *Thennan* abbat, honoured on this day in the *Aberdeen* breviary. His happy death is marked in the *Scots* calendar, anno 684. In the isle of *Inys-Cathaigh*, in *Ireland*, the commemoration of holy *Kynnera* virgin, who led a solitary life in great sanctity, in the south of *Ireland*; till understanding, by divine revelation, with how great perfection our Lord was served by S. *Senan* and his disciples in the monastery of *Inys-Cathaigh*, she went thither, desiring to live and die in their neighbourhood. But as S. *Senan*'s rule would not allow any woman to come near his monastery; she requested of him, that she might once at least receive the blessed Sacrament at his hands, and that if then she died, she might be buried there. The saint granted her petition, and she, after receiving the heavenly viaticum, presently fell asleep in the Lord, and was buried in the island. At *Hexham*, the commemoration of blessed *Alfwald*, king of the *Northumbrians*, treacherously slain by his subjects, anno 789, whose sepulchre was illustrated by miracles. *William of Malmesbury*, l. 1. de Regibus.

September 24. At *Arpine*, in the kingdom of *Naples*, the commemoration of S. *Bernard*, an

English

English pilgrim, who in his return from *Jerusalem* died in that neighbourhood; whose sepulchre has been honoured with many miracles. At *Canterbury*, the deposition of the venerable archbishop *Cuthbert*; *a man of severe morals, and made up of goodness itself,* says *Dugdale*'s abridgment. Obiit anno 758. At *Worcester* the memory of holy *Bosel*, the first bishop of that see; where, according to the ancient *Saxon* manuscript, is the burying place of many saints who were bishops there.

September 25. At *Langres* in *France*, the deposition of S. *Ceolfrid*, abbat of *Weremouth* and *Jarrow*, who departed this life, in his journey towards *Rome*, anno 706. He was illustrious for his learning and piety, and was master to our great S. *Bede*. At *Cork*, in *Ireland*, the festivity of S. *Barrus*, otherwise called *Finbarrus*, bishop of that city; a prelate eminent for sanctity, and who had divers great saints for his disciples. See *Usher*'s Antiquities, p. 503. In *Scotland*, the festivity of another S. *Barrus*, first bishop of *Caithness*; whose happy death is marked in the *Scots* calendar, anno 1074.

September 26. In the province of the *East-Angles*, the commemoration of S. *Sigebert*, king and martyr; who, being a fervent convert himself, zealously contributed to the conversion of his subjects, with the concurrence of S. *Felix* bishop, and the holy abbat S. *Fursey*; till laying down his royalty he became a monk, and was at length slain by *Penda*, the pagan king of the *Mercians*,

Mercians, anno 652. S. *Bede,* l. 3. c. 18. In *Ireland,* the deposition of S. *Colmanel,* abbat of *Linalli,* in *King's county,* whose name has formerly been illustrious amongst the *Irish* saints. Obiit anno 610. At *Westminster,* the deposition of holy *Wulsy,* who upon the restoration of the monastery there, under king *Edgar,* was for the eminence of his virtues appointed by S. *Dunstan* the first abbat. Obiit anno 960. *Matthew* of *Westminster.*

September 27. In the isle of *Hy,* the commemoration of the venerable servants of God, *Rus* and *Fethno,* brothers, disciples of the holy abbat S. *Columb,* and apostolick preachers amongst the *Picts.* In *Ireland,* the commemoration of S. *Barrindeus,* abbat of *Druim-cuillin,* in the sixth century, celebrated amongst the saints of the second class in the ancient catalogue of the saints of *Ireland.*

September 28. At *Fulden* in *Germany,* the festivity of S. *Libba,* virgin and abbess, cotemporary with the great S. *Boniface*; by whom she was invited over from the monastery of *Winborn,* for the direction of his *German* converts of the female sex, in the ways of religious perfection. She was called to our Lord, anno 757. In *Scotland,* the deposition of S. *Machan,* bishop, celebrated on this day in the *Scots* calendar, who departed to our Lord, anno 856.

September 29. The festivity of S. *Michael* the Archangel, the Guardian general of the church of of God; and of all the Angels Guardians of the *British* churches. At *Hampole*, four miles from *Doncaster* in *Yorkshire*, the deposition of the venerable servant of God *Richard Rolle*, hermit, commonly called *Richard* of *Hampole*, renowned for the sanctity of his life, and the heavenly unction, which is found in all his writings. Obiit anno 1349. At *Tinningham*, in the Marches of *Scotland*, the memory of the holy abbess *Verca*, highly esteemed by the great S. *Cuthbert*. Bede, *vita Cuthberti*, c. 35, 37.

September 30. At *Canterbury*, the deposition of S. *Honorius*, disciple of S. *Gregory* the Great, the fifth archbishop of that see, and no ways degenerating from the great saints that went before him. Obiit anno 653. In *Scotland*, the commemoration of the man of God *Thocannu* (or *Totanneus*) one of the twelve coadjutors of S. *Columba*, in the conversion of the *Picts*.

OCTOBER.

October 1. AT *Ambresbury* in *Wiltshire*, the festivity of S. *Melorus* martyr, honoured on this day in the *Sarum* breviary. At *London*, the deposition of the holy bishop *Roger*, celebrated by our historians for his sanctity and miracles. Obiit anno 1241. See *Matthew Paris*, *ad annum* 1248. At *Conde* in the *Netherlands*, the feast of S. *Wasnulf* a *British* bishop, and apostolick preacher in the seventh century: whose body reposes in the collegiate church of *Conde*, which has been rendered illustrious by his miracles.

racles. See *Baldericus* in *Chronico Cameracenſi*, l. 2. c. 42.

October 2. At *Hereford*, the feſtivity of S. *Thomas de Cantilupe*, biſhop of that ſee, and ſome time Lord High Chancellor of *England:* who went to our Lord anno 1282, and for his extraordinary ſanctity, and the innumerable miracles wrought by his interceſſion, was not long after ſolemnly canonized. See biſhop *Godwin's* catalogue of the biſhops of *Hereford*.

October 3. In *Weſtphalia*, the martyrdom of the two ſaints, of the name of *Ewalds* or *Hewalds*, brothers, and prieſts of the *Engliſh* nation: ſlain by the infidels, to whom they went to preach the faith of Chriſt. Their bodies, being caſt by the murtherers into the *Rhine*, were carried up againſt the ſtream, for about forty miles, to the neighbourhod of the place where they had left their companions; and were found by them, by the means of an exceeding great light, ſhining over them from heaven; and being taken up were tranſlated to *Cullen*, and there buried with great honour. S. *Bede*, l. 5. c. 2.

October 4. At *York*, the memory of bleſſed *Edwin*, firſt chriſtian king of the *Northern Engliſh*; who was called in a wonderful manner to the faith of Chriſt, and baptized by S. *Paulinus* archbiſhop of *York*; and after a glorious reign, in which he joined a diligent care of the peace, and welfare of his people, and the maintaining of the laws, with an extraordinary piety and
zeal

zeal for religion; he was at length slain in battle by *Penda* the *Pagan*, who had rebelled against him, anno 633. S. *Bede*, l. 2. c. 9, 10, &c. At *Rome*, the memory of holy *Coenred* or *Kenred* king of the *Mercians*, who for the love of Christ exchanged his earthly kingdom for the service of God in religious solitude.

October 5. At *Coldingham* in the kingdom of the *Northumbrians*, the commemoration of S. *Ebba* the younger, virgin and abbess; and of all her sisters, the nuns of the monastery of that town; who when the *Pagan Danes* wasted the *Northern* provinces, under *Inguar* and *Hubba* (anno 868, or 870) fearing their brutal lust, more than their savage cruelty; disfigured themselves, by cutting off their own noses, and upper lips; that they might be no occasion of temptation to the infidels: who seeing them thus embrued in their blood, set fire to their monastery, and consumed them all. *Matthew Westminster*, ad annum 870.

October 6. In *Ireland*, the commemoration of B. *Wigbert*, an *English* priest, eminent for the holiness of his life, who for the promoting the greater glory of God, and the salvation of souls, went over into the *Lower Germany*, and there preached the faith of Christ, for the space of two years: but not meeting with a correspondence from the part of the infidels; he went back to *Ireland*, to his beloved solitude; and there happily ended his days, towards the latter end of the seventh century. S. *Bede* l. 5. c. 10. In *Wales*, the commemoration of S. *Budoc* confessor, patron of the priory of *Pille* in *Pembrokeshire*. At *Cullen*, the festivity of S. *Elphius* who suffered martyrdom under *Julian* the apostate: and who according to his acts, was son to a king of the *Scots*. Also the commemoration of S. *Eucharius* bishop and martyr, brother to S. *Eliphius*; and of his virgin sisters, S. *Menna*, S. *Libaria*, and S. *Susanna*.

October 7. At *Chich* (now S. *Osiths*) near *Colchester* in *Essex*, the festivity of S. *Osithe* virgin and martyr: who was trained up to all sanctity, with other holy virgins, by S. *Modwenna*, at *Pollesworth*, near the forest of *Arden* in *Warwickshire*; and afterwards, with the help of her parents, built herself a nunnery at *Chich*, where serving her divine spouse in all purity and religious perfection, she was at length martyred by the *Danes*, when they wasted *England* in the ninth century. A fountain is said to have broke out, in the place where she was beheaded, and divers miracles to have been wrought at her sepulchre; over which was built in her honour a famous church and monastery of canon regulars, which continued till the dissolution of abbeys under *Henry* VIII. At *Lincoln*, the translation of S. *Hugh*, bishop of that see; whose body being taken up, eighty years after his death, was found incorrupt, and his very habit with which he was buried, in the same condition as when it was first put on.

October 8. In *Brecknockshire* of *Wales*, the festivity of S. *Keyna*, daughter of *Braghan* lord of *Brecknock*,

Brecknock, who for her admirable piety and sanctity is called, by the ancient *Britons*, *Keynvaire*, or *Keyna the virgin*. She led a solitary life for many years, in a wood, on the banks of the river *Avon*, (where now stands the town of *Cainsham*) where also she is said to have changed by her prayers the swarms of snakes, which infested that place, into stones; many of which were to be seen there for divers ages, perfectly representing serpents. The other wonders of her life and death may be seen in her acts, published by *John* of *Tinmouth*, and *Capgrave*. In *Scotland*, the festivity of S. *Triduana*, virgin; assigned to this day in the *Scottish* calendar; who departed to our Lord anno 532.

October 9. In *Cornwall*, the commemoration of S. *Wendrove*, confessor, in whose name there still stands a church, dedicated to God, in that province. At *Pollesworth*, in *Warwickshire*, the commemoration of S. *Line*, virgin, brought up there under S. *Modwenna*, (in the company of S. *Editha*, and S. *Ositha*) in all purity and sanctity. At *Lincoln*, the deposition of *Robert* surnamed *Grosstest*, bishop of that see, a prelate of great learning, zeal and piety.

October 10. At *Rochester*, the deposition of S. *Paulinus*, disciple of S. *Gregory* the Great, who was the first that preached the faith of Christ to the *English* beyond the *Humber*, and to those of *Lincolnshire* and *Nottinghamshire*; converting many thousands; and, amongst the rest, king *Edwin*, with his nobles: but this good king

king being slain, he was obliged to return into *Kent*, where he had care of the church of *Rochester*, till he was called to the reward of his labours in a happy eternity, anno 644. S. *Bede*, l. 2. c. 9, 12, &c. At *Burlington* in *Yorkshire*, the festivity of S. *John*, prior of the canon regulars of that town; renowned for his sanctity and miracles. Obiit anno 1379.

October 11. At *Barking* in *Essex*, the festivity of S. *Edilburge*, virgin, sister to the great S. *Earconwald*, fourth bishop of *London*, and made by him the first abbess of *Barking*; to whose admirable sanctity, as well as to that of her religious sisters, and the wonders of God wrought in that holy community, S. *Bede* gives ample testimony, l. 4. c. 6, 7, &c. At *Kilkenny*, in *Ireland*, the festivity of S. *Canicus*, abbat and patron of that church: he was first a disciple of the holy abbat *Docus*, in *Wales*, and afterwards was trained up under the discipline of S. *Finian* of *Clonard*; being one of the twelve, who, coming out of his school, were for their extraordinary sanctity called the twelve apostles of *Ireland*. He founded the famous monastery of *Achad-bho*, formerly the seat of the bishops of *Ossery*; and there reposed in our Lord, anno 599.

October 12. In the monastery of *Undale*, the deposition of S. *Wilfrid* the elder, bishop of *York*, one of the brightest lights of the ancient *English* church; who after innumerable labours for the glory of God, and the salvation of souls, accompanied with many grievous afflictions and
perse-

persecutions, passing through fire and water, went to everlasting rest, anno 709. *Heddi*, S. *Bede*, &c. In *Ireland*, the festivity of S. *Mobyus*, surnamed *Clairineach*, an abbat, illustrious for sanctity. Obiit anno 544.

October 13. At *Westminster*, the translation of S. *Edward* the confessor, whose body was taken up on this day, anno 1163, and solemnly translated by S. *Thomas Becket*, archbishop of *Canterbury*, in presence of *Henry* II. and many bishops, abbats, and other persons of distinction, who were all eye-witnesses of its being entire and without the least blemish of corruption; and his very garments fresh and sound, though it was now near one hundred years since his death. In *Austria*, the festivity of S. *Colman*, a holy pilgrim of the *Scottish* nation, who returning from the *Holy Land* was taken up upon suspicion of being a spy, and put to most cruel torments, which he bore with invincible patience and courage, still maintaining his innocence, and offering up all his sufferings to God. He was at last hanged between two thieves, *October* 13, anno 1012: God bearing testimony to his innocence and sanctity, by many miracles; by occasion of which his body was, not long after, translated to the town of *Merck*, where it is kept with great veneration to this day. In *Scotland*, the festivity of S. *Conwallan*, abbat, who flourished in the sixth century: Also of S. *Cogan*, abbat, in the eighth century.

October 14. At *Wurtzbourg* in *Franconia*, the festivity of S. *Burchard*, an *Englishman*, disciple of S. *Boniface* of *Mentz*, and consecrated by him first bishop of *Wurtzbourg*. He was eminent in all pastoral virtues, and passed to a better life anno 752. In *Scotland*, the festivity of S. *Fintana*, and S. *Findocha*, illustrious virgins, anciently honoured in the *Scots* calendar.

October 15. At *Worcester*, the translation of S. *Oswald*, bishop and confessor. In the abbey of *Kitzingen*, in *Germany*, the festivity of S. *Tecla*, virgin and abbess; who was one of the chiefest of those spouses of Christ, who were invited out of *England*, by S. *Boniface*, apostle of *Germany*, in order to propagate Christ's kingdom amongst those of their own sex; by training them up in religious discipline. She went to the embraces of her heavenly spouse, about the middle of the eighth century.

October 16. At *Mentz* in *Germany*, the festivity of S. *Lullus*, archbishop of that see, a worthy disciple and successor of S. *Boniface*; in whose steps he constantly walked, by an imitation of all his virtues. In his old age he retired to his monastery which he had founded at *Heresfeld*, to prepare himself for eternity; where he also happily reposed in our Lord, anno 787; and where his tomb was illustrated with innumerable miracles. At S. *Gall*, in the diocese of *Constance*, the festivity of S. *Gallus*, abbat, apostle of the *Switzers*: he was the favourite disciple of the great S. *Columbanus*, whom he followed from the monastery

nastery of *Benchor* into *Britain*; and from *Britain* into *France*, *Burgundy*, and *Switzerland*. He was powerful both in word and work; and having constantly served our Lord with the utmost fervour and perfection, from his very childhood to the 95th year of his age, he happily entered into his kingdom of never ending joys, anno 640. In *Ireland*, the festivity of S. *Cyra*, virgin, abbess of the famous monastery of *Kilchere*, in that part of *Munster* which was called *Muscragia*.

October 17. At S. *Andrews* in *Scotland*, the festivity of S. *Regulus*, whom the *Scots* call S. *Rule*; of whom they relate, that by divine admonition he brought away from *Greece* some part of the relicks of S. *Andrew* the apostle, and deposited them in a church, which he built in the place where now stands the city of S. *Andrews*, (which to this day is called, by the *Highland Scots*, *Kill-rule*, or the church of *Regulus*): here living in common, in a monastick way, with his disciples, he is supposed to have given origin to the ancient *Culdees*, or worshippers of God, a kind of canon regulars of whom there is frequent mention in the *Scottish* histories. S. *Regulus* has a place on this day in the *Aberdeen* breviary. In *Kent*, the commemoration of the saints *Ethelred*, and *Ethelbright*, two royal youths, who for the innocence of their lives, the violence of their death, and the prodigies that followed it, were honoured by our forefathers among the martyrs. They suffered about the year 668. At *Canterbury*, the deposition of holy *Nothelmus*, the tenth archbishop of that see: He had been a priest of the church of *London*, and assisted S. *Bede* in the compiling of his church history. He went to our Lord anno 735. At *Ely*, the translation of the incorrupted body of S. *Etheldreda* or *Audry*, queen, virgin and abbess; celebrated on this day with an office of 9 lessons, in the *Sarum* breviary.

October 18. At *York*, the commemoration of the venerable servant of God *James*, deacon of S. *Paulinus* archbishop of *York*, whom he left behind him when he was obliged to return to *Kent*; who was, says S. *Bede*, l. 2. c. 20. an ecclesiastical and holy man, who living in that church for a long time after, by teaching and baptizing rescued great numbers of souls from the power of the old enemy. On this day is also marked in the *Scots* calendar, the festivity of S. *Monon*, said there to have been martyred in *Arduena*, anno 404.

October 19. At *Oxford*, the festivity of S. *Fridefwide*, virgin, celebrated for her extraordinary sanctity, and upon this account honoured of old as patroness or tutelar saint of that city. See *Dugdale's Monasticon*, vol. 1. p. 173, 174. She flourished in the eighth century, and has an office of 9 lessons in the *Sarum* breviary. Also the commemoration of holy *Algiva* virgin, who taught S. *Fridefwide* to be a saint. In *Ireland*, the deposition of S. *Ethbin* abbat, a noble *Briton*, and for some time disciple of S. *Samson*, bishop of *Dole*; who following a divine call, and leaving all that he seemed to possess in this world, sailed over into *Ireland*, and there led a solitary

but

but most saintly life, in a wilderness called *Necten Wood:* till he was invited to the happy mansions of the heavenly paradise, some time in the ninth century.

October 20. At *Toleys*, in the confines of *France* and *Germany*, the deposition of S. *Wendelyn* abbat, of royal extraction; who going abroad, became first a monk, and afterwards abbat of a monastery there, now from him called S. *Wendelyns*, where famous for sanctity and miracles, he reposed in our Lord about the year 720. *Wilson's martyrology.* In the *Isle* of *Man*, the commemoration of S. *Bradan* and S. *Orore*, honoured heretofore with churches, which still bear their names, in that island.

October 21. At *Cullen* in *Germany*, the festivity of S. *Ursula* a noble *British* virgin, with her companions (whom their acts make to amount to the number of eleven thousand) who going abroad, either as some authors affirm, to join their countrymen in *Little Britany*, or as others suppose, to fly from the rage of the pagan *Saxons*, were drove upon the coasts of the *Lower Germany*; from whence going up the country, they fell in with an army of *Hunns*, who at that very time wasted those parts, and were all slain by them, in hatred of their faith and purity; and on this account have been ever since honoured as glorious martyrs, by the Catholick church. In *Ireland*, the festivity of S. *Fintan*, surnamed *Munnu*, abbat, much renowned by reason of his sanctity and miracles, through all the churches of the *Scots* and *Irish*. [*B. Adamnan* in the life

life of S. *Columba*] He went to our Lord, anno 634.

October 22. At *Rouen*, the deposition of S. *Melanius* or *Mellon*, said to have been a noble *Briton*, converted at *Rome*, and from thence sent by S. *Stephen* the pope, to preach the faith at *Rouen*; of which church he is accounted the first bishop. At *Cullen*, the festivity of S. *Cordula* virgin and martyr, one of the companions of S. *Ursula*: of whom it is related in the *Roman* martyrology, that being terrified with the slaughter of the other virgins, she hid herself; but repenting of her cowardice, she came forth the next day, and received, the last of them all, the crown of martyrdom. At *Fiesoli* in *Tuscany*, the festivity of S. *Donatus*, a *Scot*, bishop of that city in the 9th century; and honoured there to this day, as a principal patron.

October 23. At *Tavestock* in *Devonshire*, the commemoration of S. *Rumon* bishop; whose body in former times reposed in the church of the abbey there, where he was honoured as patron. *W. Malmesbury*. In *Cornwall*, the commemoration of S. *Columb*, virgin and martyr: of whose acts, see *Gibson's Cambden*, in *Cornwall*. In *Northumberland*, the commemoration of S. *Ywy*, deacon and disciple of S. *Cuthbert*. *Herebert Rosword*. Fast. SS.

October 24. In the *Isle* of *Jersey*, the deposition of S. *Magloir* bishop, successor to S. *Samson* in the see of *Dole*; which he afterwards exchanged for the solitude of *Jersey*, where, many resorting

resorting to him, to put themselves under his discipline, he built a monastery for them; and led with them a most heavenly life, till he was called to a better world, anno 575. His body was translated to *Paris*, in the time of the invasions of the *Normans*; where it still waits for a happy resurrection, in a church dedicated to God in his name.

October 25. At *Beverley* in *Yorkshire*, the commemoration of S. *John* bishop of *York*, commonly known by the name of S. *John* of *Beverley*, a prelate of *no ordinary erudition; and of extraordinary sanctity*, says Mr. *Wharton*. [*Anglia sacra*, vol. 1. p. 694.] Hs is solemnly commemorated on this day both in the *York* and *Sarum* missals. In *Scotland*, the festivity of S. *Marnock* bishop, patron of *Killmarnock*, honoured on this day in the *Scots* calendar. At *Ceprano* in the kingdom of *Naples*, the commemoration of S. *Ardwyne* an *English* priest, whose sepulchre there has been glorified with miracles.

October 26. At *Hexham* in *Northumberland*, the deposition of S. *Eata*, who was made bishop of that see, upon his resigning the see of *Lindisfarne* to his disciple S. *Cuthbert*. He was trained up from a boy under the discipline of the great S. *Aidan*; and was afterwards abbat, first of *Mailross*, and then also of *Lindisfarne*. His character in S. *Bede* (l. 4. c. 27.) is, that *he excelled all men living in meekness, and in christian simplicity, or candour and uprightness*. He departed to our Lord, anno 685. In the monastery of *Herefield* in *Germany*, the deposition of S. *Witta*, alias *Albuinus*,

Albuinus, an *Englishman*, a disciple and fellow-labourer of S. *Boniface* of *Mentz*; and consecrated by him first bishop of *Buraburg*, which see is since translated to *Paderborn*. He died in great sanctity, anno 786, or 787.

October 27. In *Ireland*, the festivity of S. *Abban* abbat, founder of divers churches and monasteries; and one of the chiefest propagators of monastick discipline in that island. At S. *Ives* in *Cornwall*, the commemoration of S. *Iia* or *Ivia*, a woman of singular sanctity, honoured there of old as virgin and martyr.

October 28. The feast of S. *Simon* the Apostle, surnamed *Cananeus* or *Zelotes*; whom some writers affirm to have preached the faith of Christ in *Britain*. At *Winchester*, the happy death of the great and good king *Ælfred*, who went to our Lord anno 901. In *Scotland*, the commemoration of blessed *Motifer* or *Mocufer*, one of the twelve apostolical men, who joined their labours with the great S. *Columb*, in the conversion of the *Picts*.

October 29. The day assigned for the festivity of *Venerable Bede*, priest, monk, and doctor of the church of God; who for his sanctity and learning is justly accounted the singular glory of *England*. At *Lindisfarne*, or the *Holy Island*, the commemoration of S. *Ceolulph*, some time king of the *Northumbrians*, a learned and religious prince, to whom S. *Bede* dedicated his history; who for the love of the kingdom of heaven, quitting his earthly kingdom, became a monk in the monastery

tery of *Lindisfarne*; and there happily ended his days in the exercises of religion, about the middle of the eighth century: and as *W. Malmesbury* informs us, was illustrious for miracles after his death; lib. 1. *de Regibus.* In *Scotland,* the festivity of S. *Kenneir,* virgin. At *Canterbury,* the deposition of the holy archbishop *Eadsin,* anno 1050.

October 30. In *Cornwall,* the commemoration of the saints *Arvan* and *Illogan,* confessors, who have left their names to the places which they formerly illustrated with their sanctity. In *Scotland,* the festivity of S. *Tarkin,* bishop; honoured in the *Aberdeen* breviary on this day: who went to our Lord anno 889. At *Canterbury,* the deposition of the holy archbishop *Egelnoth,* anno 1038.

October 31. In *Hainault,* the festivity of S. *Foillan,* bishop and martyr. He was brother to the saints *Fursey* and *Ultan*; and for some time abbat of the famous monastery of *Burghcastle* in *Suffolk:* afterwards going to *Rome,* he was consecrated bishop by S. *Martin* pope, and commissioned by him to preach the faith of Christ in the *Netherlands*; where at length he met with the crown of martyrdom, anno 660.

NOVEMBER.

Novemb. 1. THE general commemoration of all the *Saints* of our *British Islands*; and more especially of those great numbers, whose names, though recorded in the book of of life, are now unknown on earth; by reason of the destruction of a great part of our ancient records, together with the monasteries, which were the depositaries of them. In *Norway*, the commemoration of the holy bishop *Gotebald*, an *Englishman*, an apostolick preacher in *Norway* and *Sweden*, in the eleventh century.

November 2. In the monastery of *Clarevale*, the deposition of S. *Malachi*, archbishop of *Armagh*: whose extraordinary sanctity, and wonderful miracles, are attested by the great S. *Bernard*, his intimate acquaintance, in the book he has written of his life. Obiit anno 1148. In *Ireland*, the memory of the man of God *Imarius*, who led a recluse and most mortified life in a cell, near the great church of *Armagh*; where he first received S. *Malachi* under his discipline, and taught him to be a saint. At *York*, the memory of the holy priest *Sycar*, to whose sanctity and prophetick spirit (of which S. *Malachi* had many proofs) S. *Bernard* also gives testimony. At *Lens* in the diocese of *Arras*, the festivity of S. *Vulganius* confessor, in whose name the collegiate church of that town is dedicated: their records bearing testimony that he was of *the most christian nation of the English*. *Miræus*, Belgick calendar, p. 647. In *Scotland* the festivity of S. *Maura* virgin, honoured on this day in the *Aberdeen* breviary; whose happy death is there assigned to the year 899: her name is still retained in the town called from her *Killmaure*.

November 3. At *Holiwell* in *Flintshire*, the festivity of S. *Wenefride* virgin and martyr, honoured

noured on this day with an office of nine leſſons in the *Sarum* breviary. At *Guitherin* in *Denbighſhire*, the commemoration of the holy abbeſs *Theonia* (to whom S. *Wenefride* was recommended by S. *Elerius*) and of divers other ſaints, whoſe bodies anciently repoſed in the church of *Guitherin*. Alſo the commemoration of the holy hermit *Saturninus*, who ſerved God in a ſolitary cell at *Henthlant*. In *Scotland*, the feſtivity of S. *Englate* biſhop, who went to our Lord anno 966. See the *Calendar* of *Scots* ſaints, publiſhed by Mr. *Robert Keith*.

November 4. At S. *Clair*, in the territory of *Rouen* in *Normandy*, the martyrdom of S. *Clarus*, a *Britiſh* prieſt, eminent for ſanctity: who retiring into a wilderneſs, to avoid the ſollicitations of an unhappy woman, who was inflamed with an impure love for his perſon, was murdered by two ruffians, at her ſuggeſtion; and ſo fell a martyr of purity. At *Wincheſter*, the depoſition of S. *Birnſtan* biſhop, a diſciple of S. *Grimbald*, and eminent in all virtues; but more eſpecially excelling in chaſtity, and humility. Obiit anno 932.

November 5. In *Glamorganſhire*, the commemoration of S. *Docunus* abbat, otherwiſe called *Cungarus*; who firſt led an eremitical life in *Somerſetſhire*, then built an oratory in honour of the bleſſed Trinity, at a place from him called *Cungreſbury*; and there appointed twelve *regular canons*, to attend always on the divine ſervice: after which going into *Glamorganſhire*, he founded there a monaſtery, not far from the ſea coaſt, where he lived and died in great sanctity. Of this monastery of S. *Docunus*, and its abbats, there is frequent mention in the ancient Synods of *Landaff*; published by Sir *H. Spelman*.

November 6. The festivity of S. *Leonard*, confessor, who, though no native of *Britain*, was in a particular manner honoured by our forefathers, as appears by the many churches and monasteries dedicated in his name, in all parts of *England*. Amongst the rest there was at *Wroxhall* in *Warwickshire*, an ancient church erected in his honour; where *Hugh* Lord of *Wroxhall* afterwards founded a nunnery; who having suffered much by seven years captivity amongst the infidels, imploring in his distress the prayers and intercession of S. *Leonard*, was miraculously brought away in his chains, in the night, and found the next morning in a wood near his own house. See *Dugdale*. At *Dole* in *Little Britany*, the deposition of S. *Iltut*, first abbat of the famous monastery and school of *Llan Iltut* in *Glamorganshire*, and master of many eminent *British* saints. He flourished in the sixth century. The commemoration also of his holy disciple *Isam*, whom he appointed his successor in his school and monastery of *Llan Iltut*, when in the latter part of his life he retired into a lonesome cave, to attend wholly to divine contemplation. At S. *Winocs-Bergen* in *Flanders*, the festivity of S. *Winoc* abbat, illustrious for sanctity and miracles; who with his brother S. *Judocus* is by many reckoned amongst our *British* saints, as being at the least of *British* extraction. In *Ireland*, the commemoration of another S. *Winoc*, a *British*

bishop

bishop of eminent sanctity, in the fifth century, coadjutor of S. *Patrick* in his apostolical labours in that island. As also at *Tours*, the memory of a third *Winoc*, a *Briton*, mentioned with great honour by S. *Gregory* of *Tours*, l. 5. *Hist. Franc.* c. 21.

November 7. At the monastery of *Epternac* in the dutchy of *Luxembourg*, the deposition of S. *Willibrord* archbishop of *Utrecht*, and apostle of the *Netherlands*; who being sent, with eleven companions, all of them *English Saxons*, to preach the faith of Christ to the *Frisons*, and other infidel nations of the *Lower Germany*, after fifty years labours, and the conversion of innumerable souls, by his preaching and his miracles, was called to eternal rest anno 739. Also the commemoration of the other eleven eminent servants of God, who were associated with S. *Willibrord* in the work of the Lord. At *Strasbourg* in *Germany* the festivity of S. *Florentius*, a *Scotsman*, bishop of that see, illustrious for sanctity. Obiit anno 675.

November 8. At *Bremen* the festivity of S. *Willehad* an *Englishman*, first bishop of *Bremen*, and apostle of the *Saxons*, in the time of *Charlemagne*; who laboured in that rough field, in the midst of difficulties and persecutions, with great diligence, till he had the happiness to see duke *Witikind* embrace the faith; whose conversion was followed by that of his people; after which S. *Willehad* met joyfully with that death, which was to open to him the gates of everlasting life, anno 799. At *Caerguby* in the *Isle of Anglesey*, the festivity

festivity of S. *Kebius*, disciple of the great S. *Hilary*, and first bishop and apostle of *Anglesey*: where there remained in *Leland*'s time a college of canons, supposed to have been formerly the monastery of this saint. In *Scotland*, the festivity of the saints *Gervad* bishop, and *Morok* confessor, who flourished in the beginning of the ninth century, and have a place on this day in the *Scots* calendar.

November 9. At *Glastenbury*, the festivity of S. *Benignus* or *Benen*, disciple of S. *Patrick*, and for some time archbishop of *Armagh*; who, according to the records of *Glastenbury*, coming over into *Britain*, embraced an eremitical life in that neighbourhood, at a place called *Ferremere*, where illustrious for sanctity and miracles he finally reposed in our Lord. His relicks were translated to the abbey of *Glastenbury*, anno 1091, where innumerable miraculous cures were wrought at his tomb. *William of Malmesbury*, Antiquit. Glast. At *Glastenbury* also, the commemoration of S. *Patrick the younger*, nephew of the great S. *Patrick*; whose body was found there in the old church, on the right side of the altar, anno 1184.

November 10. At *Canterbury*, the deposition of S. *Justus*, disciple of S. *Gregory* the Great, first bishop of *Rochester*; and translated from thence, after the death of S. *Mellitus*, to be the fourth archbishop of *Canterbury*: which see when he had administered in a most saintlike manner for some years, he was, as S. *Bede* expresses it, *taken up to the heavenly kingdoms* (anno 627.) At *Mecklen-*

Mecklenbourg in *Germany*, the festivity of S. *John* bishop and martyr, an *Irishman* by birth, who preached the faith of Christ in the north of *Germany*; and was there put to a cruel death, by the infidels, anno 1066. In *Ireland*, the festivity of S. *Ædus* bishop in *Meath*, who has a place amongst the most celebrated saints of the *Irish* nation, in the ancient catalogue published by *Usher*, p. 498. Obiit anno 589. Also a commemoration of S. *Ilaud* abbat, under whose discipline S. *Ædus* was from his youth trained up, and taught to be a saint. *Usher, ibidem.*

November 11. In *Holderness* of *Yorkshire*, the commemoration of S. *Wilgis* confessor, father to S. *Willibrord*; who after leading, with his whole family, a very religious life in the world, became a monk, and at length an hermit, passing the remainder of the days of his mortality in very great sanctity, in a little oratory which he had made for himself, in a neck of land, running out between the *Ocean* and the *Humber*. *Alcuin, in vita Willibrordi.* In *Ireland*, the festivity of S. *Sinellus* abbat, who founded the monastery of *Cluain-Inys*, in the lake of *Fermanagh*; where he received S. *Columban*, when very young; and trained up S. *Mumnu*, whose name, in succeeding times, was so famous amongst all the churches of the *Scots* and *Irish*.

Nov. 12. At *Daventer* in the *Netherlands*, the festivity of S. *Lebwin*, an *English* priest, and apostolical preacher in the *Lower Germany*, who flourished in the eighth century; whose body reposes in a church dedicated in his name, which is now the cathedral of *Daventer*. At *Ghent* in *Flanders*, the festivity of S. *Livinus* bishop and martyr, a *Scot* or *Irishman* by birth; who going over to the *Low Countries* to preach the faith of Christ, was there martyred by the unbelievers, at a place called *Asche*, between *Ghent* and *Brussel-les*, anno 633. He is held in great veneration in all that country; and this day is kept holy, on his account, in the city of *Ghent*. In *Scotland*, the festivity of S. *Machan* bishop of *Moray*, anno 887.

November 13. In the diocese of *Arras*, the festivity of S. *Kilian* or *Killen*, confessor and apostolical preacher in *Artois*, to which he was sent by S. *Faro* bishop of *Meaux*. He was a near relation of S. *Fiacre*, and a close imitator of his virtues; and after many labours reposed in our Lord, in the seventh century, at *Aubigny*, where there is a church and monastery of canon regulars, which bears his name. In *Scotland*, the deposition of S. *Devinike*, bishop in the ninth century.

November 14. At *London*, the translation of the body of S. *Erkonwald*, bishop and tutelar saint of that city and diocese; whose relicks were translated on this day to a more honourable place in the church of S. *Paul*, and being laid in a coffin of great price, were buried in the east part of the church, above the high altar, where they remained till the change of religion. Of this saint, *Dugdale* writes, *That neither the course of a thousand years, nor the voracious flames, which attempted it in vain, nor the fury of the populace,*

when

when faith was quite extinguished, could ever efface the memory of Erkonwald. In the isle of *Enlly* or *Bardsey*, the deposition of S. *Dubricius* archbishop of *Caerlion*, one of the most celebrated of the *British* saints; and the father and master of many saints. In his old age he resigned his archbishoprick to S. *David*, and retired to the island above named; where he happily reposed in our Lord, some time in the ninth century. At *Eu* in *Normandy*, the deposition of S. *Lawrence O Tuathail*, archbishop of *Dublin*; who with his admirable sanctity illustrated, not only our *British* islands, but also the whole church of God. Obiit anno 1181. In *Scotland*, the festivity of S. *Medan* or *Middam*, bishop in the sixth century.

November 15. In *Little Britain*, the festivity of St. *Machutus* or *Maclovius*, vulgo S. *Malo*, bishop of *Aleth*; nearly related to S. *Samson* and to S. *Magloir*; and trained up from his infancy under the discipline of S. *Brendan*, in the monastery of *Llancarvan* in *Glamorganshire*. He was a saint from his childhood, carefully avoiding every thing in which he apprehended sin; and continually thirsting after true wisdom, and the fountain of it, which is God himself: Him he loved with his whole soul, when as yet a boy; and was even then so strong in faith, as to be already favoured with miracles. As he advanced in age, he advanced in sanctity; and much more after he was made priest, and then bishop; still *going on from virtue to virtue*, in the midst of labours and persecutions, till he was happily called from his earthly banishment, *to see the God of gods* in his heavenly *Sion*, anno 630. He has a place this

this day in the *Sarum, York,* and *Aberdeen* calendars, as well as in the Roman Martyrology.

November 16. At *Pontigny* in *France,* the deposition of S. *Edmund,* archbishop of *Canterbury;* renowned through all Christendom, for the purity of his heart, and sanctity of his life. He departed to our Lord, anno 1240; and by reason of the many evident miracles wrought at his tomb, was solemnly canonized within seven years after his death.

November 17. At *Lincoln,* the deposition of S. *Hugh,* who from a *Carthusian* monk, and prior of their first establishment at *Witham,* in *Selwood* forest, was made bishop of *Lincoln;* which see he administered, for many years, with that faith, zeal and sanctity, which might have been admired, even in a prelate of the apostolick age; till he happily exchanged this dying life below, for the true and everlasting life above; anno 1200. In *Scotland,* the festivity of S. *Fergus,* bishop, and of S. *Midana,* virgin; who have a place on this day in the *Scots* breviaries.

November 18. In the monastery of *Streanshall,* now *Whitby* in *Yorkshire,* the deposition of S. *Hilda* virgin and abbess; she was trained up to all sanctity by S. *Aidan,* and other servants of God; and founded, or directed, divers religious houses, in which she became the spiritual mother and mistress of many great saints. S. *Bede,* l. 4. c. 23. She passed from death to life eternal, anno 680; and her departing soul was seen ascending, with an immense light, to the mansions of everlasting

lasting light, by blessed *Begu* virgin, in the monastery of *Hakeness*, which was 13 miles distant from that of *Whitby*. At *Lucca* in *Tuscany*, the festivity of S. *Frigdianus* bishop, illustrious for sanctity and miracles; who, as his acts affirm, was a native of our *British* islands. At *Santo Padre* in the kingdom of *Naples*, the commemoration of S. *Fulk* an *English* pilgrim; whose body reposes in the church of that place, and has been illustrated with many miracles.

November 19. In *Kent*, the festivity of S. *Ermemburge* queen, (whom some have called *Dompneva*) wife to *Merowald* son of king *Penda*, and mother to the saints *Mildred*, *Milburge*, &c. who with the consent of her husband, retiring from this stormy sea of the world into the quiet haven of religion, there lived in a most saint-like manner, and died happily some time in the seventh century. At *Glastenbury*, the commemoration of S. *Wenta* virgin; whose relicks were formerly kept in the abbey of *Glastenbury*. See *Dugdale*'s Monasticon, vol. 1. fol. 4.

November 20. At S. *Edmunds-Bury* in *Suffolk*, the festivity of S. *Edmund* king of the *East Angles*, martyred by the *Danes*, anno 870. His body was found without the least blemish of corruption 57 years after his death, and translated to *Bury*, where a noble church and monastery was afterwards built in his honour. On the same day, the martyrdom of S. *Humbert* bishop of *Helmham*, who suffered with S. *Edmund*. See *Matthew* of *Westminster*. [anno 870, and 855.] At *London*, the commemoration of the holy bishop *Theodred*,
sur-

surnamed *the good*, who translated the body of S. *Edmund*, and built over it the great church of *Bury*, anno 927.

November 21. In *Lombardy*, the deposition of S. *Columbanus* abbat; who all his life long was most renowned for sanctity, and miracles. He was disciple of S. *Comgall*, in his monastery of *Benchor*; from whence he passed over, with twelve other companions, (amongst whom were the saints *Gallus* and *Deicola*) into *Britain*, and from thence into *France*: where he founded the famous monastery of *Luxeuil*, &c. to which he gave an excellent rule, followed by many saints. At length going into *Italy*, he founded the monastery of *Bobbio*, upon mount *Apennine*; from whence he passed to the mountain of an happy eternity, anno 615. In the territory of *Arras*, the memory of S. *Obedius* hermit, an *Irishman* by birth; honoured as patron in the village of *Wancourt*.

November 22. At *Pont S. Maxence* in *France*, the commemoration of S. *Maxencia* a *Scottish* virgin and martyr, honoured as tutelar saint of that town, to which she gives the name. She was, according to her acts, daughter to a king of the *Scots*; and for the preservation of her virginity, privately retired beyond the seas, choosing for her abode a solitude, where now stands the town of *Pont*. To this place her lover followed her, and not being able to prevail upon her to consent to his lust, slew her upon the spot. Thus she fell a martyr to purity; and is honoured on the 20th of *November* with a proper office, in the

the diocese of *Beauvais* in *France*, and in the *Scots* breviary.

November 23. At *Bangor* in *Caernarvonshire*, the festivity of S. *Daniel* the first bishop of that see about the year 516; he was consecrated by S. *Dubricius*, and was so renowned amongst the ancient *Britons*, for his sanctity, that the cathedral of *Bangor* was dedicated in his name. Obiit anno 545.

November 24. At *Lismore* in *Ireland*, the commemoration of S. *Malchus*, some time master to the great S. *Malachi*; who from a monk of *Winchester* was made bishop of *Lismore*, and by reason of his sanctity was resorted to, as an oracle, from all parts both of *Ireland*, and *Scotland*. He was co-temporary with S. *Bernard*, who (in his life of S. *Malachi*) bears testimony both to his sanctity, and to his miracles.

November 25. At *York*, the commemoration of the holy archbishop *Egbert*, illustrious for his birth, being brother to a king; but more illustrious for his piety, and wisdom. He enriched his church with a famous library, wrote himself several learned and godly tracts; and opened a school at *York* for learning, in which amongst others he had for his disciple the great *Alcuin*, preceptor to the emperor *Charlemagne*. This holy prelate departed to our Lord, anno 766. Also the memory of holy *Eadbricht*, brother to archbishop *Egbert*, to whom his kinsman S. *Ceolulph* resigned the kingdom of the *Northumbrians*, anno 738; which after a glorious reign of twenty ty years, he exchanged for a religious solitude, in the service of the King of kings; to whom he went, anno 768.

November 26. In *Scotland*, the happy decease of S. *Margaret*, queen; or to speak more properly, the day in which she began truly to live; by dying here, to live for ever with God. In the monastery of *Rumsey* in *Hampshire*, the commemoration of holy *Christina* virgin and abbess, sister to S. *Margaret*, who entering into that religious community, together with her holy mother *Agatha*, concluded there a saintly life with the death of the saints, anno 1080.

November 27. At *Glastenbury*, the commemoration of S. *Ealswithe*, virgin; the purity of whose soul and body was evidenced by her incorruption after her death. See *Dugdale.* At *Rode* in *Brabant*, the festivity of S. *Ode* a *Scottish* virgin, of royal blood; who having miraculously recovered her sight, by making a pilgrimage to the tomb of S. *Lambert*, at *Liege*, took a resolution, upon the spot, to consecrate her virginity by vow to God: and instead of returning home, embraced and followed a most religious life, in a solitude of *Taxandria* (now called *Brabant*) and there finally reposed in our Lord anno 713. Her relicks are kept in the collegiate church of *Rode*, which is dedicated to God in her name; and she has a place on this day in the *Scots* calendar.

November 28. At *Cerne* in *Dorsetshire*, the commemoration of S. *Edwold* confessor, brother to S. *Edmund* king and martyr; who fleeing the dangers

dangers of the world, chose for himself a lonesome cell, in the neighbourhood of *Shaftsbury*; where, *bearing in mind the eternal years*, he passed the days of his mortality in such wonderful sanctity, as to deserve to be enrolled amongst the saints, and to be enshrined in the church of the abbey of *Cerne*. See *William* of *Malmesbury*, p. 250, 251.

November 29. At *Athelingay* in *Somersetshire*, the commemoration of S. *Egelwin* confessor, honoured of old as patron of the abbey of *Athelingay*, and illustrious for many miracles. He was brother to *Kennewalch*, king of the *West Saxons*; but more ennobled by his virtue than by his blood. He was continually afflicted with sicknesses; but these hindered him not from a fervent application of his soul to the love and service of his God. He concluded a holy life by a happy death; and now shews himself ever ready to succour (by his prayers) such as call for his assistance, says *William* of *Malmesbury*, p. 255.

November 30. The festivity of S. *Andrew* the apostle, tutelar saint of the kingdom of *Scotland*; and not much less honoured by the ancient *English*; as appears from the divers cathedrals, and other churches dedicated to God in his name: which devotion seems to have been originally derived from our first preachers, who came from the monastery of S. *Andrew* in *Rome*; and were disciples of S. *Gregory* the *Great*, the founder of that monastery, who was particularly devoted to S. *Andrew*. In *Ireland*, the festivity of S. *Brendan* abbot of *Birra*, most illustrious for his wisdom

dom and sanctity, in the ninth century. He was joined in the band of a most strict friendship with the great S. *Columkille*; who also, as we learn from S. *Adamnan*, l. 3. c. 15. at the time of S. *Brendan*'s death, saw heaven open, and a multitude of angels going forth to meet his soul, with so great light, and such incomparable brightness, as to illuminate the whole earth.

DECEMBER.

Decemb. 1. IN the isle of *Enlly* or *Bardsey*, the memory of a great multitude of ancient *British* martyrs and confessors, whose bodies there wait for a glorious resurrection; from whom that isle was anciently named by the *Britons*, *The island of twenty thousand saints*. In the monastery of *Oundle* in *Northamptonshire*, the burying place of S. *Cett*, commemorated in the ancient *Saxon* manuscript of the sepulchres of *English* saints.

December 2. In *Ireland*, the commemoration of the holy bishops, and apostolick preachers, *Auxilius, Secundinus*, and *Isserninus*; all *Britons* by birth; and the first and principal assistants of S. *Patrick*, in bringing over the *Irish* to the faith of Christ. See the acts of the councils held by S. *Patrick*; and *Usher*, p. 430, 438. In *Wales*, the memory of S. *Publicus*, confessor; of whose church see *Cambden* in *Carnarvonshire*.

December 3. At *Dorchester* in *Oxfordshire*, the festivity of S. *Birinus* first bishop and apostle of the *West Saxons*, sent into *Britain* by pope *Honorius*,

rius, in the seventh century. S. *Bede*, l. 3. c. 7. At *Coire* or *Chur* in the land of *Grisons*, the festivity of S. *Lucius*, said to have been a *British* prince; who through the zeal of the glory of God, and of the conversion and salvation of souls, going abroad, preached the faith of Christ among the *Switzers* and *Grisons*; where he was made bishop of *Coire*; and at length ended his days by martyrdom. His feast is solemnly kept, with an octave, in the diocese of *Coire :* where there is, not far from the city, an ancient monastery, which bears his name.

December 4. At *Salisbury*, the festivity of S. *Osmund* bishop of that see, soon after the conquest; illustrious for his wisdom and sanctity. He built the cathedral there; and compiled the *Sarum* office, adopted afterwards by most of the churches in *England* and *Wales*. He departed to our Lord anno 1099. At *Coire*, the festivity of S. *Emerita* virgin and martyr, sister to S. *Lucius*. In *Ireland*, the feast of S. *Berchan*, an abbat of eminent sanctity in the sixth century; who having lost the sight of his bodily eyes, was wonderfully favoured with prophetick light in his soul.

December 5. At *Solenhoff* in *Germany*, the commemoration of S. *Sola*, an *Englishman*, disciple of S. *Boniface*, archbishop and martyr; who was first an apostolick preacher, and afterwards an hermit at a place in the diocese of *Eychstadt*, which now from him is called *Solenhoff*; where he lived and died in great sanctity, about the year 768. In *Ireland*, the commemoration of the holy abbat *Cummian*, author of an excellent letter,

(published

(published by *Usher*) in which he endeavoured to bring over the monks of S. *Columba* to the catholick observance of Easter. He flourished in the seventh century.

December 6. At *Leominster* in *Herefordshire*, the burying place of S. *Ethelred*, confessor, commemorated in the ancient *Saxon* manuscript of the sepulchres of the *English* saints. In *Scotland*, the commemoration of *Constantine* III, king of the *Scots*, who leaving all for the love of Christ, made a happy end among the *Culdees*, or regular clerks of S. *Andrews*, anno 943. In *Ireland*, the festivity of S. *Nessan*, abbat; named amongst the most illustrious saints of that island, as well as in the ancient catalogue, published in *Usher's Antiquities*, as in the epistle of abbat *Cummian* to abbat *Segenius*. Also in *Ireland*, the commemoration of another S. *Nessan*, bishop, famed for sanctity, in the sixth or seventh century.

December 7. In the territory of *Carlile* in *Cumberland*, the commemoration of blessed *Alrick*, alias *Godwin*, who led for many years a most saintly life in a lonesome cave in that neighbourhood. He was visited two years before his happy death by S. *Godrick*, who put himself under his discipline; and saw his departing soul, in the shape of a most beautiful sphere, as it were, of resplendent crystal, taking her journey towards the heavenly mansions. At *Charlebury* in *Oxfordshire*, the burying place of S. *Dionia*, commemorated in the *Saxon* manuscript of the sepulchres of the *English* saints.

December

December 8. The *Conception* of the blessed Virgin, a feast which some say, first began to be celebrated in the kingdom of *England,* in the days of S. *Anselm.* At *London,* the commemoration of the holy bishop *Vodinus*; slain by *Hengist* the *Saxon*; because he had reprehended king *Vortigern,* for putting away his lawful wife, and marrying the daughter of *Hengist.* Also a commemoration of many other *Britons* of all degrees, who suffered martyrdom for the faith of Christ, under the *Pagan Saxons.*

December 9. In the kingdom of the *East-Angles,* the commemoration of holy king *Anna, an excellent and most religious man,* says S. *Bede,* and happy in a most holy and saint-like offspring. He was slain by the *Pagan Penda* anno 654. At *Barking* in *Essex,* the festivity of S. *Wulfhilde* abbess, greatly renowned for her sanctity and miracles. She departed to our Lord anno 985. Her body was taken up thirty years after her death; and was found whole and sound, as if it had been but just then buried. In *Cornwall,* the commemoration of the saints *Moscea* and *Veepe,* honoured of old amongst the *Cornish* saints.

December 10 At *Clonard* in *Westmeath,* the commemoration of S. *Finian* bishop; who after he had for thirty years illustrated *Great Britain* with the rays of his sanctity, returning into *Ireland,* his native country, in order to raise up religion there, which had suffered some decay after the death of S. *Patrick*; opened for this purpose his famous school of *Clonard*; out of which, innumerable great men came forth, most eminent

H both

both for their learning and piety; and amongst the rest, the twelve, who for their extraordinary sanctity were called the twelve apostles of *Ireland*. S. *Finian* flourished in the sixth century; and was the father of no fewer than 3000 monks. In *Ireland* also the commemoration of S. *Fortchern* bishop, and S. *Cayman* abbat, under whose discipline S. *Finian* received his first education in christian piety.

December 11. At *Streanshall*, now *Whitby*, in *Yorkshire*, the commemoration of the holy virgin *Elfleda*, or *Elfreda*, daughter to king *Oswi*; and by him consecrated to God from her infancy, under the discipline of S. *Hilda*; to whom she afterwards succeeded in the government of that illustrious congregation. S. *Bede* l. 4. c. 26. Also the commemoration of the holy queen *Eanflede* mother of the royal virgin *Elfleda*; who after her husband's death, became a nun in the same monastery; and there lived, and died in the odour of sanctity.

December 12. In the monastery of S. *Columkille*, in the isle of *Hy*, the commemoration of the man of God *Grillaan* or *Gallan*; one of the twelve apostolick preachers, whom S. *Columkille* associated to himself in preaching the word of life to the *Northern Picts*. In *Ireland*, the festivity of S. *Cormac* abbat; whose name is set down in the ancient catalogue, amongst the most celebrated saints of that kingdom. He is also numbered by B. *Adamnan* in the life of S. *Columkille*, l. 3. c. 117, amongst the holy founders of religious communities; who visited that saint

in

in his monastery of *Y-Combkille*: and as the same father informs us, through a desire of being more retired from the world; he three times attempted to find in the *Northern* ocean a solitude, where he might fix his abode for the remainder of his life; but could not effect it. He flourished in the sixth century.

December 13. In *Ireland*, the festivity of S. *Columba*, abbat of *Tyrdaglas* in *Munster*, who was one of those eminent saints, who were called the twelve apostles of *Ireland*; and was himself the master and teacher of many saints. At *Caster* two miles from *Peterborough*, the festivity of S. *Tibba* virgin and anchoress; kinswoman to the saints *Kinisdred*, and *Kiniswide*, and joined in burial with them. Their relicks were afterwards translated to the abbey of *Peterborough*, where also according to the ancient *Saxon* Manuscript was the burying place of many other saints.

December 14. In the monastery of *Lyming* in *Kent*, the deposition of S. *Ethelburge*, daughter to S. *Ethelbert*, and widow to S. *Edwin*, two most christian kings: who after the death of her husband, consecrated her widowhood to God, in the monastery of *Lyming*, of which she was abbess; and departed to our Lord, in the sweet odour of sanctity, towards the close of the seventh century. At *Lyming* also the burying place of S. *Eadburge* virgin. *Saxon MS*. In *Scotland*, the festivity of S. *Drostan* abbat, whose relicks were honoured of old at *Aberdeen*. In *Cornwall*, the martyrdom of S. *Fingar* alias *Guinger*, and his companions: who being some of the first converts of S. *Patrick* in *Ireland*, sailed over to *Cornwall*, in quest of a proper place of retirement, in which they might attend to God alone: but upon their landing there, they were all massacred, in hatred of their religion, by *Teudrick*, a *Pagan* prince of the *Danmonians*; about the year 455. They are honoured on this day in the cathedral of *Vannes*, in *Little Britain*; to which, 'tis probable, some part of their relicks was translated. Also the festivity of S. *Piala* virgin, sister of S. *Fingar* and martyred with him.

December 15. At *Whitby*, in *Yorkshire*, the translation of the body of S. *Hilda* virgin and abbess, illustrious for sanctity. On this day is also commemorated S. *Palladius* or *Padie*, ordained by S. *Celestine* pope, bishop for the *Scots*: to whom the *North Britons* are greatly indebted for the propagating amongst them the kingdom of Christ; and the *South Britons* for being particularly instrumental in banishing from among them the *Pelagian* heresy. See S. *Prosper* in *Chronico* & l. *Contra Collatorem*.

December 16. In *Scotland*, the festivity of S. *Bean* bishop of *Murthlac*; honoured on this day both in the *Aberdeen* breviary, and in the *Roman* Martyrology. He flourished under king *Malcolm* the second, in the former part of the eleventh century. At *Litchfield*, the commemoration of the holy bishop *Sexulf*, who was the first abbat of *Medehamsted*, now called *Peterborough*; and was afterwards by S. *Theodore* translated

lated to the bishoprick of *Litchfield*. He flourished in the seventh century. Also in the neighbourhood of the isle of *Ely*, the commemoration of S. *Alnoth* hermit and martyr.

December 17. At *Winchester*, the commemoration of the holy bishop *Daniel*, who succeeded S. *Hedda* in that see, anno 703; which he most worthily administered for 42 years, and then retired to the monastery of *Malmesbury*, where he happily reposed in our Lord, anno 745. At *Winchester* also the commemoration of the royal virgins *Elflede* and *Ethelhild*, daughters to king *Edward* the elder, and sisters to S. *Edburge*, and the holy queen S. *Editha*; who for the love of God despised the world, and consecrated their virginity to Jesus Christ; and being faithful to his love till death, received from him the crown of life, about the middle of the tenth century.

December 18. In the monastery of *Heidenheim* in *Bavaria*, the festivity of S. *Winibald* abbat, son to S. *Richard*, and brother to S. *Willibald* and to S. *Walburge*; and no less allyed to them in sanctity than in blood. He departed to our Lord, anno 706. In *Scotland*, the festivity of S. *Manes* or *Manere*, bishop; honoured on this day in the *Aberdeen* breviary, where he is said to have departed to our Lord, anno 824. In the neigbourhood of *Exeter*, the burying place of S. *Sithefulla* virgin. *Saxon* MSS.

December 19. At *Shaftsbury* in *Dorsetshire*, the commemoration of blessed *Ethelgive* virgin and abbess, daughter to the great king *Ælfred*; and celebrated for the holiness of her life. Obiit anno 896. At *Wurtzbourg* in *Germany*, the commemoration of holy *Macharius* abbat of the *Scots* monastery in that city; who flourished in sanctity of life in the twelfth century. *Wilson*'s Martyrology.

December 20. At *Hexham* in *Northumberland*, the commemoration of holy *Acca* bishop, disciple and individual companion to the great S. *Wilfrid*; to whom he also succeeded in the bishoprick of *Hexham*. He was cotemporary to S. *Bede*, who assures us, l. 5. c. 21. ' that he was a man ' most learned in the scriptures; most pure in ' the confession of the catholick faith; most skil- ' ful in the rules of ecclesiastical discipline; most ' strenuous and industrious in all good; and a ' doer of great things both before God and man.' He held his bishoprick 24 years, and departed to our Lord anno 740.

December 21. In *Wales*, the commemoration of S. *Juthwara*, virgin and martyr; and of her holy sisters *Edware*, *Willgith* and *Siaewell*, all celebrated for sanctity. At *Gallinaro*, a village in the kingdom of *Naples*, the commemoration of S. *Gerard* an English pilgrim, whose sepulchre is renowned for the miracles there wrought. On this day also are commemorated in the *English* martyrology two royal virgin saints of the name of *Edburge*; the one a daughter of king *Penda*, abbess of *Dormuncaster*; the other of king *Ethelwolf*, abbess of *Winchester*.

December 22. In *Scotland,* the feſtivity of S. *Ethernan,* kinſman and companion of S. *Columkille,* in his apoſtolical expedition for winning over the nation of the *Picts* to Chriſt. His name has been very illuſtrious of old both in the *Scottiſh* and *Iriſh* churches. He has a place on this day in the *Aberdeen* breviary, where he is ſtiled a biſhop; and is ſaid to have gone home to our Lord, anno 592. In *Ireland,* the commemoration of S. *Mugenocus Killecumuli,* one of the moſt eminent amongſt the diſciples of S. *Finian* of *Clonard.* See *Uſher*'s Antiquities, p. 498.

December 23. In *Scotland,* the feſtivity of S. *Carannus,* biſhop; and of S. *Majota,* virgin; who have a place on this day in the *Scots* breviary. In the dioceſe of *Landaff,* the commemoration of the ſaints *Febric* and *Jarmen,* whoſe churches are mentioned in the acts of the ſynods of *Landaff.* In *Cornwall,* the commemoration of S. *Colon* or *Cullan,* in whoſe name a church was anciently dedicated to God in that province.

December 24. At *Rome,* the commemoration of holy king *Offa,* who in the flower of his age, and in the midſt of the flatteries of the world, being the darling of his people, leaving his kingdom, (of the *Eaſt Saxons*) his virgin ſpouſe S. *Kyneſwide,* (by whoſe prayers and addreſſes to the Queen of virgins this happy change was effected), and all his worldly hopes and poſſeſſions, for the love of God; went to *Rome* in the company of *Coenred,* king of *Mercia*; and there becoming a monk, conſecrated the remainder of his days to religion, in order to ſecure to himſelf a better and eternal

eternal kingdom. An example which was afterwards followed by many others of the *English* nation, of all conditions: as our venerable historian informs us towards the close of his history. In *Cornwall*, the commemoration of S. *Levan* and S. *Mellin*, who have left there their names to the places where their bodies repose in expectation of a glorious resurrection.

December 25. The temporal birth-day of our eternal King, *Jesus Christ* the Son of God, the King of all nations. At *Glastenbury*, the commemoration of many saints, as well externs as natives, whose relicks were formerly honoured in that ancient monastery, the catalogue of which may be seen in the first volume of *Dugdale*'s Monasticon. Also in many other places, the commemoration of divers other foreign saints, whose sacred remains have been deposited in these islands; and who shall one day arise from hence in glory, to meet the Son of God, and to be taken up to his heavenly kingdom. At *Wurtzbourg*, in the monastery of S. *Megingard*, the commemoration of S. *Gregory* priest and monk of royal *English* blood, celebrated on this day in *Wilson*'s *English* martyrology: who departed to our Lord about the middle of the tenth century. At *Wilton*, the commemoration of S. *Alburgha* sister to king *Egbert*, foundress of the monastery of *Wilton*. *Tanner*'s *Notitia*, p. 592.

December 26. In *Monmouthshire*, the festivity of S. *Tathai* confessor, who from his hermitage in the mountains of *Wales*, was invited by king *Caradoc* to the city of *Gwent*, where he opened a
famous

famous school, in which he trained up S. *Cadocus* and many other excellent men. He was an *Irishman* by birth, and flourished in the fifth century. At *Tuam* in *Ireland*, the festivity of S. *Jarlaithe*, the founder and first bishop of the church of *Tuam*; the cathedral of which is dedicated in his name. He is celebrated in the ancient catalogue as one of the chiefest of the *Irish* saints of the second class. He flourished in the beginning of the sixth century. In *Ireland* also the commemoration of another S. *Jarlaithe* a disciple of S. *Patrick*, who succeeded S. *Benignus* in the see of *Armagh* anno 465; and departed to our Lord anno 482.

December 27. In *Ireland*, the commemoration of S. *Coman* or *Comman*, founder of the church of *Rofscommon* in the sixth century; in which he had many disciples, and successors, illustrious for sanctity. In *Ireland* also the commemoration of divers other saints, of the name of *Coman* or *Coeman*: of which number were S. *Coeman* disciple of S. *Columba* of *Tyrdaglafs*; abbat of *Enach-truim*; S. *Coeman* brother to S. *Coemgen*; S. *Coeman* of *Kill-Choemain*, in the third isle of *Aran*, &c. In *Cornwall* the commemoration of S. *Auftel* and S. *Kevern*, formerly honoured in that province, as appears by the places called to this day by their names. In *Bedfordshire* the commemoration of S. *Arnulph* hermit, who is supposed to have given name to *Arnulphsbury*, in that county.

December 28. At *Canterbury* the translation of the uncorrupted body of S. *Alphege* archbishop;

martyred by the *Danes* anno 1012. In *Wales*, the commemoration of divers ancient *British* faints, whose names are retained by the places, where they were formerly honoured: such as S. *Athan*, S. *Aylvew*, S. *Breuile*, S. *Goven*, S. *Katterus*, S. *Melan*, S. *Mongan*, &c. &c. who were all renowned in their days for the sanctity of their lives; and however little thought on at present upon earth, shine most gloriously in heaven. In *Ireland* the commemoration of S. *Ludeus* and S. *Moditeus*, celebrated amongst the faints of the second class in the ancient catalogue. Also the commemoration of S. *Ernaan* abbat, illustrious for sanctity. On the same day the festival of S. *Umba* virgin, markt on this day in our ancient calendars.

December 29. At *Canterbury* the solemnity of S. *Thomas Becket*, archbishop of that see; who for his constancy in maintaining the liberties of the church, was slain in his own cathedral, anno 1170; and by reason of the innumerable miracles wrought at his tomb was, three years after, canonized for a saint, by pope *Alexander* III. At *Lanthony* in *Monmouthshire*, the memory of the holy hermits *Hugh* and *Ernisius*, who first inhabited that solitude. In *Staffordshire*, the memory of the religious matron *Wulfruna*, foundress of *Wolverhampton*.

December 30. At *Dormundcaster* near *Peterborough*, the commemoration of S. *Weede* or *Eve* virgin and abbess, celebrated for sanctity. She is said in *Wilson*'s Martyrology (*Dec.* 2.) to have been daughter of king *Penda*, and the youngest of

BRITISH PIETY. 179

of five fisters, all faints; to have been the third abbess of *Dormundcaster*, after her sisters S. *Kyneburge*, and S. *Edburge*; and to have passed to a better life, anno 692. Also a commemoration of S. *Genetrude* virgin, whose name occurs in an ancient manuscript litany, amongst our *English* virgin saints. Also the memory of holy *Wulfi*, a recluse, illustrious for sanctity in the days of S. *Edward* the confessor.

December 31. At *Chertsey* in *Surrey*, the commemoration of the saints *Beocca* abbat, and *Ethor* priest; whose bodies formerly reposed in the monastery of *Chertsey*, with fourscore monks who were slain with them (by the *Danes*) and honoured amongst the martyrs. *Saxon* MSS. Also a commemoration of S. *Alun*, confessor; and of S. *Kumerick*, confessor; of whose priory see *Dugdale*'s abridgment, p. 124. In the *Isle of Wight*, the commemoration of the man of God, *Paulinus* disciple of S. *Germanus*: who opened in that island a school of christian piety and divine learning, in which he trained up amongst other eminent disciples, the great S. *David* of *Menevia*. And in other places of many other holy martyrs, confessors, and virgins, *Britons*, *English*, *Scots*, and *Irish*, whose names are in the book of life.

Soli DEO *honor & gloria.*

THE BURIAL PLACES OF THE ENGLISH SAINTS;

Translated from Two ancient SAXON MANUSCRIPTS, in *Bennet* Library, *Cambridge*, Volume 284. p. 147, and 149.

The FIRST MANUSCRIPT.

Chiefly relating to the SAINTS of *Kent*.

A Narration of the SAINTS *who repose in the Land of the* English, *in the Name of our Lord* JESUS CHRIST.

S. AUGUSTIN baptized *Æthelbert* king of *Kent*, with all his people.

Æthelbert's queen was named *Bertha:* his son was *Eadbald*; and his daughter was *Æthelburga*, surnamed *Tata*. This lady was given in marriage to *Eadwin* king of the *Northumbrians:* and was accompanied by S. *Paulinus*, who baptized that king and all his people. After the death of
Eadwin,

Eadwin, *Æthelburga* returned to *Kent*; where her brother king *Eadbald* gave her land in *Limene* (*Liming*) where she built a church: and there she reposes, together with S. *Eadburga*.

Eadbald had for wife *Emma* daughter of the king of the *French*: of this marriage was born S. *Eanswithe*, who reposes at *Folkstone*: and two sons, *Earcombercht* (who succeeded in the kingdom) and *Eormenred Clito* (*i. e.* prince of the blood.) *Eormenred* had two sons, S. *Æthelred* and S. *Æthelbright*, and two daughters *Eormenburga* and S. *Eormengitha*.

King *Earcombercht* had two sons by his queen *Sexburga*, king *Ecgbert* and king *Lotharius*; and two daughters, S. *Eormenilda* and S. *Eorcongota*.

S. *Eormenburga*, otherwise called *Dompneva*, married to *Merwald* the son of king *Penda*: To these were born S. *Milburg*, S. *Mildred*, S. *Milgith*, and S. *Mervin* (*Meresin*). All these for the love of God disposed of their whole estate, in their life-time, for pious uses.

Dompneva afterwards went into *Kent*, to receive from king *Ecgbert* the *weregeld* (or fine) which he desired to pay her, on occasion of the death of her two brothers, slain by his orders, in the isle of *Thanet*, and privately buried in the royal palace of *Estrey*, where they were miraculously discovered, by a bright pillar of light, shining at midnight over the place of their burial; which the king seeing was greatly terrified;
and

and being made thereby sensible of his crime, sent for their sister *Dompneva*, and gave her eighty *carucats* of land: where she built a monastery, in which prayers might be said for their souls; the king assisting her in this work. She also sent her daughter *Mildred* beyond the seas, to be instructed in monastick disciplines: which she learnt in so perfect a manner, as to make a great progress in all sanctity; the proofs of which are still to be seen. To her care her mother committed the monastery which she had erected: And thus S. *Mildred* received from archbishop *Theodore* the sacred veil, in company with seventy other virgins; with whom continuing to advance, according to the will of God, in all virtues, she merited eternal life: and was afterwards illustrious for frequent miracles.

S. *Eormengitha* passed the days of her mortal life in the same monastery with her niece (S. *Mildred*), and after her death was buried, as she had desired, at the distance of one mile to the east of S. *Mildred*'s monastery; where wonderful works were heretofore frequent and famous: yea and are celebrated to this day.

S. *Mildred* had for successor in the government of her monastery S. *Eadburga*, who built the church there; in which also she lies buried.

Sexburga queen of *Kent* founded the monastery of S. *Mary* in the isle of *Shepey*, and placed nuns there.——S. *Sexburga*, S. *Ætheldryda*, and S. *Withburga* were daughters of *Anna* king of the *East Angles*. S. *Ætheldryda* was married to *Ecgfrith*

frith king of the *Northumbrians*; which notwithstanding she always preserved her virginity. She was buried in the great church of *Ely*, where she has been illustrated with miracles. In the same church also reposes her sister S. *Withburga*.

S *Eormenilda* daughter of *Earcombercht* and *Sexburga*, was married to king *Wulfere* the son of *Penda* king of the *Mercians*; under whose reign the nation of the *Mercians* received baptism. Of this marriage was born S. *Werburge* a sacred virgin, who was buried in the monastery of *Heanburh (Hanbury)*. She was afterwards taken up, and now reposes at *Legecester (Chester)*. But S. *Eormenilda* reposes at the borough of *Ely*, together with her mother, and her aunt S. *Ætheldryda:* where she shines with many miracles.

Her sister S. *Eorcongota* was sent beyond the seas, to be trained up by her aunt S. *Ethelburga*, the abbess of the place: and there by the will of God she made great progress in virtue; and having finished her days, was quickly illustrious for miracles.

King *Withred*, son of king *Ecgbert*, built a monastery at *Dover*, in honour of S. *Martin*; the saint himself marking the place where he would have this monastery erected: which was accordingly executed. He also placed monks here, and appointed them lands for their maintenance to this day. This king reposes near S. *Augustine*, within the porch, on the south side of the church of S. *Mary*; which his great-grand-father, king *Eadbald*, had built in honour of God, and S. *Mary*.

The SECOND MANUSCRIPT.

Here begins a Narration *of the* SAINTS *who repose in* England.

S. ALBAN, the first martyr of *Britain*, reposes near *Watlingchester*, by the water called *Werlam.*

S. *Columkille* reposes in the place called *Duncaban*, by the river *Tau.*

S. *Cuthbert* at *Durham.* The head of St. *Oswald* is with the body of S. *Cuthbert*; his right arm is at *Bebbanbyrig (Bamborow)*: The rest of his body in the new monastery of *Gloucester.*

S. *John* the bishop reposes at *Beverley*, by the little river *Hull.*

S. *Ecbert*, and S. *Wilfrid* bishop, and S. *Withburga*, repose at *Rippon*, on the river *Earwe.*

S. *Chad*, S. *Cedd*, and S. *Ceatta*, lie in the church of *Litchfield*, near the water called *Onkel.*

S. *Æthelred* king, and S. *Ostrythe* sister of S. *Oswald* king, rest in the monastery of *Bardney*, by the river *Wightam (Witham).*

S. *Eadburge* reposes at *Southwell* upon *Trent.*

S. *Guthlake* at *Crowland*, which monastery is situated in the midst of the fenns of *Gyrwie.*

S. *Alkmund* at *Northworthig (Derby)*, on the river *Derwent.*

S. *Botulf*

S. *Botulf* lies buried at *Medeshamsted*, on the river *Nen*.

S. *Æthelbert* reposes in the cathedral of *Hereford*, by the river *Wy*.

S. *Cett* in the monastery called *Undola (Oundle)*, by the river *Nen*.

S. *Winburga (Milburge)*, in the monastery of *Wenlock* upon the *Severn*.

S. *Winstan* in the monastery of *Repedune* upon the *Trent*.

S. *Dionia* in the place called *Ceorlingburgh (Charlebury)*, by the little river *Wenrisk (Winrush.)*

S. *Eadgith (Editha)* reposes at *Pollesworth*, near the river *Onker*.

S. *Rumbold* at *Buckingham* upon the *Ouse*.

S. *Æthelred* at *Leominster* upon the *Lug*.

S. *Eadmund* the king, at *Bedricksworth (Bury)*, amongst the *East Angles*.

S. *Osgyth (Osith)*, at *Chich*, in the church of S. *Peter* by the sea.

S. *Æthelburga*, in the monastery of *Barking* upon the *Thames*.

S. *Erconwald* the bishop reposes at *London*.

S. *Neot* priest, at *Einulfsbury*.

S. *Ivo*, S. *Æthelred* and S. *Æthelbright* repose at *Ramsey*.

S. *Florentius* martyr, S. *Kyneswitha* and S. *Kyneburge* rest at *Peterborough*, with many others; though

though now unknown: for miracles are not wrought by all that are saints.

At *Thorney* repose S. *Botulf*, and S. *Athulf*, and S. *Huna*, and S. *Thancred*, and S. *Torthred*, and S. *Herefarth*, and S. *Cissa*, and S. *Benedict* (*Biscop*), and S. *Toua*.

At *Abbandune* (*Abington*), S. *Vincent* martyr.

At *Canterbury*, S. *Dunstan*, and S. *Augustine*, with very many other saints.

At *Rochester*, S. *Paulinus*.

At *Winchester*, in the old minster repose S. *Birinus* the *Roman* bishop, and S. *Hedda*, and S. *Swithun*, and S. *Æthelwold*, and S. *Ælfeage*, and S. *Birnstan*, and S. *Fritheslane*, and S. *Justus* martyr, with many other saints. In the new minster S. *Judocus* and S. *Grimbald* lye buried; and in the church of the nuns, S. *Eadburga*.

At *Rumsey* reposes S. *Merwinna*, the first abbess of that place; as also S. *Balthild* the queen, and S. *Æthelfleda*, with a number of other saints.

At *Wilton*, S. *Iwy* bishop, and S. *Eadgythe* (*Editha*).

At *Shaftsbury*, S. *Edwin* (*Edward*) king, and S. *Ælfgyva*.

At *Glastenbury*, S. *Aidan*, and S. *Patrick*, and many other saints.

At *Congresbury*, S. *Congar*.

S. *Sithefulla* the virgin, near *Exeter*.

S. *Ruman* bishop, at *Tavestock*.

S. *Petrock* in *West Wales* (*Cornwall*), at the bay of the sea called *Hailemouth*.

In *Adelmſbury (Malmeſbury)* reſt S. *Maildun*, S. *Aldelm*, and S. *John the Sage*.

At *Worceſter*, S. *Oſwald* the archbiſhop; and with him a great many biſhops, ſaints.

At *Eveſham* upon the *Avon*, S. *Ecgwin* biſhop.

At *Winchelcomb*, S. *Kenelm* the royal child.

In *Wimborn* minſter repoſe S. *Cuthburga*, and S. *Quenburga*: the former of which inſtituted that way of life and diſcipline, which is to this day in vigour there among the nuns.

S. *Fritheſwoed (Fritheſwide)* repoſes at *Oxford*.

At *Middleton (Milton* abbey in *Dorſetſhire)*, are the head of S. *Brangwallador* biſhop; and the arm of S. *Samſon* biſhop; as alſo the croſier of the ſame.

At *Stæning* on the river *Bramber*, among the *South Saxons*, repoſes S. *Cuthman*.

S. *Beocca* abbat, and S. *Ethor* prieſt, reſt in the monaſtery of *Chertſey*: where alſo fourſcore others were ſlain with them.

Praiſe and glory be to our Lord Jeſus Chriſt, for his goodneſs, to all ages, and to all eternity. *Amen*.

I shall here subjoin the testimony given by Mr. *Cambden*, in his *Britannia* (published anno 1695, col. cxxxii) to the great multitude, as well as to the fervour, zeal, and unfeigned piety of our ancient *English* Saints, in these words:

"NO sooner (says he) was the Name of Christ preached in the *English* nation, but with a most fervent zeal they consecrated themselves to it, and laid out their utmost endeavours to promote it, by discharging all the duties of christian piety, by erecting churches and endowing them; so that no part of the christian world could shew either more or richer monasteries. Nay even some kings preferred a religious life before their very crowns. So many holy men did it produce, who for their firm profession of the christian religion, their resolute perseverance in it, and their unfeigned piety, were sainted; that in this point it is equal to any country in the whole christian world.—— So *England* might justly be called an island fruitful in saints."

A TABLE

[191]

A TABLE

OF THE
NAMES of the SAINTS, &c.

Commemorated in this
BRITISH MARTYROLOGY.

AB. stands for archbishop; *Ab*. for abbat; *ab*. for abbess; *B*. for bishop; *C*. for confessor; *D*. for doctor; *H*. for hermit; *K*. for king; *M*. for martyr; *P*. for priest; *Q*. for queen; *V*. for virgin; *W*. for widow; *& co.* signifies, that there are divers other saints, companions or disciples of the saint there named.

A.

Aaron *M*. July 1.
Abban *Ab*. October 27.
Acca *B*. December 20.
Achebran *C*. April 8.
Adalbert *C*. June 25.
Adamnan *Ab*. September 3.
Adamnan *C*. January 28.
Adelhare *M*. April 20.
Adrian *Ab*. January 10.
Adrian *B. M. & co.* March 4.
Adrian *P*. April 2.

Adulph

Adulph B. June 18.
Ædan B. January 31.
Ædus B. November 10.
Ælfrick AB. April 9.
Ælfred K. October 28.
Aelgar H. July 9.
Aelgiva Q. May 12.
Aelred Ab. January 12.
Ængufs B. March 11.
Æthelred C. December 6.
Agatha V. June 6.
Agatha Q. November 26.
Aidan B. August 31.
Ailbeus B. September 12.
Airedan Ab. September 6.
Alban M. June 22.
Albinus Ab. January 10.
Albuinus B. October 26.
Alburgha Q. December 25.
Alchilda V. March 28.
Alcmund M. March 19.
Alcmund B. June 19.
Alcuin Ab. May 19.
Aldate C. June 14.
Aldewin Ab. May 3.
Aldhelm B. May 25.
Alexander C. April 12.
Alfreda V. August 8.
Alfwald K. September 23.
Alfwold B. March 25.
Algiva V. October 19.
Alice V. August 10.
Allan C. February 22.
Almedha V. M. August 2.
Alnoth M. December 16.

Alphege

Alphege *AB. M.* April 19.
Alrick *H.* December 7.
Alto *Ab.* February 10.
Alun *C.* December 31.
Amnichade *C.* January 30.
Amphibalus *M.* June 26.
Andrew *Apostle,* November 30.
Anna *K.* December 9.
Anselm *AB. D.* April 21. July 5.
Aran isle (SS. of) March 21.
Arbogast *B.* July 21.
Ardwyne *C.* October 25.
Aristobulus *C.* March 15.
Arnulph *H.* December 27.
Arvan *C.* October 30.
Asaph *B.* May 1.
Athelard *AB.* May 11.
Athy *V.* September 5.
Athilda *V.* March 28.
Attracta *V.* February 9.
Audoenus *AB.* August 24.
Audry *Q. V. ab.* June 23.
Angulus *B. M.* February 7.
Augustine *AB.* May 26.
Austel *C.* December 27.
Auxilius *B.* December 2.

B.

BAGNA *C.* June 5.
Baithen *Ab.* June 11.
Baldred *B.* March 6.
Balther *C.* February 18.
Bardsey Saints 20000, December 1.
Barrindeus *Ab.* September 25.
Barrus *B. & co.* September 27.

Barforarius *Ab*. February 13.
Bartholomew *H*. June 24.
Baruch *H*. February 27.
Bathildis *Q*. January 27.
Bean *B*. February 8.
Bean *B*. December 16.
Beatus *C*. May 9.
Bede *C. D*. May 27. October 29.
Bega *V*. September 6.
Begu *V*. May 4.
Benchor *MM*. May 10.
Benen *or* Benignus *B*. November 9.
Bennet Bifcop *Ab*. January 12.
Bennow *or* Beuno *C*. January 14.
Beocca *Ab. & co. MM*. December 31.
Bercham *B*. April 7.
Berchan *Ab*. December 4.
Bercthun *Ab*. May 22.
Bernach *Ab*. April 7.
Bernard *C*. September 24.
Bertelin *H*. Auguft 12.
Beye *V*. November 1.
Bilfrid *H*. February 19.
Birinus *B*. December 3.
Birnftan *B*. November 4.
Bithius *C*. May 13.
Blaine *B*. Auguft 10.
Blafius *B. M*. February 3.
Blathmake *& co. MM*. January 20.
Boifil *C*. July 5.
Boniface *AB. & co. MM*. June 5.
Bofa *B*. March 9.
Bofel *B*. September 24.
Botuid *M*. July 28.
Botulph *Ab*. June 17.

Botulph

Botulph *B.* May 31.
Bradan *C.* October 20.
Brandubh *B.* February 17.
Branwallador *B.* June 3.
Bregwin *AB.* August 26.
Brendan *Ab.* May 16.
Brendan junior *Ab.* November 30.
Briavel *C.* August 7.
Brigide *V. ab.* February 1.
Brigide *V.* March 14.
Brigide *V.* May 28.
Briocus *B.* April 30.
British Prelates, January 1.
Brithwald *AB.* January 9.
Brithwald *B.* January 22.
Budgualan *C.* August 26.
Budoc *C.* October 6.
Burchard *B.* October 14.
Buriene *V.* May 29.

C.

Cadoc *Ab.* } January 24.
Cadoc *B. M.*
Caidoc *P.* April 2.
Camin *or* Cammin *Ab.* March 22.
Canicus *Ab.* October 11.
Canoc *C.* February 11.
Caradoc *P. H.* April 13.
Carannus *B.* December 23.
Carantac *C.* May 16.
Carthac *Ab.* March 5.
Carthac junior *Ab. & co.* May 14.
Cataldus *B.* May 10.
Cathmael *Ab.* May 13.
Cayman *Ab.* December 10.

Ceadda (Chad) B. March 2.
Ceadwall K. April 20.
Cedda B. January 7.
Cedmon *monk*, February 12.
Celestine *pope*, April 6.
Celin C. January 8.
Celsus AB. April 6.
Ceolfrid Ab. September 25.
Ceolulph K. October 28.
Cett C. December 1.
Chebeus C. June 28.
Christiana V. July 26.
Christina V. November 26.
Cissa C. May 12.
Clarus M. November 4.
Clitanc K. August 19.
Coelan Ab. September 11.
Coeman Ab. } December 27.
Coeman C.
Coemgen Ab. } June 3.
Coemgen sen.
Coenred K. October 4.
Cogan Ab. October 13.
Colan *or* Colon C. December 23.
Colm B. June 6.
Colin Ab. May 9.
Colman B. August 8.
Colman B. September 3.
Colman M. October 13.
Colman's SS. 230. June 29.
Colmoc B. June 7.
Colmonel Ab. September 26.
Columb V. M. October 23.
Columba *or* Columkille Ab. June 19.
Columba Ab. December 13.

Columban

Names of the SAINTS, &c.

Columban *Ab*. November 21.
Coman *or* Comman *Ab*. December 27.
Comgall *Ab*. May 10.
Comgall jun. *Ab*. May 12.
Congellus *Ab*. April 7.
Conlaeth *B*. February 2.
Conſtantine *K. M*. March 11.
Conſtantine III. *K*. December 6.
Conwall *C*. May 18.
Conwallan *Ab*. October 13.
Cordula *V. M*. October 22.
Cormac *Ab*. December 12.
Corniſh Saints, March 5, &c.
Corpreus *B*. February 17.
Corpreus jun. *B*. March 7.
Cortill *B*. April 28.
Cronan *Ab*. April 28.
Cronan *C*. June 3.
Croniack *C*. January 4.
Cuanus *C*. April 2.
Culan *B*. February 18.
Culdees, March 29.
Cullan *C*. December 23.
Cumian *B*. June 11.
Cummian *Ab*. December 5.
Cungar *Ab*. November 5.
Cuthbert *B*. March 20. September 4.
Cuthbert *AB*. September 24.
Cuthburge *V*. September 7.
Cuthman *C*. February 8.
Cybthak *C*. September 22.
Cynibil *P*. January 8.
Cyra *V*. October 16.
Cyriol *C*. January 2.

D.

Daniel *B.* of Bangor, November 23.
Daniel *B.* of Winchester, December 17.
Darerca *W.* July 22.
Darlugdacha *V. ab.* February 1.
David *AB.* March 1.
David *Ab.* July 15.
David *K.* May 29.
Daye, January 15.
Declan *B. & co.* Jul. 23.
Decuman *H. M.* February 27.
Deicola *Ab.* January 18.
Dega *B.* August 18.
Deifer *H.* March 16.
Deruvian *C.* January 3.
Devinike *B.* November 13.
Deusdedit *AB.* June 30.
Dicul *AB.* } January 28.
Dicul *C.*
Dionia, December 7.
Diormit *C.* June 30.
Disen *B.* September 8.
Diuma *B. & co.* February 18.
Docus *C.* May 4.
Docuinus *Ab.* November 15.
Dogmael *Ab.* June 14.
Domangart *B.* March 24.
Dominic *B.* February 13.
Dompneva *W.* November 19.
Donan *Ab.* April 7.
Donatus *B.* October 22.
Donatus *C.* February 13.
Donewald *C. & co.* July 15.
Drithelm September 1.

Drostan

Droftan *C.* December 14.
Dubritius *AB.* November 14.
Dunnius *Ab.* May 14.
Dunftan *AB.* May 19. September 7.
Duthake *B.* March 8.
Dwywan *C.* January 3.
Dymma *C.* February 17.
Dympna *V. M.* May 15.

E.

EADBERT *B.* May 6.
Eadbert *K.* November 25.
Eadburge *or* Edburge *V.* of Ailefbury, July 18.
Edburge *V.* of Lyming, } September 8.
Edburge *ab.* of Menftrey, }
Edburge *V.* of Winton, June 15.
Edburge *ab.* of Cafter, } December 21.
Edburge *ab.* of Winton, }
Eadgithe *or* Editha *V. ab.* May 15.
Editha *V.* of Wilton, September 16.
Editha *V.* of Ailefbury, July 18.
Editha *V.* of Pollefworth, September 16.
Editha *Q.* July 15.
Editha of Hafting, June 7.
Eadfin *AB.* October 29.
Ealfwitha *V.* November 27.
Eanfleda *Q.* December 11.
Eanfwide *V.* September 14.
Earcongota *V.* February 25.
Eafterwin *Ab.* March 6.
Eata *B.* October 26.
Ebba *V. ab.* October 25.
Ebba jun. *& co. MM.* October 5.
Edelburge *ab.* of Barking, } October 11.
Edelburge *Q. ab.* }

Edel-

Edelburge *ab*. of Brie, July 12.
Edgar *K*. May 24.
Edilhun *C*. April 25.
Edilwald *P. H.* March 23.
Ediltrudis. *See* Audry.
Edmund *K. M.* November 20.
Edmund *AB*. November 16.
Edward *K. C.* January 5. October 13.
Edward *K. M.* March 18.
Edwin *K*. October 4.
Edwold *H*. November 28. August 29.
Egbert *P*. April 25.
Egbert *P*. April 11.
Egbert *AB*. November 25.
Egelnoth *AB*. October 30.
Egelwin *C*. November 29.
Egwin *B*. January 11.
Elerius *Ab*. June 13.
Eleutherius *pope*, May 26.
Elfleda *V. ab.* January 23.
Elfleda *V*. December 17.
Elfreda *V. ab.* December 11.
Eliphius *M. & co.* October 6.
Ellenius *Ab*. January 24.
Elphage *AB. M.* April 19.
Elphage *B*. September 1.
Elvan *B*. January 2.
Emerita *V*. December 4.
Enda *Ab. & co.* March 21.
Eneon Bhrenin *K*. January 14.
Engelmund *Ab*. June 21.
Englate *B*. November 4.
Eoban *B. M.* June 5.
Eochoid *C*. January 26.
Eogain *B*. August 23.

Erchod

Erchod *B.* August 24.
Erconwald *B.* April 30. November 14.
Ercus *B.* April 16.
Ermemburga *Q.* November 19.
Ermengithe *V.* July 30.
Ermenilda *Q. ab.* February 13.
Ernaan *Ab.* December 28.
Ernisius *H.* December 29.
Eskill *B. M.* April 10.
Etchen *B.* February 11.
Etha *V.* September 6.
Ethbin *Ab.* October 19.
Ethelbert *K. C.* February 24.
Ethelbert *K. M.* May 20.
Ethelbright } *MM.* October 17.
Ethelred
Ethelburga *Q.* May 24.
Etheldreda *Q. V. ab.* June 23.
Ethelfleda *W.* April 14.
Ethelgive *V.* December 19.
Ethelred *C.* December 6.
Ethelred *K. M.* April 22.
Ethelred *K. C.* May 5.
Ethelwin *B.* May 3.
Elthelwold *B.* of Winchester, August 1.
Ethelwold *B.* of Lindisfarne, February 12.
Ethelwolph *K.* April 14.
Ethernan *B.* December 22.
Ethor *P. M.* December 31.
Etto *& co.* July 10, 11.
Evan *B.* August 18.
Everildis *V.* July 9.
Euurcius *B.* September 7.
Ewalds *MM.* October 13.

F.

Fagan *C.* January 3.
Failan *C. Ab.* September 6.
Fanchea *V. ab.* March 21.
Fara *V. ab.* April 3.
Febric *C.* December 23.
Fechin *Ab.* January 20.
Felix *B.* March 8.
Fergus *B.* November 17.
Fethno *C.* September 27.
Fiaker *H.* August 30.
Filan *Ab.* January 9.
Finan *B.* February 16.
Finbarrus *B.* September 25.
Findoche *V.* October 14.
Fingar *& co. MM.* December 15.
Finian *B.* December 10.
Finian *C.* March 16.
Fintan *Ab.* February 17.
Fintan jun. *Ab.* October 21.
Florentius *B.* November 7.
Foillan *B. M.* October 31.
Forannan *B.* April 27.
Fortchern *B.* December 10.
Fredegand *C.* July 17.
Fredolin *C.* March 6.
Fremund *M.* May 11.
Frideswide *V.* October 19.
Frigdianus *B.* November 18.
Frithstane *B.* April 9.
Frothmund *M.* February 25.
Fulk *C.* November 18.
Fursey *Ab.* January 16.

G.

Gallus *Ab.* October 16.
Genetrude *V.* December 30.
Genocus *C.* May 13.
George *M.* April 23.
Gerald *B. & co.* March 13.
Gerard *C.* December 21.
Gerebern *M.* May 15.
Germanus *B.* July 31.
Germanus *B.* of Man, July 3.
Germanus *B. M.* May 2.
Gervad *B.* November 8.
Gibrian *C.* May 8.
Gilbert *C.* February 4.
Gilbert *B.* April 1.
Gilbert *B.* August 11.
Gildas *Ab. & co.* ⎫ January 29.
Gildas jun. *Ab.* ⎭
Glastenbury Saints, December 25.
Godrick *H.* May 21.
Godwin *H.* December 7.
Golven *B.* July 1.
Gotebald *B.* October 31.
Gregory *pope,* March 12.
Gregory *C.* December 25.
Grillaan *C.* December 12.
Grimbald *C.* July 8.
Gudwall *B.* February 22.
Guerir *C.* April 4.
Guinocus *B.* April 13.
Guithelin *AB.* January 8.
Gundleus *C.* March 29.
Guronus *H.* January 4.
Guthagon *C.* July 3.
Guthlake *H. & co.* April 11.

HAMUND

H.

Hamund B. M. March 22.
Hardulf C. August 6.
Hedda B. July 7.
Heiu V. ab. January 23.
Helen empress, August 18.
Hemelin C. March 10.
Henry B. M. January 19.
Henry H. January 16.
Henry VI. K. M. May 22.
Herebald Ab. May 7.
Herebert P. March 22.
Hereferth C. May 12.
Herefrid C. June 2.
Hereswide Q. September 21.
Hilda V. ab. November 18.
Hildelid V. ab. March 24.
Hismael B. March 27.
Honorius AB. September 30.
Honorius H. August 23.
Hugh B. October 7. November 17.
Hugh M. July 27.
Hugh H. December 29.
Humbert B. M. November 20.
Huna C. May 12.
Hygbald Ab. September 20.

J & I.

James C. October 18.
Janbercht AB. August 11.
Jarlaith B. } December 26.
Jarlaith Tuam }
Jarmen C. December 23.
Jaruman B. February 18.
Ibar B. April 23.

Idaberge *V.* July 25.
Ieron *M.* August 17.
Iia *or* Ivia *V. M.* October 27.
Illogan *C.* October 30.
Iltut *Ab.* November 6.
Ilund *Ab.* November 10.
Imarius *P.* November 2.
Ina *K.* April 1.
Inan *C.* August 18.
Indractus *& co. MM.* February 5.
John *B.* May 7.
John *B.* June 19.
John Scot *B.* August 19.
John *B. M.* November 10.
John *P.* June 27.
John *C.* October 10.
John *Ab.* February 21.
Joseph of Arimathea, July 27.
Irchard *B.* August 24.
Irish SS. in three classes, March 17.
Isam *Ab.* November 6.
Isserninus *B.* December 2.
Ita *or* Mida *V.* January 15.
Ithamar *B.* June 10.
Julius *M.* August 1.
Ivo *B.* April 26.
Jurmin *C.* May 31.
Justinian *H. M.* August 23.
Just *C.* January 22.
Justus *AB.* November 10.
Juthwara *V. M. & co.* December 23.
Ivy *B.* July 16.

K.

KADROE *Ab.* March 7.
Kebius *B.* November 8.

Keivin

Keivin *Ab.* June 3.
Kellach *B.* May 1.
Kellen *C.* March 27.
Kenan *C.* January 17.
Kenelm *K. M.* July 17.
Kenneire *V.* October 29.
Kennoche *V.* March 13.
Kenred *K.* October 4.
Kentigern *B.* January 13.
Kentigerna *W.* January 9.
Kertennus *B.* August 15.
Kevern *C.* December 27.
Kewe, August 27.
Keyna *V.* October 8.
Kiaran *or* Keran *B.* March 5.
Kiaran jun. *B.* September 9.
Kilian *& co. MM.* July 8.
Kilian *C.* November 13.
Kined *or* Kinedvau *Ab.* August 1.
Kumerick *C.* December 31.
Kyneburge *Q.* March 6.
Kynedride *V.* } February 14.
Kyneswide *V.* }
Kynnera *V.* September 23.
Kyrinus *B.* March 17.

L.

LACTIN *Ab.* March 18.
Laisrean *Ab.* September 13.
Laisrean *B.* April 18.
Lanfrank *AB.* March 24.
Laudatus *Ab.* January 14.
Lawrence *AB.* of Canterbury, February 2.
Lawrence *AB.* of Dublin, November 14.
Lebwin *C.* November 12.

Leonard

Leonard *C.* November 6.
Leonorius *B.* June 30.
Lethardus *B.* February 24.
Levan *C.* December 24.
Leufred *Ab.* June 21.
Lewine *V. M.* July 25.
Lily *C.* March 3.
Line *V.* October 9.
Lioba *V. ab.* September 28.
Livinus *B. M.* November 12.
Lolan *B.* September 22.
Loman *B.* } September 3.
Loman *B.* }
Luan *or* Molua *Ab.* August 4.
Lucius *K. C.* December 3.
Ludeus *C.* December 28.
Ludger *B.* March 26.
Lugadius *Ab.* April 18.
Lugeus *or* Lugidus *Ab.* August 4.
Luitphard *B. M.* February 4.
Lullus *AB.* October 16.
Luman *C. & co.* July 22.
Lupus *B.* July 28.

M.

MACARIUS *Ab.* December 19.
Maccalleus *B.* February 6.
Macglaftian *B.* January 30.
Machan *B.* November 12.
Machutus *or* Maclou *B.* November 15.
Mackeffog *B.* March 10.
Madern *or* Maddren *C.* May 17.
Magloir *B.* October 24.
Magnus *M.* April 16.
Maidoc *B.* January 31.

Maidulf *or* Maildun *Ab*. May 25.
Mailoc &c *co*. January 30.
Main *B*. June 16.
Majota *V*. December 23.
Makwolock *B*. January 29.
Malachi *AB*. November 2.
Malcallan *Ab*. January 21.
Malchus *B*. November 24.
Malcolm III. *K*. June 1.
Malcolm IV. *K*. June 18.
Maldod *Ab*. May 13.
Malrube *H. M.* August 27.
Man Isle SS. July 3.
Manere *B*. December 18.
Marcellus *B. M.* September 4.
Marchelm *C*. July 14.
Margaret *Q*. June 10. November 16.
Margaret *V*. August 16.
Marnan *B*. March 1.
Marnok *B*. October 25.
Marnok *C*. May 3.
Many Martyrs, January 4. September 17.
Martyrs by the Saxons, December 8.
Martyrs by the Danes, March 31.
Matildes *Q*. August 7.
Maura *V*. November 2.
Maxencia *V. M.* November 22.
Mecthildis *V*. April 12.
Medan *B*. November 14.
Medran *C*. July 7.
Mel *B*. February 6.
Melchi *B*. February 6.
Meldan *B*. February 8.
Mellin *C*. December 24.
Mellitus *AB*. April 24.

Mellon-

Mellon *B.* October 22.
Melorus *M.* October 1.
Merefin *C.* January 17.
Merwenna *V. ab.* March 30.
Mida *V.* January 15.
Midan *C.* February 4.
Midana *V.* November 17.
Midwyn *C.* January 2.
Milburge *V. ab.* February 23.
Mildred *V. ab.* February 20
Milwide *V.* January 17.
Minnan *C.* March 1.
Mirinus *B.* September 4.
Mobyus *Ab.* October 12.
Mochoemoc *Ab.* March 14.
Mochteus *B.* August 22.
Mochua *Ab.* April 2.
Modan *Ab.* April 4.
Moditeus *C.* December 28.
Modoch *B.* January 31.
Modwenna *V. ab.* July 5.
Molacus *C.* January 20.
Moling *B.* June 17.
Molonach *B.* June 25.
Monennius *Ab.* April 5.
Monon *M.* October 18.
Moroc *C.* November 8.
Mofcea, December 9.
Motifer *C.* October 28.
Muganocus *C.* December 22.
Mundus *Ab.* April 15.
Mungo *B.* January 13.
Munis *B.* February 6.
Munnu *Ab.* October 21.
Muran *B.* March 12.
Murgeus *B.* Sept. 3.

NECTAN

N.

Nectan *C.* January 22.
Nennidhius *Ab.* January 16.
Nennio *B.* May 9.
Neot *C.* July 31.
Neſſan *B.* } December 6.
Neſſan *Ab.* }
Neſſan *C.* June 25.
Nethalen *B.* January 17.
Nicolas *B. M.* June 12.
Ninian *B. & co.* September 16.
Nonna *W.* March 2.
Nothelm *AB.* October 17.
Novatus *P.* June 20.

O.

Obodius *C.* November 21.
Ode *V.* November 27.
Odhrain *C.* July 7.
Odilia *V.* July 17.
Odo *AB.* } July 4.
Odo *Ab.* }
Offa *K.* December 24.
Olave *K. M.* July 29.
Olcan *B.* February 20.
Orore *C.* October 20.
Ortrude *V.* June 27.
Oſburga *V. ab.* March 28.
Oſithe *V. M.* October 7.
Oſmund *B.* July 16. December 4.
Oſtfor *B.* April 4.
Oſtrythe *Q.* August 5.
Oſwald *K. M.* August 5.
Oſwald *AB.* February 28. October 15.
Oſwin *K.* August 20.

Otger

Otger *C.* September 11.
Oudoceus *B.* July 2.
Owen *AB.* August 24.
Owini *C.* March 4.

P.

Padie *or* Palladius *B.* July 6. December 15.
   Pandwyne *V.* August 24.
Paternus *B.* April 15.
Paternus *C.* April 10.
Patrick *B.* March 17.
Patrick junior, November 9.
Patricianus *B.* May 31.
Patto *B.* March 30.
Paul *apostle,* January 25. June 29.
Paul *B.* March 12.
Paulinus *AB.* October 10.
Paulinus *C.* December 31.
Pega *V.* April 12.
Peter *apostle,* June 29.
Peter *Ab. & co.* January 6.
Petranus *B.* September 6.
Petrock *Ab. & co.* } June 4.
Petrock *B.*
Piala *V. M.* December 15.
Piran *B.* March 5.
Piro *Ab.* June 2.
Plebeias *C.* September 16.
Plechelm *B.* July 20.
Plegmund *AB.* August 2.
Probus *C.* February 5.

Q.

Quenburge *V.* August 28.
   Queranus *Ab.* September 9.

R.

REGULUS *or* Rule *Ab.* October 17.
Richard *B.* April 3.
Richard *B.* of Andr. August 21.
Richard *K.* February 7.
Richard *H.* September 29.
Ringen *B.* September 16.
Rioch *Ab.* February 6.
Robert *Ab.* June 7.
Robert *H.* May 23.
Robert *B.* April 13.
Robert *B.* October 9.
Rodan *Ab.* April 15.
Roger *B.* October 1.
Ronald *C.* February 20.
Ronan *B.* February 7.
Ruffin *M.* July 24.
Ruffus *M.* August 27.
Rumon *B.* October 23.
Rumwold *B.* June 24. July 1.
Rumwold *C.* August 28.
Rus *C.* September 27.

S.

SALVIUS *B.* March 15.
Sampson *B.* July 28.
Saturninus *H.* November 3.
Saxon Saints 100. March 13.
Scandalius *C.* May 5.
Scottish Saints, March 29. September 15.
Sebbi *K.* August 29.
Sebert *K.* January 5.
Secundinus *B.* December 2.
Segenius *Ab.* April 8.

Senach *B.* September 2.
Senan *B.* March 8.
Senan *C.* June 28.
Serapion *M.* June 16.
Servanus *B.* July 1.
Sethryd *V. ab.* May 28.
Sexburga *Q. ab.* July 6.
Sexulf *B.* December 16.
Siburgis *V.* March 15.
Sigebert *K.* September 26.
Sigefrid *B. & co.* February 15.
Sigfrid *Ab.* August 22.
Silaus *B.* May 21.
Simon Stock *C.* May 16.
Sinellus *Ab.* November 11.
Sithefulla *V.* December 19.
Socrates *M.* September 17.
Sola *H.* December 5.
Stephen *M.* September 17.
Stephen *Ab.* March 28. April 17.
Swibert *B.* } March 1.
Swibert *B.* jun. }
Swithin *B.* July 2, & 15.
Suneman *H.* September 20.
Sycar *P.* November 2.
Syra *V.* June 8.

T.

Tarkin *B.* October 30.
Tarnan *B.* June 12.
Tathai *C.* December 26.
Tatwine *AB.* July 30.
Tecla *V. ab.* October 15.
Tetta *V. ab.* August 12.
Thancred *M.* September 18.

Thean *B.* January 1.
Theliau *B.* February 9.
Thenaw *W.* July 18.
Thennan *Ab.* September 23.
Theodore *AB.* September 19.
Theodred *B.* November 20.
Theonia *V. ab.* November 3.
Thocannu *C.* September 30.
Thomas *AB. M.* July 7. December 29.
Thomas *B.* August 20. October 2.
Thomas *archdeacon,* August 17.
Thomas *monk,* August 6.
Tibba *V.* December 13.
Tigernake *B.* April 5.
Timotheus *P.* June 20.
Torchgyth *V.* January 26.
Torthred *C.* September 18.
Tova *V.* September 18.
Triduana *V.* October 8.
Trumwine *B.* January 25.
Tuda *B.* February 16.
Tyshei *M.* March 27.

U. V.

Veepe, December 9.
Verca *ab.* September 29.
Vimin *B.* January 21.
Vincent *C.* April 5.
Ulfad *M.* July 24.
Ulfrid *M.* January 21.
Ulfrick *P.* February 21.
Ultan *B.* September 4.
Ultan *Ab.* } May 2.
Ultan *C.*
Vodinus *AB. M.* December 8.
Vouga *B.* June 15.

Ursula

Ursula & co. *VV. MM.* October 21.
Vulgan *C.* November 2.
Umba *V.* December 28.

W.

WALBURGA *V. ab.* February 26. May 1.
Walstan *C.* May 30.
Walter *Ab.* August 13.
Waltheof *Ab.* August 3.
Wasnulf *B.* October 1.
Weede *V. ab.* December 30.
Welch Saints, December 28.
Wendelyn *Ab.* October 20.
Wendrove *C.* October 9.
Wenefride *V. M.* November 3. June 24.
Wenta *V.* November 19.
Wereburge *V. ab.* } February 3.
Wereburge *Q. W.* }
Werenfrid *C.* August 14.
Wigbert *Ab.* August 13.
Wigbert *P.* October 6.
Wilfrid *B.* October 12.
Wilfrid jun. *B.* April 29.
Wilgis *C.* November 11.
Willehad *B.* November 8.
Willeik *C.* March 2.
William *AB.* June 8.
William *B.* September 2.
William *M.* March 25.
William *M.* May 23.
William *Fr.* March 7.
William *P.* June 28.
Willibald *B.* July 8.
Willibrord *B. & co.* November 7.
Willibald *B.* December 18.

Winewald

Winewald *Ab.* May 22.
Winfrid *AB. M.* June 5.
Winnin *B.* September 10.
Winoc *B.* }
Winoc *Ab.* } November 6.
Winoc *P.* }
Winwaloc *Ab.* March 3.
Wiro *B.* May 8.
Wiſtan *K. M.* June 1.
Withburge *V.* July 19.
Witta *B.* October 26.
Woolgam *C.* March 15.
Wulfhilde *V. ab.* December 9.
Wulſtan *B.* January 19.
Wulſy *Ab.* September 6.
Wulſy *recluſe,* December 30.
Wulfruna *matron,* December 29.

Y.

Ywy *C.* October 23.

THE END.

A SUPPLEMENT.

OR

Additions and Amendments

TO THE

BRITISH MARTYROLOGY.

JANUARY.

Jan. 1. AT *Llanvaelrhys* in *Carnarvanshire*, the festivity of St. *Maelrhys*, an ancient British Saint, honoured in the church of that place, as long as the old religion maintained its ground. In like manner at *Llanwynnodl*, in the same county, the feast of St. *Gwynnoydyl*, and at *Llanfachreth* in *Merionethshire*, the feast of S. *Machreth*, or *Macaritus*, in whose names the churches of those parishes were dedicated. [See *Browne Willis*'s Survey of *Bangor*.] In *Ireland* the festivity of S. *Munchin*, first bishop of *Limerick*,

Limerick, illustrious for his wisdom and sanctity. [*Ware.*] As also of S. *Cuan*, or *Mochua*, of which name there were two holy abbots in that kingdom. [*Colgan.*]

Jan. 2. At *Abor* in *Carnarvanshire*, the festivity of S. *Boduan*, Confessor, honoured of old in the church of that parish. [*Br. Willis.*]

Jan. 3. At *Llanwenog* in *Cardiganshire*, the feast of S. *Gwenog*, Confessor, in whose name the church there is dedicated. [*Willis.*]

Jan. 4. At *Tavestock* in *Devonshire*, the feast of S. *Rumon*, an ancient British bishop; in whose honour divers churches have been erected in the diocese of *Exeter*. He was tutelar Saint of the abbey of *Tavestock*, where his body waited for a happy resurrection. In *Scotland*, the memory of that venerable Servant of God *Vigian*, a monk of *Clugny*, who for his great merits and virtues, was raised to the dignity of a bishop in that kingdom. Obiit Anno 1002. [*Chatelain*'s Universal Martyrology.]

Jan. 6. In the diocese of *Bangor*, the memory of the Saints *Howyn*, *Meryn*, *Ylched*, and *Eigrad*, all of them honoured heretofore with churches amongst the ancient Britons. [*Willis*'s Survey of *Bangor*.]

Sunday within the octave of the Epiphany. At *York*, the translation of the body of S. *William*, archbishop of that See; the memory of which was solemnly kept on this day. He
was

was canonized by pope *Honorius* III. and his name was inserted in the new Roman Martyrology by *Benedict* XIV, of glorious memory (*June* 8.) with this elogium, that *amongst the rest of the miracles wrought at his tomb, he had raised three dead persons to life.*

Jan. 7. At *Llangwilloc* in the Isle of *Anglesey*, the feast of S. *Gwilloc*, an ancient British Confessor. [*Willis.*] Also in the diocese of S. *David's*, the memory of St. *Synin*, honoured on this day at *Capell Llangain* in *Carmarthenshire*. [*Idem.*]

Jan. 8. At *Sherborn* in *Dorsetshire*, the memory of S. *Wulsin*, who was appointed by S. *Dunstan* first abbot of *Westminster*, and afterwards was made bishop of *Sherborn:* To the sanctity of whose life and death our historians bear testimony. As they do also to that of his successor *Alfwold*. [See *W. Malmesbury de Pontiff.*] At *Rome*, the memory of S. *Pega*, an *English* virgin, illustrious for sanctity. [*Chatelain.*] In *Ireland*, the festivity of S. *Ergnate*. [*Idem.*] In *Ireland* also, the decease of S. *Molibba*, bishop of *Glendaloch*, and of S. *Erard*, bishop of *Ardagh*. [*Ware.*] In *South Wales*, the feast of S. *Kinwill* (or *Conwill,*) honoured at *Conwilgaio* in *Carmarthenshire*. [*Willis.*]

Jan. 10. At *Armagh* in *Ireland*, the decease of the venerable servant of God *Thomian*, fifteenth archbishop of that See from S. *Patrick*. [*Ware.*]

Jan. 12. At *Ridale* in *Yorkshire*, the festivity of S. *Aelred*, abbot, of the order of the *Cistertians*, or *Bernardins*, whose name is inserted on the second of *March* in the *Cistertian* Martyrology, (published with the Roman by *Benedict* XIV.) with this ample elogium; that he was *illustrious for his knowledge in the sacred letters, for the integrity of his manners; for his contempt of himself; for his wonderful patience; for his prophetical spirit; for his heavenly conversation; and for his exceeding great miracles.* In *North Wales*, the feast of S. *Llwychaiarn*, honoured of old, by reason of his eminent sanctity, with two parish churches, still standing in the hiocese of S. *Asaph*. [*Willis.*] In the monastery of *Cluain-Ferta-Molua* in *Ireland*, the happy decease of S. *Laidgen*, monk. At *Druin-Druith*, in the same island, the memory of S. *Cumein*, Confessor. [*Chatelain* Martyrologe Universel.]

Jan. 13. At *Armagh*, the decease of that holy prelate *Ailild* I the sixth archbishop of that see. [*Ware.*] At *Landygwyd* in *Cardiganshire*, the feast of S. *Dygwyd*, Confessor.

Jan. 14. In the Isle of *Bardsey*, the memory of S. *Laudat*, or *Lowdhad*, first abbot of the monastery there. He was nearly allied to S. *Kentigern* and S. *Beuno* : And his abbey subsisted under a peculiar rule till the change of religion. [Mr. *Vaughan*'s MSS.]

Jan. 15. In the monastery of *Lindisfarne*, or the *Holy Island*, the festivity of S. *Ceolulph*, king of the *Northumbrians*, or *Northern English*; who for

for the love of Chrift exchanged his crown and fcepter for the habit of a monk, in that holy folitude; and there happily ended his days in religious exercifes, in the eighth century. In *North Wales*, the memory of S. *Saeran*, Confeffor, whofe feaft was formerly celebrated there on the Sunday after St. *Hilary*. [*Willis.*] At *Kildare*, the deceafe of the holy bifhop *Forannan*. [*Ware.*]

Jan. 16. In *North Wales*, the feftivity of S. *Maurice*, (*Murog*) Confeffor, honoured of old on this day in the church of *Llanfwrog* in *Denbighfhire*, and in a chapel of the fame name in *Anglefey*. [*Willis.*] In *South Wales*, the memory of S. *Lawdog*, Confeffor, who has four churches dedicated in his name in the diocefe of S. *David*. [*Willis.*] Quere, whether this Saint be not the fame as S. *Laudat*, abbot of *Bardfey*.

Jan. 23. At *Mombeliard* in *Franchecounté*, the feftivity of S. *Maymbod*, an *Irifhman*, flain by robbers in the neighbourhood of *Dampierre*, who by reafon of the fanctity of his life, and the violence of his death is honoured there amongft the martyrs. [*Chatelain.*] In *South Wales*, the feaft of S. *Elliew*, who is honoured with churches in the diocefe of S. *David*: As is alfo S. *Elidere*, or *Eliere*, as may be feen in Mr. *Eckton*'s Thefaurus, and Mr. *Willis*.

Jan. 25. In the Ifle of *Anglefey*, the feftivity of S. *Dwynwen*, honoured of old on this day in the church of *Llandwynne*. [*Willis.*] At *Pendennis* in *Cornwall*, the feaft of S. *Ithia*, who joined with a married life the exercifes of all

A 3

chriftian

christian virtues in such perfection, as to be honoured after her death amongst the Saints in a church erected in her name. [*Chatelain.*] In *Galloway*, the festivity of S. *Eoglodius*, Confessor, disciple of S. *Columkille*, and associated with him in preaching Christ to the *Picts*. [*Idem.*]

Jan. 27. In *Ireland*, the memory of S. *Naal*, or *Natalis*, abbot of *Killnamanach* in *Ossory*; and sometime master of the great S. *Senan*. [*Chatelain.*]

Jan. 29. In *Ireland*, the commemoration of S. *Dallan*, honoured there as a martyr, in some churches dedicated in his name. [*Chatelain.*] In *Wales*, the festivity of S. *Tybie*, honoured at *Llandebie* in *Carmarthenshire*. [*Willis.*]

Jan. 31. In *Carnarvanshire*, the festivity of S. *Gwinning*, titular Saint of the parish of *Dwygyfylche*. [*Willis.*] At *Llandissel* in *Cardiganshire*, the feast of S. *Tyssill*; in whose name that church is dedicated. [*Idem.*]

FEBRUARY.

Feb. 1. IN *Ireland*, the commemoration of S. *Kinnia*, virgin. [*Chatelain.*] At *Lacock* in *Wiltshire*, the memory of that venerable Servant of God *Ela*, countess of *Salisbury*, who was so devoted to religion, that she founded two monasteries in one day, *viz.* that of the Carthusians at *Henton* in *Wiltshire*, and that of the Canonesses of S. *Austin*, at *Lacock*. In this latter leaving the world and all its vanities, she

took

took the habit of religion, Anno 1236, was made abbefs Anno 1240; refigned her office Anno 1257; and went to our Lord in a good old age, Anno 1261. [*Dugdale.*] At *Llanina* in *Cardiganshire*, the feaſt of S. *Ina*, titular faint of that church. [*Willis.*]

Feb. 3. In *Ireland*, the happy deceafe of the holy prelate S. *Colman Mac Duach*, firſt biſhop of *Kilmachough*, in the ſeventh century. [*Ware.*] In the iſle of *Anglefey*, the feſtivity of S. *Meirian*, Confeffor, honoured in the pariſh of *Llanfeirian*. [*Willis.*]

Feb. 4. In *Ireland*, the memory of S. *Cuannach*, abbot, in the ſeventh century. [*Chatelain.*]

Feb. 8. In *Ireland*, the deceaſe of the holy prelates *Fiachre* and *Colman*, biſhops of *Clonard*, in the ſeventh century. [*Ware.*]

Feb. 9. At *Llan-Ennion Vrenin* in *North Wales*, the feſtivity of S. *Anian*, or *Eneon Bhrenin*, king of *Cumbria*, who about the beginning of the ſeventh century, leaving his royalty, retired to that folitude, and built there a church, which was afterwards called by his name, where he dedicated the remainder of his days to divine Love. [Mr. *Vaughan*, and *Willis*.] In *Ireland*, the feſtivity of S. *Cronan*, biſhop of *Liſmore*, who departed to our Lord Anno 717. [*Ware.*]

Feb. 10. In the dioceſe of *Landaff*, the feſtivity of S. *Fagan*, whoſe name is ſtill retained by a pariſh and church in *Glamorganſhire*. [*Willis.*]

In *Ireland*, the commemoration of S. *Gobnate*, virgin, abbefs in *Munster*, in the seventh century. [*Chatelain.*]

Feb. 11. At *Armagh*, the feſtivity of S. *Jarlaith*, diſciple of S. *Patrick*, third archbiſhop of that See; who went to our Lord Anno 432; and was illuſtrious amongſt the *Iriſh* ſaints of the firſt claſs. In a little iſland on the eaſt ſide of *Angleſey*, the feſtivity of S. *Cyriol*, or *Seiriol*, of whoſe church and monaſtery there. See *Tanner*'s Notitia Monaſtica, p. 699.

Feb. 12. In *Ireland*, the memory of S. *Sedulius*, abbot, in the neighbourhood of *Dublin*. [*Chatelain.*]

Feb. 13. At *Llanrhaidar* in *Denbighſhire*, the feſtivity of S. *Dyfnog*, Confeſſor, of whoſe church there, and his famous well, ſee *Willis*'s Survey of *Bangor*, p. 329.

Feb. 15. At *Ghent*, the feſtivity of S. *Columban*, Confeſſor, who coming out of *Ireland*, led a recluſe and penitential Life in a cell near the church of S. *Bavon*, and died happily Anno 859. [*Chatelain.*]

Feb. 17. In *Ireland*, the feſtivity of S. *Cormac*, fourth Biſhop of *Armagh*, illuſtrious for ſanctity; who went to our Lord, Anno 497. [*Ware.*] Alſo in *Ireland*, the feaſt of S. *Luroch*, biſhop of *Ardfrathen*, the See of which is now at *Derry*. [*Chatelain.*]

Feb. 18. In *Ireland*, the festivity of S. *Culan*, or *Culaneus*, bishop, disciple of S. *Patrick*. [*Tyrechanus.*]

Feb. 21. In *Ireland*, the festivity of S. *Fintan*, bishop of *Clonfert*, in the ninth century. As also the memory of S. *Senach Garbh*, and of S. *Colman*, the son of *Comgel*, successors of S. *Fintan*, in that See. [*Ware.*]

Feb. 28. In the Isle of *Anglesey*, the festivity of S. *Libio*, Confessor, honoured in the church of *Llanlibio*. [*Willis.*]

MARCH.

March 1. IN *South Wales*, the feast of S. *Tyfaelog*, and of S. *Caffeliak*, both of them honoured with churches in the diocese of S. *David*. [*Willis.*] In *Ireland*, the festivity of S. *Moena*, or *Monennius*, the first bishop of *Clonfert*, who departed to our Lord Anno 571. [*Ware.*]

March 2. In *Ireland*, the decease of S. *Lugad*, abbot, brother of S. *Munnu*, who was called to our Lord on this day. In *Wales*, the feast of the holy Confessors of Christ, S. *Caron*, and S. *Gwynnio*. [*Willis.*]

March 3. In *Ireland*, the feast of S. *Foilenna*, virgin, in whose name a church was erected in the province of *Connaught*. [*Chatelain.*] In *Little Britain*, the feast of S. *Jacutus*, abbot, honoured with divers churches in that province.

He

He was a native of *Great Britain*, as were moſt of the other ſaints, of the *Leſſer Britany*, in the ſixth century. [Dom. *Lobineau Saints de Bretagne.*]

March 7. In the iſle of *Angleſey*, the feſtivity of S. *Cyngar*, Confeſſor. [*Willis.*]

March 8. At *Llanrhyian* in *Pembrokeſhire*, the feaſt of S. *Rheanus*, Confeſſor, in whoſe Name the church of that pariſh is dedicated. [*Willis.*]

March 9. In *Ireland*, the feaſt of S. *Mella*, widow and abbeſs. [*Chatelain.*] In *Ireland* alſo, the memory of the holy abbot *Caſſidus*, maſter of the great S. *Senan*.

March 12. The depoſition of S. *Elphegus*, ſurnamed the *Bald*, biſhop of *Wincheſter*, in the tenth century. In *Little Britain*, the memory of S. *Joavan*, diſciple of S. *Paul* of *Leon*, and ordained biſhop by him: as alſo of his two ſucceſſors *Tiernomail* and *Cetomerin*, diſciples of the ſame ſaint. [*Lobineau.*]

March 13. In *Ireland*, the feſtivity of S. *Conchenna*, ſiſter to the holy abbots S. *Lugad*, and S. *Munnu*, and not unworthy of two ſuch brothers. [*Chatelain.*]

March 16. In *Cornwall*, the memory of S. *Columba*, virgin, and martyr. [*Chatelain.*] In *Ireland*, the feaſt of S. *Neſſan*, biſhop of *Cork*, in the ſeventh century. [*Ware.*] At *Langronog* in *Cardiganſhire*, the feſtivity of S. *Granog*, Confeſſor,

March 27. In *Ireland*, the decease of S. *Suarlack*, the first bishop of *Foure*, who exchanged this mortal life, for a happy immortality, Anno 745. [*Ware.*] In *Ireland* also, the decease of the holy archbishop *Gelasius*, successor of S. *Malachi*, in the See of *Armagh*.

March 29. In *Ireland*, the memory of S. *Fulartach*, bishop of *Clonard*, who went to our Lord Anno 774. [*Ware.*]

March 30. In *Ireland*, the festivity of S. *Fergus*, bishop of *Downe*, who was called to a happy eternity Anno 583. [*Ware.*]

APRIL.

April 1. AT *Lewes* in *Sussex*, the memory of venerable *Lauzon*, prior of the *Cluniack* monks, of the abbey of S. *Pancrace*, in that town, who is commemorated on this day in the Universal Martyrology of *Chatelain*.

April 3. At *Llandyrnog* in *Denbighshire*, the feast of S. *Tyrnog*, Confessor. [*Willis.*]

April 4. In *Anjou*, the festivity of S. *Alman*, honoured as an *English* bishop, in a village bearing his name near *Angers*. [*Chatelain.*]

April 5. At *Llandervell* in *Merionethshire*, the feast of S. *Derfel Gadern*, to whose memory the church of that place is dedicated. [*Willis.*]

April 6.

April 6. At *Breteuil,* in the diocese of *Beauvais,* the festivity of S. *Lisold,* a *British* confessor, honoured there in the church of the abbey of S. *Constantian.* [*Chatelain.*]

April 9. In the north of *England,* the memory of the holy virgins *Gisla* and *Rictrudis,* illustrious for piety and religion, in the eighth century.

April 12. In *North Wales,* the festivity of S. *Jestyn,* or *Justin,* honoured with two churches bearing his name in the diocese of *Bangor.* [*Willis.*]

April 13. In *South Wales,* the feast of S. *Ismael,* or *Hismael,* bishop and Confessor, much revered by the ancient Britons. There remains to this day a parish which bears his name in the diocese of S. *David.* [*Willis.*]

April 21. At *Clynnoc Vawr* in *Carnarvonshire,* the festivity of S. *Beuno* or *Bennow,* abbot, honoured with many churches in *North Wales;* and himself founder of many churches. His last foundation was that of the famous monastery of *Clynnoc Vawr;* from whence he was called to the land of the living, Anno 623. He lyes buried in the old church or chapel there, of which Mr. *Willis* has published an accurate description in his survey of *Bangor,* p. 299, 300, where also may be seen the great veneration the people have still for his memory; and that to this day they attribute miracles to his sepulchre.

April 22.

April 22. At *Llandyfnan* in the isle of *Anglesey,* the feast of S. *Dyfnan,* confessor, honoured of old on this day in the church of that place. [*Willis.*]

April 24. At *Armagh* in *Ireland,* the decease of S. *Flannan,* or *Florence,* abbot, who went to our Lord anno 704. In *Ireland* also, the festivity of S. *Hubright,* or *Hubriton,* hermit, brother of S. *Gerald* of *Mayo.* [*Chatelain.*] At *Weremouth* in the bishoprick of *Durham,* the memory of the venerable abbot *Huethbercht,* who succeeded S. *Ceolfrid* in the administration of the united monasteries of *Weremouth* and *Gyrwy.* S. *Bede, de abbatibus,* &c.

April 25. In *Ireland,* the festivity of S. *Macaldus,* or *Macalleus,* bishop, who gave the veil to S. *Brigide,* in the fifth century. [*Chatelain.*]

April 27. In *Ireland,* the feast of S. *Asicus,* disciple of S. *Patrick,* and consecrated by him first bishop of *Elphin.* [*Ware.*]

April 28. In the neighbourhood of *Tuam* in *Ireland,* the Feast of S. *Luctigernus,* abbot, renowned in the sixth century for sanctity. [*Chatelain.*]

April 30. At *Ferden* in the lower *Saxony,* the deposition of S. *Swibert,* or *Suidbercht,* the younger, first bishop of *Ferden,* who passed to a happy eternity anno 807. He is counted by *Ven. Alcuin,* jointly with S. *Viro,* amongst the Saints of *York*. [*Carmine de Sanctis, Eboracensibus*, published by *Gale*.]

MAY.

May 1. IN *North Wales*, the festivity of S. *Valacinian*, confessor. [*Willis*.] In the diocese of *Landaff*, the feast of S. *Tocho*, confessor, honoured of old in the church of *Landogh*. [*Willis*.] Also in *Wales*, the festivity of S. *Tyfredoc*, who has divers churches dedicated in his name. [*Idem*]

May 3. In *Ireland*, the festivity of S. *Conlaeth*, first bishop of *Kildare*, illustrious for his sanctity and miracles; whom S. *Brigide* invited out of his solitude, to be the director and father of all the religious men who embraced her institute. He was called to the reward of his labours anno 519. [*Ware*.]

May 4. In *Ireland*, the festivity of S. *Briand*, Bishop of *Clonfert*, honoured in a particular manner at the town of *Dally ne Rilly*, where there is a well called by his name, the water of which is in great repute for the curing of various diseases. [*Chatelain*.]

May 7. In *Ireland*, the memory of S. *Brocan*, or *Breccan*, confessor, anciently honoured at *Echdruim*. [*Chatelain*.]

May 8. The feast of S. *Wiro*, bishop. He is called *Viro*, or *Vira*, by *Ven. Alcuin*, and jointly with S. *Suidbert*, is numbered by him amongst the saints of *York*, who carried the gospel of
Christ

Chrift amongft the Infidels. [*Carmine de Sanctis Eboracenfibus.*]

May 9. In *Wales*, the feftivity of S. *Tyddwg*, honoured on this day in the diocefe of *Landaff*. [*Willis.*]

May 10. At *Pontoife*, the memory of S. *William*, an *Englifh* prieft, who went to our Lord anno 1193. [*Chatelain*] His tomb was illuftrious for many miracles. [S. *Antonin.*] In *Ireland*, the feftivity of S. *Ædus*, bifhop of *Kildare*, obiit anno 638. [*Ware.*]

May 11. At *Canterbury*, the paffion of many holy ecclefiafticks, and religious men, who were flain by the *Danes*, when they took that city, anno 1011, and are commemorated on this day in the martyrology of the *Canon Regulars*, publifhed by authority of *Benedict* XIV.

May 14. In *Wales*, the feftivity of S. *Damian*, or *Dwywan*, honoured in the church of *Llanendwyn* in the diocefe of *Bangor*. [*Willis.*]

May 18. At *Clonard* in *Ireland*, the feftivity of S. *Branus*, confeffor, who flourifhed in fanctity in the fixth century. [*Chatelain.*]

May 19. At *Tours*, the deceafe of the venerable *Alcuin*, præceptor to the emperor *Charlemagne*, by whom he was invited over from *York*; where he was mafter of that great fchool famous for divine and human learning, which had been brought to perfection by his predeceffor archbifhop archbishop *Æilbert*, whom he so much extols in his poem *de Sanctis Eboracensibus*. Obiit anno 804.

May 20. Amongst the ancient Britons, the festivity of S. *Collen*, or *Cullan*, honoured of old with churches both in *Wales* and *Cornwall*, as may be seen in Mr. *Willis*'s Parochial.

May 23. At *Knaresborough* in *Yorkshire*, the memory of S. *Robert Flower*, hermit; who forsaking his lands and worldy goods, for the love and service of God, embraced a solitary life, amongst the rocks near the river *Nidd*: where others resorting to him, upon the opinion of his sanctity, he established a religious community of *Trinitarians*, for the redemption of captives out of the hands of infidels. See *Leland*'s Itinerarium, vol. I. p. 96. and *Dugdale*'s Monasticon, vol. 2.

May 27. At *Pennant* in *Montgomeryshire*, the feast of S. *Melangel*, confessor. [*Willis.*]

May 30. In *Carnarvanshire*, the festivity of S. *Tydclud*, tutelar saint of the church of *Penmachno*. [*Willis.*]

JUNE.

June 1. IN *Little Britany*, the feast of S. *Ronan*, or *Renan*, an *Irish* bishop; who leaving his native country to flee from the honour and esteem which the eminence of his virtues had there acquired him, hid himself in a solitude

tude of *Armorica*: but the lustre of his sanctity, and the glory of his miracles, would not suffer him to lie long concealed; but have procured him an extraordinary veneration in that province, amongst the most illustrious of their saints. He flourished in the sixth century. [Dom. *Lobineau.*]

June 2. In *North Wales*, the feast of S. *Gwyfer*, confessor, in whose name the church of *Dissert* in *Flintshire*, is dedicated. [*Willis.*]

June 3. In *North Wales*, the festivity of S. *Gwyvena*, virgin. [*Willis.*]

June 4. In *Little Britany*, the feast of S. *Ninnoca*, a *British* virgin and abbess. [*Lobineau.*]

June 5. At *Llandudno* in *Carnarvanshire*, the festivity of S. *Tudno*, confessor, honoured of old on this day in the church of that place. [*Willis.*]

June 6. At *Llangurnock* in *Montgomeryshire*, the festivity of S. *Cuno Gurnock*, confessor. [*Willis.*] In *Ireland* in the province of *Meath*, the memory of S. *Choca*, virgin. [*Chatelain.*]

June 8. In *Ireland*, the deposition of the holy bishop *Bronus*, one of those who were ordained by S. *Patrick*, and are ranked in the first class of the *Irish* saints. [*Tirechanus.*]

June 9. In *North Wales*, the festivity of S. *Madryn*, confessor. [*Willis.*]

June 10. In *Carnarvanshire*, the memory of S. *Rhochwyn*, honoured on this day in the chapel of *Llanrhochwyn*. [*Willis.*]

June 12. In *Ireland*, the memory of S. *Mochulleus*, confessor. [*Chatelain.*] At the abbey of *Lure* in *Burgundy*, the memory of holy *Columbin*, abbot, disciple and successor of S. *Deicola.*

June 13. In *Wales*, the festivity of S. *Sanan*, or *Sannam*, honoured with churches among the ancient Britons. [*Willis.*]

June 16. In *Wales*, the festivity of S. *Trygan*, alias *Trillo*, and of S. *Elidan*, each of them honoured with divers churches by the ancient Britons. [*Willis.*] Also at *Porthkerig* in *Glamorganshire*, the feast of S. *Kerig*. [*Idem.*]

June 17. Among the ancient Britons, the festival of S. *Myllin*, or *Mellan*, honoured of old with churches, both in *Wales* and *Cornwall*. [See *Willis*'s Dedications.]

June 21. At the abbey of S. *Meen*, in *Little Britain*, the festival of S. *Meen*, or *Mevennius*, a *British* abbot, and disciple of S. *Brendan*, illustrious for his sanctity, and the miracles which still continue to be wrought at his sepulchre. [*Chatelain.*]

June 25. In *Wales*, the festivity of S. *Devodog*, or *Divodug*, confessor, in whose name divers

divers churches have anciently been dedicated. [*Willis.*]

June 26. In *North Wales*, the festivity of S. *Tauricius*, or *Twrog*, confessor, disciple of S. *Beuno*. [*Willis.*] In the Lower *Germany*, the memory of S. *Corbican*, an *Irish* priest, in the eighth century. [*Chatelain.*]

June 29. In *Little Britany*, the deposition of S. *Gunthiern*, confessor, prince of some part of *Wales*; who privately withdrawing himself from his earthly principality, for the love of a heavenly kingdom, embraced an eremitical life in *Armorica*, from whence he passed to the happy mansions of eternal glory, some time in the sixth century. [*Lobineau.*]

J U L Y.

July 2. IN *Brecknockshire*, the feast of S. *Gewydh*, formerly honoured with two churches in that county. [*Willis.*]

July 4. At *Llanbeblig* in *Carnarvanshire*, the feast of S. *Publicius*, confessor, of whose church see *Willis*'s survey of *Bangor*, p. 272.

July 6. In *Wales*, the festivity of S. *Ervill*, confessor, honoured with a church in the diocese of S. *Asaph*. [*Willis.*]

July 11. In the diocese of S. *Asaph*, the Festivity of S. *Gowsr*, confessor, of whose church see *Willis*'s survey.

July 13.

July 13. In *Wales*, the festivity of S. *Doguan*, honoured as a martyr at *Mertherdivan*, in the diocese of *Landaff*. [*Willis*.]

July 16. In *Little Britain*, the feast of S. *Tenedan*, or *Tinidor*, bishop and confessor, in the sixth century. [*Lobineau*.]

July 18. In *Little Britain*, the feast of S. *Genery*, confessor. [*Lobineau*.]

July 22. In *North Wales*, the festivity of S. *Sulian*, honoured with churches both in the diocese of *Bangor*, and in that of S. *Asaph*. [*Willis*.]

July 25. At *Langenderin* in the diocese of S. *David*, the feast of S. *Cynderin*, confessor. [*Willis*.]

July 26. In *Ireland*, the feast of S. *Gotalmus*, confessor. [*Chatelain*.]

July 27. In *Scotland*, the memory of S. *Pumice*, virgin. [*Chatelain*.] In *Ireland*, the commemoration of S. *Nathinæus*, priest, honoured as patron in the diocese of *Achadh-Conar*, in the county of *Sligo*.

AUGUST.

August 4. AT *Bodvuan* in *Carnarvanshire*, the festivity of S. *Buan*, or *Vean*, honoured of old in that parish. [*Willis*.] In *Little Britain*,

Britain, the feast of S. *Lugidianus*, an *Irish* abbot, renowned for sanctity in the sixth century. [*Lobineau.*]

August 8. In *Wales*, the festivity of S. *Illhog*, confessor. [*Willis.*] He was, I believe, the same as was honoured in *Cornwall* by the name of S. *Illogan*. Also, at *Llanhychan* in *Denbighshire*, the memory of S. *Hychan*, confessor, [*Willis.*]

August 9. In *Ireland*, the festivity of *S. Fedlimid*, founder of the church of *Kilmore*, in the sixth century: as also the feast of *S. Nathy*, bishop of *Achonry*, in the same century. [*Ware.*]

August 12. In *Ireland*, the feast of S. *Muredach*, disciple of *S. Patrick*, and first bishop of *Killala*. [*Ware.*]

August 13. In *Lincolnshire*, the feast of *S. Hybald*, or *Hygbald*, abbot, to whose sanctity *S. Bede* gives testimony, l. iv. c. 3. and whose ancient veneration is attested by the dedications of divers churches in that county. [*Willis.*]

August 14. In *Ireland*, the feast of *S. Fachnan*, first founder of the church and school of *Ross*, in the sixth century; in which he had for his successor *S. Finchad*, disciple of *S. Barrus*, [*Ware.*] In *Wales*, the memory of *S. Owen*, confessor. [*Willis.*] In *Northumberland*, the memory of *S. Betta*, who preached the gospel to the midland English. *S. Bede*, l. iii. c. 21.

August 15. In *Little Britain*, the feast of *S. Armel*,

Armel, abbot, illustrious for sanctity and miracles, in the sixth century; and one of the leaders of that colony of saints, who going forth from *Great Britain*, peopled *Armorica* with so many holy ones, who have left their names to a great part of the parishes of that province. [*Dom. Lobineau.*]

August 22. In *North Wales*, at *Dolwythelan* in *Carnarvanshire*, the memory of S. *Gwythelan*, confessor. [*Willis.*]

August 23. In *Wales*, the festivity of S. *Tydvill*, martyr, honoured with churches in the diocese of *Landaff*. [*Willis.*]

August 26. The festivity of S. *Pandwyne*, or *Pandionia*, a Scottish virgin, honoured at *Elterslie* in *Cambridgeshire*; where retiring from the tyranny of her father, she led a solitary life in great sanctity, till she was called to a happy eternity, anno 904. *Richard*, parson of *Elterslie* in her life.

August 27. At *Llanvedhyd* in *Denbighshire*, the festivity of S. *Vodhyd*, confessor. [*Willis.*]

SEPTEMBER.

Sept. 1. IN the diocese of *Landaff*, the feast of S. *Lythao*, alias *Thaw*, in whose name two churches are there dedicated. [*Willis.*]

Sept. 2. In *Cornwall*, the festivity of S. *Maws*, a British bishop, of whose chapel, chair, and well, see *Leland*'s Itinerary, vol. 3. In *Wales*, the

the memory of *S. Julien*, honoured heretofore at *Capell Julien* in *Cardiganshire*. [*Willis.*]

Sept. 3. In *Ireland*, the feast of *S. Ballon*, confessor, brother to *S. Gerald* of *Mayo*. [*Chatelain.*]

Sept. 4. In *Anglesey*, the memory of *S. Rhuddlad*, in whose name the church of *Llanrhuddlad* is dedicated. [*Willis.*]

Sept. 5. At *Strat-margel* in *Montgomeryshire*, the festivity of *S. Marcella*; in whose name the church and monastery there is supposed to have been dedicated. *Leland* also in his Itinerary, vol. 5. speaks of a parish church of *S. Marcella*. [*Willis.*]

Sept. 6. At *Llanidlos* in *Montgomeryshire*, the feast of *S. Idlos*, confessor. [*Chatelain.*] In *Ireland*, the feast of *S. Bacconna*, confessor. In the north of *England*, the decease of *S. Bilfrid*, anchoret, who glorified God by a most saintly life, in the eighth century. [*Idem.*]

Sept. 9. In *North Wales*, the festivity of the holy confessors, *S. Tanoc*, and *S. Eelrhyw*. [*Willis.*] In *Little Britain*, the feast of *S. Osmana*, a British or Irish virgin; who fleeing from the contagion of the world, embraced a solitary life in that province, in the sixth century, where she has ever since been honoured amongst the saints. [*Lobineau.*]

Sept. 11. In *Wales*, the memory of *S. Deiniel*,
or

of *Daniel* the younger, surnamed *the Carpenter*, honoured with churches both in *North Wales* and *South Wales*. [*Willis*.]

Sept. 14. At *Llandockwyn* in *Merionethshire*, the festivity of S. *Teckwyn*, confessor. [*Willis*.]

Sept. 18. In a little island near *Anglesea*, the memory of S. *Dunwen*, virgin, whose church gives name to the island.

Sept. 21. In the kingdom of *Northumberland*, the commemoration of the holy queen *Ethrith*, who quitting the pomps and pleasures of the world, entered into religion, where she was made abbess: and after many years tending to religious perfection, was called to the embraces of her heavenly spouse, anno 786. [*Hoveden*.]

Sept. 24. In *Yorkshire*, the memory of S. *Ebba*, anchoret, illustrious for sanctity, whose blessed soul took her flight from his hermitage at *Coln*, ten miles distant from the city of *York*, to the happy mansions of the heavenly paradise, anno 767. *Alcuin de Sanctis Eborac. Hoveden.*

Sept. 25. At *Ruthin* in *Denbighshire*, the festivity of S. *Meugan*, confessor. At *Croyland*, the passion of the venerable abbot *Theodore*, with many of his monks slain by the *Danes*, anno 810. [*Ingulphus*.] On this day was also honoured in *Wales*, S. *Caian*, confessor. [*Willis*.]

Sept. 26. In *Wales*, the festivity of S. *Barrog*, or *Barwg*, confessor, honoured with a church

in

in the deanery of *Newport*, *Monmouthshire*. [*Willis*.]

Sept. 27. In *Ireland*, the feast of *S. Lupite*, virgin. [*Chatelain*.]

Sept. 28. In *Wales*, the festivity of *S. Ginod*, honoured in the church of *Llangunwyd*, in the diocese of *Landaff*. [*Willis*.]

OCTOBER.

October 1. IN the diocese of *S. David*, the feast of *S. Milers*, confessor, to whose memory the church of *Llys-y-fran* in *Pembrokeshire*, is dedicated. [*Willis*.]

October 2. In *Ireland*, the memory of *S. Fiechus*, disciple of *S. Patrick*, and archbishop of *Leinster*; of whom *Jocelin* writes, c. 117. that he sent to heaven before him no fewer than sixty Saints of the number of his disciples.

October 5. At *Llangynhavel* in *Denbighshire*, the festivity of *S. Cynhaval*, confessor. [*Willis*.]

October 6. The memory of *S. Budoc*, confessor, greatly honoured amongst the Ancient Britons, as appears from the churches dedicated in his name. *Leland* informs us, that he came out of *Ireland* into *Cornwall*, and there happily ended his mortal pilgrimage. Itinerary, 3d vol. He had also formerly a church in *Oxford*.

October 7. In *Wales*, the festivity of *S. Keinwen*, virgin, honoured with two churches in the

Isle of *Anglesey*. [*Willis.*] Also in the diocese of *Landaff*, the memory of S. *Tydder*, confessor, [*Idem.*]

October 8. In *Wales*, the festivity of S. *Cadwallador*, confessor, honoured with two churches among the Ancient Britons; who affirm, that he was their last crowned king, who being disgusted with this wretched and deceitful world, withdrew himself from it, and wholly dedicated the remainder of his life to religious solitude and divine love. In *Wales* also, the feast of S. *Kynog*, alias *Gynog*, in whose name many churches were dedicated. [*Willis.*]

October 10. In the diocese of *Landaff*, the feast of S. *Melan*, honoured with a church, bearing his name, in the archdeaconry of *Landaff*. [*Willis.*]

October 13. At *Trim* in *Ireland*, the memory of S. *Finsecha*, virgin; whose relicks are honoured there, with those of seventeen other saints. [*Chatelain.*]

October 14. At *Darowen* in *Montgomeryshire*, the feast of S. *Tydyr*, confessor, in whose name the church of that parish is dedicated. [*Willis.*]

October 15. In *Little Britain*, the festivity of S. *Cadoc*, a British bishop and confessor, who flourished in the sixth century. [*Lobineau.*]

October 16. In *Little Britain* also, the feast of S. *Vitalis*, or *Vial*, confessor, in the same century. [*Lobineau.*] He was also honoured with a church in *Wales*, as may be seen in *Willis's* dedications.

October 18.

October 18. In *Wales*, the festivity of S. *Gwendilina*, abbess, in whose honour divers churches have been dedicated. [*Willis.*] Also the memory of S. *Brothen*, honoured in the parish of *Llanfrothen* in *Merionethshire*. [*Idem.*]

October 21. In *Carnarvanshire*, the festivity of S. *Tudwen*, virgin, honoured in the chapel of *Llandudwen*. [*Willis.*]

October 24. At *Penegoes* in *Montgomeryshire*, the festivity of S. *Cadmarch*, or S. *Cadfarch*, in whose name that church is dedicated. [*Willis.*]

October 25. At *Llangan* in the diocese of *Landaff*, the feast of S. *Gan*, confessor; honoured also with a church in the diocese of S. *David's*. [*Willis.*]

October 26. At *Llanwnog* in *Montgomeryshire*, the feast of S. *Gwinnog*, confessor. [*Willis.*]

October 27. At S. *Ives* in *Cornwall*, the memory of S. *Iia*, honoured there of old, as virgin and martyr. She was according to her acts (quoted in *Leland's Itinerary*, vol. 3.) daughter to a nobleman of *Ireland*, and a disciple of S. *Barricus*, a companion of S. *Patrick*; and came from *Ireland* with S. *Elwin*, and many others, into *Cornwall*, the great refuge of the antient *Irish* saints. With her, or at least about the same time, came over also S. *Breach*, virgin, S. *Sinxin*, abbot, S. *Maruan*, monk, &c. together with the holy virgins, *Crewenna*, *Helena*, and *Tecla*. As also S. *Germok*, an *Irish* prince, honoured

A SUPPLEMENT

October 30. At *Gloucester*, the commemoration of *S. Arilda*, virgin and martyr, illustrious for miracles. Her Body was translated from *Kington*, near *Thornbury*, (where she suffered death in defence of her purity) to the Abbey of *Gloucester*. [*Leland's* Itinerary vol. 4. p. 78.] The church of *Oldberry*, or *Odbury* in *Gloucestershire*, is dedicated in her name. [*Willis*.]

October 31. In *Wales*, the festivity of *S. Dewael*, or *Dogmael*, abbot; and of *S. Howel*, confessor, honoured by the ancient Britons on this day. [*Willis*.]

NOVEMBER.

Nov. 1. THE commemoration of divers ancient British saints, whose festivity is marked on this day, by Mr. *Willis*, in his survey of their churches; viz. *S. Elhaiarn*, *S. Kedol*, *S. Morhaiarn*, *S. Peulan*, *S. Rhaydrys*, *S. Kigilium*, *S. Wria*, &c. most of all whom we know little more at present than their names.

Nov. 3.

Nov. 3. In *Wales*, the festivity of *S. Christiolus*, confessor, whose name has been very illustrious amongst the ancient British saints, as appears by the many churches dedicated to his memory. [*Willis.*] In *Ireland*, the festivity of *S. Macnisi*, the first bishop of *Connor*, who reposed in our Lord anno 513. [*Ware.*] At *Clodock* in *Herefordshire*, the feast of *S. Cloddocus*, confessor. [*Willis.*]

Nov. 5. In *Anglesey*, the feast of *S. Gwenvaen*, honoured in the parish church of *Rhoscolyn*. [*Willis.*] In *Little Britain*, the feast of *S. Colledoc*, confessor, and of *S. Kerrian*, hermit: As also the memory of *S. Guethenoc*, a holy solitary, said to have been brother of *S. Winwaloc*, and disciple of *S. Budoc*. [*Lobineau.*]

Nov. 6. At *Ceidio* in *Carnarvanshire*, the memory of *S. Ceidiaw*. [*Willis.*] At *Llanwnda* in *Pembrokeshire*, the feast of *S. Wnda*. [*Idem.*]

Nov. 7. In *North Wales*, the festivity of *S. Cynfur*, or *Cynfarwy*, honoured with divers churches in the dioceses of *Bangor* and *S. Asaph*. [*Willis.*]

Nov. 8. In *Wales*, the festivity of *S. Keby*, renowned for wisdom and sanctity amongst the ancient Britons. There are many churches in *Wales* and *Cornwall* dedicated in the name of *S. Cuby* or *Guby*, which probably all belong to the same saint. It is also the day of *S. Tyssilio*, whose name in like manner has been illustrious amongst the ancient Britons, as appears from the

the dedications of divers churches, in Mr. Willis's surveys.] It is also the feast of S. Salvi, abbot, honoured in Little Britain. [Lobineau.]

Nov. 18. At Llanbabo, the decease of that saint of Anglesey, the memory of S. Pabo, in whose name is dedicated the chapel of Llanbabo. [Willis.] Also, in the same island, the feast of the saints Marcellus and Marcellinus, honoured in the church of Llandeusant. [Idem.] Also, at Tregynnan in Montgomeryshire, the memory of S. Knonla, confessor. [Idem.] In Ireland, the feast of S. Medunnu, confessor. [Chatelain.]

Nov. 10. At Llanelth in Anglesey, the feast of S. Eleth, confessor. [Willis.] In the county of Tyrconnel, the memory of S. Sodelbia, virgin. [Chatelain.] At Llangiveynowr in Carmarthenshire, the memory of S. Gwynow, confessor. [Willis.]

Nov. 11. In Carnarvanshire, the festivity of S. Cynfran, and of S. Crechw, both of them marked on this day by Mr. Willis in his survey of Bangor. In Ireland, the feast of S. Cumin, abbot, surnamed the Long; and of S. Duban, priest. [Chatelain.]

Nov. 12. At Llanarth in Cardiganshire, the feast of S. Wen. [Willis.]

Nov. 13. At Pennmynith in Anglesey, the feast of S. Credivael, alias Gradivael, honoured heretofore as tutelar saint of that parish. [Willis.]

Nov. 14.

honoured in Little Britain. [Labineau.]

Nov. 18. At *Lambeth*, the deceafe of that truly great and good man, *Reginald Pole*, cardinal and archbiſhop of *Canterbury*, obiit anno 1558. [*Willis*.] Alſo, in the ſame iſland, the feaſt of S. *Thomas*, Anchoret, and Abraham, confeſſor. [*Wilkins*.] Alſo, at *Tregunon*, in *Montgomeryſhire*, the memory of S. *Mailig*, confeſſor. [*Willis*.]

Nov. 20. At *Llangolman* in *Pembrokeſhire*, the feaſt of S. *Colman*, of which name there were two hundred and thirty *Iriſh* ſaints. [*Uſher*.]

Nov. 21. At *Aberporth*, in *Cardiganſhire*, the feaſt of S. *Cynfilli*, confeſſor. [*Wilkins*.]

Nov. 22. In *Wales*, the feſtivity of S. *Coiniin*, confeſſor; and of S. *Deyniolen*, virgin, honoured with divers churches in that principality. [*Willis*.]

Nov. 24. In *Ireland*, the feſtivity of S. *Kinan*, firſt biſhop of *Duleth*, a prelate of extraordinary ſanctity, who went to enjoy his Lord, anno 488. [*Ware*.]

Nov. 25. At *York*, the memory of the holy archbiſhop *Eegbert*, brother to king *Eadbert*, illuſtrious for his piety and learning. Alſo the commemoration of the venerable *Aelbert*, ſucceſſor to archbiſhop *Eegbert*, who brought that famous ſchool to perfection, which his predeceſſor had opened at *York*, for divine learning; where, amongſt others, he had the great *Alkwine*, or *Alcuin*, for his ſcholar, who was afterwards preceptor

ceptor of the emperor *Charlemagne*, and founder of the university of *Paris*. He was succeeded by archbishop *Lanbald*, who no ways degenerated from the virtues of the holy prelates that went before him. Of all these, see *Alcuin*'s poem *de Sanctis Eboracensibus*. In the diocese of *Landaff*, the feast of *S. Dockoe*, honoured at *Llandogo* in *Monmouthshire*. [*Willis*.] He is probably the same as that famous *S. Docus*, or *Docus*, called the *Doctor of the Britons*, and the master or teacher of the *Irish* saints of the second class. [*Usher*.]

November 27. At *Saltzburgh* in *Bavaria*, the festivity of *S. Virgilius*, bishop and confessor. He was a native of *Ireland*, who going abroad to propagate the kingdom of Christ, was for the eminence of his virtues, at the desire of king *Peppin*, promoted to the bishoprick of *Saltzburgh*, which he administred worthily of a successor of the apostles; and after having brought over the *Carinthians* to the faith of Christ, went to receive from him the reward of his labours, anno 780. In the isle of *Anglesey*, the memory of *S. Gallgo*, confessor. [*Willis*.]

Nov. 30. The festivity of *S. Tugdual*, first bishop of *Treguire* in *Little Britain*, who went over from *Great Britain* with many other saints in the sixth century, to propagate the kingdom of Christ. Also, the memory of *S. Pompeia*, widow, mother of *S. Tugdual*, and of holy *Seulis*, his virgin sister. [*Lobineau*.] At *Henllan* in *Denbighshire*, the festivity of *S. Sadwrn*, or *Saturnius*, hermit, in the seventh century; to whom

S. Winefride

DECEMBER.

Dec. 1. AT *Bangor*, the feast of *Daniel*, commonly called by the *Britons*, *Dainiel*, or *Deinol*, first bishop of that see, in the time of *S. David*; and so renowned for sanctity, that both the cathedral of *Bangor*, and many other churches, have been dedicated in his name: [*Willis*]

Dec. 2. At *Llanllechid*, in *Caernarvonshire*, the memory of *S. Llechida*, virgin, tutelar saint of that church. [*Willis*.] Also, at *Edern*, in the same county, the feast of *S. Edern*, confessor. [*Idem*.]

Dec. 5. In *Wales*, the festivity of *S. Gardin*, or *Cywrda*, whose memory has been in great veneration amongst the *Welch*, as appears by the dedication of divers churches in *Willis's* Parochial.

Dec. 9. In *Little Britain*, the feast of *S. Budoc*, bishop, master of many saints. At *Glanfanfre* in *Scotland*, the memory of *S. Lu—*, anchoret. [*Chatelain*.]

Dec. 11. In *North Wales*, the feast of *S. Peris*, surnamed the *Cardinal*, illustrious amongst the ancient *British* saints: [*Willis's* survey of *Bangor*, p. 272.]

p. 272.] Also, in the isle of Anglesey, the memory of S. Flewin, honoured in the chapel of Llanfleuin. [Jan. p. 286.]

Dec. 12. At *Quimper Corentin* in *Little Britain*, the feast of *S. Corentin*, first bishop of that see, and apostle of the neighbouring country. [*Lobineau*.] He has a place in the ancient British litany of the 7th century published by *Mabillion*.

Dec. 13. At *Rihall* in *Rutland*, the burying place of *S. Tibba*, virgin and anchoress, whose body was afterwards translated to *Peterborough*. She flourished in sanctity in the seventh century.

Dec. 16. In *Ireland*, the memory of *S. Berikel*, anchoret, brother to *S. Gerald of Mayo*. [*Chatelain*.]

Dec. 17. In *Wales*, the festivity of *S. Avan*, or *Afan*, honoured with divers churches amongst the ancient Britons: also, the feast of *S. Tydecho*, honoured with a church in *Anglesey*. [*Willis*.] In *Little Britain*, the feast of *S. Briac*, abbot, in the sixth century. *Lobineau*.]

Dec. 18. At *Exeter*, the memory of *Sithewella*, or *Sithfled* (Silvola) honoured as virgin and martyr in a church bearing her name in the suburbs of that city; where also her sepulchre was seen in *Leland*'s time. [*Itinerary*, vol 3 p. 49.] In the Isles of *Scilly*, the memory of *S. Lide*, virgin, whose sepulchre was honoured of old in a little island bearing her name.

name. [*Leland*.] In *Ireland*, the feast of S. *Flannan*, first bishop of *Kilaloe*, to which see he was promoted, anno 639. [*Karre*.]

Dec. 23. At *Hexham*, the memory of the venerable bishop *Erithebert*, who succeeded S. *Ace*, in that see, and had for his successor S. *Alchmundy*; as also of S. *Gilbert*, bishop, who succeeded S. *Alchmund*, anno 781. [*Hoveden*.]

Dec. 26. In *Wales*, the memory of S. *Maethly*, honoured with a church in the diocese of *Bangor*. [*Willis*.] At *Wythern* in *Galloway*, the memory of the holy bishops *Pecthelm*, cotemporary with S. *Bede*, and mentioned by him in his history; and *Pecwine*, who went to our Lord, says *Hoveden*, anno 777.

Dec. 31. At *Llanvaeloc* in *Anglesey*, the feast of S. *Maeloc*, confessor, observed there heretofore on this day. [*Willis*.] In *Carnarvanshire*, the feast of S. *Goning*, confessor. [*Idem*.]

A TABLE

A TABLE

OF THE

NAMES of the SAINTS, &c.

Commemorated in this

SUPPLEMENT.

A

ÆDUS, *B.* May 10
Aelbert, *A. B.* Nov. 25
Aelred, *Ab.* Jan. 12
Ailild, *A. B.* Jan. 13
Alcuin, May 19
Alfwold, *B.* Jan. 3
Alman, *B* April 4
Anian, *K.* Feb. 9
Arilda, *V. M.* Oct. 30
Armell, *Ab.* Aug. 16
Aficus, *B.* April 27
Avan, *C.* Dec. 17

B.

Ballon, *C* Sept. 3
Barrog, *C.* Sept. 26
Beriket, *C.* Dec. 16
Betta, *P.* Aug. 14
Beuno, *P.* April 21
Bilfrid, *H* Sept. 6
Boduan, *C.* Jan. 2

Branus, *C.* May 18
Breaca, *V.* Oct. 27
Braccan, or Bracan, *C.* May 7
Briac, *Ab.* Dec. 17
Briand, *B.* May 4
Bronus, *B.* June 8
Brothen, *C.* Oct. 18
Buan, or Vean, Aug. 4
Budoc, *B.* Dec. 9
Budoc, *C.* Oct. 6.

C.

Cadfarch, *C.* Oct. 24
Cadwalladore, Oct. 8
Caian, *C.* Sept. 25
Caron, *C.* March 2
Ceidiaw, *C.* Nov. 6
Celynin, *C.* Nov. 22
Ceolulph, *K.* Jan. 15
Ceromarin, *B.* March 12
Choca, *V.* June 6
Cladocus, *C.* Nov. 3

Colledoc,

Names of the SAINTS. 37

Calledoc, *B.* Nov. 5
Collan, *C.* May 20
Colmans, Nov. 20
Colman, *B.* Feb. 3, 8, 21.
Columba, *V. M.* March 16
Columban, *C.* Feb. 15
Columbin, *Ab.* June 12
Conchenna, *V.* March 13
Conlaeth, *B.* May 13
Conogan, *B.* Oct. 15
Corbican, *C.* June 26
Corentin, *B.* Decemb. 12
Cormac, *B.* Feb. 17
Credival, *C.* Nov. 13
Credyw, *C.* Nov. 11
Cristiolius, *C.* Nov. 3
Cronan, *B.* Feb. 9
Cuan, *Ab.* Jan. 1
Cuannach, *Ab.* Feb. 4
Culan, *B.* Feb. 18.
Cumein, *C.* Jan. 12.
Cumin, *Ab.* Novemb. 11.
Cynderin, *C.* July 25
Cynfar, *C.* Nov. 7
Cynfran, *C.* Nov. 11
Cynfill, *C.* Nov. 21
Cyngar, *C.* March 7
Cynhaval, *C.* Oct. 4.
Cyriol, *C.* Feb. 11

D.

Daconna, *C.* Sept. 6
Dallan, *M.* Jan. 29
Damian, *C.* May 14
Daniel, *B.* Dec. 1
Daniel, *C.* Sept. 11
Derfel Gadern, April 5
Devodog, *or* Divodug, *C.* June 25
Deyniolen, *V.* Nov. 22
Dockoe, *C.* Nov. 25
Deguan, *M.* July 13
Duban, *P.* Nov. 11
Dogvael, *Ab.* Oct. 31
Dwynwen, Jan. 25
Dwywau, *C.* May 14
Dunwan, *V.* Sept. 18

Dyfnan, *C.* April 22
Dyfnog, *C.* Feb. 12
Dygwyd, *C.* Jan. 13

E.

Eanbald, *A. B.* Nov. 25
Ecgbert, *A. B.* Nov. 25
Edern, *C.* Dec. 2
Eigrad, *C.* Jan. 6
Eelrhyw, *C.* Sept. 9
Ela, *W.* Feb. 1.
Eleth, *C.* Nov. 9
Elidan, *C.* June 16
Elidere, Elliere, *C.* Jan. 23
Elphegus, *B.* March 12
Eoglodius, *C.* Jan. 25
Elhaiarn, *C.* Nov. 1
Elwin, Oct. 27
Erard, *B.* Jan. 8
Ergnate, *V.* Jan. 8
Ervell, *C.* July 6
Etha, *H.* Sept. 24

F.

Fachnan, *C.* Aug. 14
Fagan, *C.* Feb. 10
Fedlimid, *B* Aug. 9
Fergus, *B.* March 30
Fiacre, *B.* Feb. 8
Fiechus, *A. B.* Oct. 2
Finchad, *B.* Aug. 14
Finsecha, *V.* Oct. 13
Fintan, *B.* Feb. 21
Flannan, *B.* Dec. 18
Flannan, *Ab.* April 24
Flewyn, *C.* Dec. 11
Foilenna, *V.* March 3
Forannan, *B.* Jan. 15
Frithebert, *B.* Dec. 23
Fulartach, *B.* March 29

G.

Gaffaliak, *C.* March 1.
Gallgo, *C.* Nov. 27
Gan, *C.* Oct. 25
Gelasius, *A. B.* March 27
Germok, *H.* Oct. 27

Gewydh,

A TABLE

Gewydb, July 2.
Gilbert, B. Dec. 23.
Gilla, V. April 1.
Gobnate, V. Feb. 10.
Goning, C. Dec. 31.
Gonod, C. Sept. 28.
Gonory, C. July 18.
Gonvill, Jan. 8.
Gordia, or Gwrda, Dec. 5.
Gower, C. July 11.
Gotalzeus, C. July 25.
Granog, C. March 6.
Grebi, B. Nov. 8.
Gruithelan, C. Aug. 22.
Gunthiern, C. June 29.
Gurneck, C. June 6.
Gwendolina, Ab. Oct. 18.
Gwenog, C. Jan. 3.
Gwenvaen, Nov. 5.
Gwethenoc, H. Nov. 5.
Gweynow, Nov. 10.
Gwyfer, C. June 2.
Gwylloc, C. Jan. 7.
Gwynfill, Nov. 2.
Gwynning, C. Jan. 31.
Gwinnin, C. March 2.
Gwynno, C. Oct. 26.
Gwynnoyde, Jan. 1.
Gwyven, V. June 3.
Gynos, M. Oct. 8.

H

Howel, C. Oct. 31.
Howyn, C. Jan. 6.
Hubright, H. April 24.
Huetbercht, Ab. April 24.
Hygbald, Ab. Aug. 12.

I and J.

Jacutus, Ab. March 2.
Jarlaith, B. Feb. 11.
Idlos, C. Sept. 6.
Jeftin, C. April 12.
Jia, V. 3rd C. Oct. 27.
Illhog, or Illogan, 6th Aug. 2.
Ina, Feb. 5.
Joavan, B. and C. March 1.

Martyrs of Canterbury, Mar. 11.
Maurice, C. Dec. 22.
Juliar, Sept. 2.
Maws, B. Sept. 2.
Meen, Ab. June 21.

K

Kedal, C. Nov. 7.
Keinwen, V. Oct. 8.
Kenan, B. Nov. 24.
Kerrian, H. Nov. 8.
Kinnia, V. Feb. 1.
Kinwill, Jan. 8.
Kirig, June 16.
Knonkell, Nov. 9.
Kynoc, M. Oct. 8.

L

Laingen, C. Jan. 8.
Laudat, Ab. Jan. 16.
Lawdoge, C. Jan. 18.
Lauzon, Prior, April 13.
Lechilda, V. Dec. 2.
Lefmon, H. Dec. 9.
Libio, C. Feb. 28.
Lide, V. Dec. 18.
Listid, C. April 6.
Luctigern, Ab. April 28.
Lugad, Ab. March 2.
Lugidianus, Ab. Aug. 10.
Lupite, V. Sept. 22.
Luroch, B. Feb. 17.
Lwychairi, C. Jan. 2.
Lwybidan, C. Nov. 19.
Lythao, Sept. 1.

M

Macaldus, B. April 25.
Macbreth, C. Jan. 3.
Machalleus, C. June 2.
Macnifi, B. Nov. 3.
Madryn, C. June 9.
Maeloc, C. Dec. 11.
Maelrhys, V. Jan. 1.
Maethly, Dec. 26.
Maimbod, M. Jan. 23.
Marcella, Sept. 5.
Manchin, B. Jan. 1.
Marcellinus Ad March 1.
Nov. 9.

Names of the SAINTS.

Martyrs of Canterbury, May 11
Maurice, C. Jan. 16
Maws, B. Sept. 2
Meen, Ab. June 21
Meilig, C. Nov. 14
Meirian, C. Feb. 3
Melan, C. Oct. 10
Melangel, C. May 27
Mella, W. March 9
Mellan, or Myllin, C. June 19
Meryn, C. Jan. 6
Meugan, C. Sept. 25
Mevennius, Ab. June 21
Milers, C. Oct. 1
Mochua, Ab. Jan. 1
Moconna, C. Nov. 9
Molibba, B. Jan. 8
Monennius, B. March 1
Morhaiarn, C. Nov. 1
Muredach, B. Aug. 12

N.
Natal, Ab. Jan. 27
Nathinæus, P. July 27
Nathy, B. Aug. 9
Nessan, B. March 16
Ninnoca, V. June 4

O.
Owen, C. Aug. 14
Osmana, V. Sept. 9

P.
Pabo, C. Nov. 9
Pandwyne, V. Aug. 26
Pecthelm, B. } Dec. 26
Pectwine, B. }
Pega, V. Jan. 8
Peris, C. Dec. 11
Peulan, C. Nov. 8
Pompeia, M. Nov. 19
Publicius, C. July 4
Pumice, V. July 27

R.
Regna, & Ranan, C. June 1
Rheaus, C. March 8

Rhochwyn, June 10
Rhuddlad, Sept. 4
Rictrith, Q. Ab. Sept. 21
Rictrudis, V. April 9
Robert, H. May 23
Rumon, B. Jan. 4
Rhwddrys, Nov. 1

S.
Sadwrn, H. Nov. 30
Saeran, C. Jan. 15
Sanan, or Sannam, C. June 14
Sedulius, Ab. Feb. 12
Senach, B. Feb. 21
Seuve, V. Nov. 30
Sithefulla, V. Dec. 18
Sodelbia, V. Nov. 10
Suarleck, B. March 27
Suibercht, B. April 30
Sulian, C. July 22
Sulian, Ab. Nov. 8
Synin, C. Jan. 7

T.
Tanoc, C. Sept. 9
Tauricius, C. June 26
Tenedan, B. July 17
Teckwyn, C. Sept. 14
Tibba, V. Dec. 13
Tiernemail, B. March 12
Theodore and Co. M. Sept. 24
Thoman, B. Jan. 10
Tocho, C. May 1
Trygan, or Trillo, C. June 26
Tudno, C. June 5
Tudwen, V. Oct. 21
Tugdual, B. Nov. 3
Tybie, Jan. 30
Tydclud, May 30
Tyddwg, May 9
Tydder, C. Oct. 7
Tydecho, C. Dec. 17
Tydvill, M. Aug. 13
Tydyr, C. Oct. 14
Tyfaelog, C. March 1
Tyfridoc, C. May
Tyrnog, C. April 3

S. *Auzel*, hermit, gave a name to a church and town in Cornwall

S. *Athan*, A. *Buduic*, William P., May 10, or *Wife*, B. May 8

Wnda, V. Nov. 6
Wrin, Nov. 1
Walon, B. Jan. 3, honoured with a church in diocese of Landaff

S. *Baff Hanat* dedicated at Builth in the diocese

S. *Beuzited* is honoured with a church at Glyn in North Wales

S. *Berchur* has a church in the diocese of Gloyn

S. *Breock* has two churches

S. *Bleuzyad* has a church

S. *Bruard* has a church

Tyfill, Jan. 3

V.

V Alscinian, C. May 1
Vigian, B. Jan 4
Virgilius, B. Nov. 27
Vitalis, C. April 16
Vylltygg, Nov. 12

An APPENDIX *of the Names of other* SAINTS *honoured by our British Ancestors, whose proper Days we have not been able to find out.*

A.

S. *ADEWELE* is honoured with a church at *Aldingham*, in the diocese of *Lincoln*

S. *Adeline* has a church at *Sudbury* in *Gloucestershire*

S. *Aldwyn* has also a church in *Gloucestershire*

S. *Aithan*, *Athan*, or *Tathan*, has a church in the diocese of *Landaff*

S. *Alleyn*, or *Allen*, has a church in *Cornwall*

S. *Almund* is honoured with a church in *Herefordshire*

S. *Alweys* has a church at *Lansalweys* in *Cornwall*

S. *Arvan* has a church in the diocese of *Landaff*

S. *Armen*, or *Harmon*, has a church in *Brecknockshire*, where great pilgrimages and offerings were formerly made. *Leland*

S. *Audonei* is honoured with a church in *Gloucestershire*

S. *Auſtel*,

An APPENDIX, &c.

S. *Auſtel*, hermit, gives name to a church and town in *Cornwall*

S. *Athawin*, or *Adws*, gives also name to a church in *Cornwall*

B.

S. *Baglan* is honoured with a church in the dioceſe of *Landaff*

S. *Baiſil* has a church at *Baiſlegg* in the ſame dioceſe

S. *Benediced* is honoured with a church at *Gyffin* in *North Wales*

S. *Bertoline* has a church in the dioceſe of *Cheſter*

S. *Bledrws* has a church in *Cardiganſhire*

S. *Brannock* is honoured with a church at *Braunton* in *Devonſhire*

S. *Breock* has two churches in *Cornwall*

S. *Blenwydd* has a chapel in *Angleſey*

S. *Bruard* has a church in *Cornwall*

S. *Byry* at *Senburie* in *Glouceſterſhire*

C.

S. *Cadwin* has a church at *Llangedwin* in *Merionethſhire*

S. *Candida* is honoured at *Whitchurch* in *Dorſetſhire*

S. *Caredog* at *Lawrenny* in *Pembrokeſhire*

S. *Caſſion* has a church at *Chapley* in *Worceſterſhire*

S. *Caſtey* at *Llangaſtey* in *Brecknockſhire*

S. *Cannock*, and S. *Carde*, are honoured with churches in *Cornwall*

S. *Celer* is honoured with a church in *Carmarthenſhire*

S. *Cirick* has a church at *Newton* in *Devonſhire*

42   *An* APPENDIX, &c.

S. *Cleer*, or *Clair*, has a church in *Carmarthenshire*, and another in *Cornwall*

S. *Clether* has also a church in *Cornwall*: as have also S. *Cornelius*, S. *Coriant*, S. *Creed*, and S. *Crewenna*, or *Crowenna*

S. *Clydwin* is honoured with a church in *Carmarthenshire*

S. *Conning*, and S. *Colwyn*, have also churches in *Wales*

S. *Culborn* is honoured with a church in *Somersetshire*

S. *Cyr* has a church at *Lansulian* in *Cornwall*

S. *Cynon*, S. *Cynfelin*, and S. *Cymbryd*, have churches in *Wales*

S. *Cynbaiern* is honoured in the church of *Lwyn Cynbaiern*, *Merionethshire*

S. *Cyriac* has a church at *Leycock* in *Wiltshire*

D.

S. *Deverex* has a church in *Herefordshire*

S. *Digat*, and S. *Dingat*, have churches in *Carmarthenshire*

S. *Dilp* is honoured at *Landilpb* in *Cornwall*

S. *Dhetty* has a church at *Llandhetty* in *Brecknockshire*

S. *Dinebo* is honoured with a church in *Herefordshire*

S. *Dominica* has a church in *Cornwall*

S. *Dona* is honoured with a church at *Llandona* in *Anglesey*

S. *Deguay* has a church in the diocese of S. *Asaph*

S. *Donat* has a place amongst the British confessors, in a litany of the seventh century, and

and is probably the same as was honoured at S. *Donats* in *Glamorganshire*

S. *Dunoke* was honoured in *Wales*, *Leland*, vol. 5. speaks of his well, which he says is a mighty spring

E.

S. *Edi* was honoured in the church of *Llanedi*, *Carmarthenshire*

S. *Egwad* had a church at *Llanegwade* in the same county

S. *Elgyn*, and S. *Emeldis*, were honoured with churches in *Yorkshire*

S. *Ella* had a church in the diocese of *Chester*

S. *Endelian*, S. *Ennoder*, S. *Erney*, S. *Ermett*, S. *Essy*, S. *Ewe*, S. *Ewny*, and S. *Eval*, had each of them a church in *Cornwall*

S. *Esperit* was honoured with a church in *Warwickshire*

S. *Elveis* had a church at *Llanelfw* in the diocese of S. *Davids*

S. *Erwene*, or *Erbene*, is honoured with a church in *Cornwall*

S. *Ewen* has a church in *Bristol*

F.

S. *Felack* was honoured with a church at *Filake* in *Cornwall*

S. *Feokk* had a church at *Feek* in the same county

S. *Florence* had a church in *Pembrokeshire*

S. *Fourson* was honoured at *Cliff* S. *Fourson* in *Devonshire*

S. *Gaffe*

44 An APPENDIX, &c.

S. *Gaffo* has a church at *Llangaffo* in *Anglesey*.

S. *Genyse*, or *Ginnis*, is honoured in *Cornwall*: S *Genevese* in the diocese of *Norwich*; and *S. Genewys* in that of *Lincoln*. Quere, Whether this be not the same as S. *Genesius*?

S. *Geduin* has a church in the diocese of S. *Asaph*.

S. *Gerens*, (whom *Leland* calls *Geron*,) and S. *Geran*, have churches in *Cornwall*: as have also S *Ginoke*, S. *Gothian*, S. *Gluvias*, and S *Grada*.

S. *Gwick*, S. *Gweitho*, S. *Gwythian*, S. *Gwrci*, S. *Gwinen*, S. *Gwinnock*, S. *Gwynner*, S. *Gwynnis*, S. *Gwinning*, and S. *Gwyfan*, have each of them a church in *Wales*.

S. *Gynlo* and S. *Gynedor*, have also churches in *Wales*.

H.

S. *Heged* was honoured with a church in *Carnarvonshire*.

S. *Hychan* has a church at *Llanhychan* in *Denbighshire*.

S. *Hydroc*, at *Lanhydroc* in *Cornwall*.

I.

S. *Januarius*, (different I suppose from the martyr of *Naples*,) has a church in *Cornwall*.

S. *Ide*, or *Eade*, and S. *Ifs*, have also churches in *Cornwall*.

S. *Jeffrey*,

An APPENDIX, &c.

Jeffrey, at *Jeffreyston* in *Pembrokeshire*: and S. *Ismael*, if this latter be not the same as S. *Ismael*

K

S. *Kine* gives name to a church and town in *Cornwall*.

S. *Kean*, S. *Kenwen*, S. *Knee*, (the same as S. *Kewly* or *Keverne*, and S. *Kewis*, have also each of them a church in *Cornwall*.

S. *Kerian* has a church in *Exeter*; S. *Kiberd* in *Cornwall*; S. *Kinemark*, S. *Koffig*, and S. *Kinlloc*, in *Wales*.

L

S. *Lany* is honoured in the dedication of two churches in *Cornwall*

S. *Ladoca* has also a church at *Ladock* in the same county

S. *Levan* gives also his name to a church and parish of *Cornwall*

S. *Llonio* has a church at *Llandinam* in *Montgomeryshire*

S. *Ludgran* is honoured at a place called by his name in *Cornwall*

S. *Llwny's* church is at *Llanllwyny* in *Carmarthenshire*

M

S. *Mabe* has a chapel at *Lavappa* in *Cornwall*; S. *Mabena* is honoured at *Mabyn* in the same county

S. *Mucra* has also a church in *Cornwall*, and S. *Machell* in *Anglesey*

S. *Madec*

S. *Madoc* has three churches in *Wales*; S. *Malteg*, one; S. *Mapley*, one; and S. *Margaret Marlos*, two.

S. *Marvan*, or *Marvenne*, S. *Marnarch*, S. *Mauditus*, S. *Maugan*, S. *Mawnan*, S. *Mauwan*, or *Mevan*, S. *Melian*, or *Mellyn*, S. *Melania*, S. *Merin*, S. *Mevy*, S. *Minever*, and S. *Moran*, have each of them a church in *Cornwall*.

S. *Manugban*, S. *Melid*, S. *Mougban*, and S. *Mwrthell*, have churches in *Wales*.

S. N*Ewlina*, and S. *Nonnita*, are honoured with churches in *Cornwall*, where there are also three churches of S. *Nunn*, probably the same as S. *None*, the mother of S. *David*.

S. O*lgain* is honoured with a church in the diocese of S. *Asaph*.

S. *Osanna* of *Hoveden*, a royal virgin, sister to king *Ofred*, was also honoured by our ancestors amongst the Saints. *Giraldus Cambrensis*.

S. P*Adarn* was honoured at *Pencarreg* in *Carmarthenshire*, *March* 5.

S. *Padock* had a church at *Haroldston-West*, *Pembrokeshire*.

S. *Paulin* has a church at *Paul* in *Cornwall*. *Pauleus*, at *Llangors* in *Brecknockshire*.

APPENDIX.

S. *Peirio* is honoured with a church at *Rhos-peirio* in *Anglesey*.

S. *Pratt* has a church at *Blisland* in *Cornwall*

S. *Pynnock*, at *Pynnock*, in the same county

R.

R. *Estitutus* has a church dedicated in his name at *Llanrysted* in *Cardiganshire*; S. *Rhoddrad*, in *Carnarvanshire*; and S. *Roche* in *Cornwall*, at a parish church bearing that name

S. *Rowsio* is honoured in the dedication of the church of *Hampsted*, near *London*

S.

S. *Amlet* is honoured with a church in the diocese of S. *David*

S. *Sancred* gives name to a church and parish in *Cornwall*

S. *Sarik*, in *Leland*'s time, had a church at *Sunning*: whither of late time, (says he, vol. 2. p. 3.) many folks resorted in pilgrimage for the disease of madness

S. *Sawell* was honoured with a church in *Carmarthenshire*

S. *Savan* had a church in *Glamorganshire*, and another in *Anglesey*

S. *Senar*, or *Sennar*, and S. *Sennan*, had churches in *Cornwall*

S. *Sithney*, and S. *Stythian*, or *Sradian*, had also churches in *Cornwall*, where there were likewise churches of S. *Symphorianus*, (probably the martyr of *Autun*) and of S. *Symphoriana*

S. *Sywall* had a church dedicated in his name in *Wales*   S. *Tallan*

T.

S. T*Allen* has a church in *Cornwall*: fo has S. *Tethe*, and S. *Tidy*, or *Tudy*

S. *Tooleda*, and S. *Terney*, and S. *Tue*, alias *Eve*, have alfo churches in *Cornwall*

S. *Theoderick* is honoured as a martyr in the church of *Matherne* in *Glamorganfhire*

S. *Theobald* has a church in the diocefe of *Litchfield*, another in the diocefe of *Carlifle*, and a third in the diocefe of *Norwich*. Quere, Whether this be a Britifh or a French Saint?

S. *Tygai*, and S. *Trygarn*, are honoured with churches in *North Wales*

S. *Tyrafies* has a church in *Shropshire*

S. *Twinnel*, alias *Winoc*, is honoured with a church in *South Wales*

U. and V.

S. U D Y has a church in *Cornwall*: fo has S. *Uni*, martyr, and S. *Unine*

S. *Urian*, and S. *Uval*, have alfo each of them a church in *Cornwall*

S. *Urithe* has a church at *Chedelhampton* in *Devonfhire*

S. *Veep* gives name to a parifh and church in *Cornwall*

S. *Vorek* is alfo honoured with a church in *Cornwall*

W.

S. W*Aynard* has a church in *Herefordfhire*

S. W *Wednack* is honoured with a church in *Cornwall*: where alfo S. *Wenapa*, S. *Wendrona*,

An APPENDIX, *&c.*

drona, S. *Wenna,* S. *Widnock,* S. *Wilow,* S. *Wittir,* and S. *Wynnoh, or Wynnotts,* have each of them a church.

S. *Wendred* has a church in the diocese of *Ely*

S. *Wenlyffo,* or *Wennhoyfo,* was honoured in North *Wales*

S. *Womar,* or *Wymer,* has a church in *Pembrokeshire*

S. *Wonno,* or *Wonnow,* and S. *Wynith,* have churches in *Radnorshire*

S. *Woolo,* has a church in the diocese of *Landaff*

S. *Wolfride* has a church at *Horton* in *Dorsetshire*

Y.

S. *Ylched,* and S. *Ynghenedel,* have each of them a church in the Isle of *Anglesey.*

N. B. The names of almost all these Saints, with the dedications of their churches, are found in the Parochial published by the late Mr. *Browne Willis.*

Here follow the names of divers Saints, invocated in an ancient litany, used in *England* in the seventh century; which that learned antiquarian Dom. *Mabillon* has published in his *Vetera Analecta,* p. 669, *&c.*

Amongst the Confessors,

S. *Donatus,* S. *Gregory,* S. *Augustin,* S. *Samson,* S. *Briocus,* S. *Melorus,* S. *Branwalatrus,* S. *Patrick,* S. *Brindan,* S. *Carnachus,* S. *Gildas,* S. *Paternus,* S. *Petranus,* S. *Guinwalocus,* S. *Courentinus,* S. *Citawus,* S. *Guoidia-*

nus, S. *Munnas,* S. *Serwanus,* S. *Seracinus,* S. *Guiniaw,* S. *Tutwal, (Tugdual,)* S. *Germanus,* S. *Columeille,* S. *Paul, (de Leon,)* S. *Judicail,* S. *Mevinnius, (Meen,)* S. *Guoidwal, (Gudwall,)* S. *Dircillus,* S. *Backlas,* S. *Rawclus,* S. *Racatus,* S. *Loutiernus,* S. *Riacatus,* S. *Toninnanus.*

Amongſt the Women Saints,
S. *Columba,* S. *Ninnoca,* S. *Ticiawa,* S. *Corona,* S. *Benedicta,* S. *Senentina,* S. *Menna,* S. *Mathitbia,* S. *Trifma,* and S. *Brigida.*

F I N I S.

www.ingramcontent.com/pod-product-compliance
Lightning Source LLC
Chambersburg PA
CBHW032132230426
43672CB00011B/2311